Living with the European Union

Also by Dennis Kennedy

THE WIDENING GULF: Northern Attitudes to the Independent Irish State, 1919–49

NORTHERN IRELAND AND THE EUROPEAN UNION (*co-editor*)

Living with the European Union
The Northern Ireland Experience

Edited by

Dennis Kennedy
Lecturer
Institute of European Studies
Queen's University
Belfast

First published in Great Britain 2000 by
MACMILLAN PRESS LTD
Houndmills, Basingstoke, Hampshire RG21 6XS and London
Companies and representatives throughout the world

A catalogue record for this book is available from the British Library.

ISBN 0-333-75380-1

 First published in the United States of America 2000 by
ST. MARTIN'S PRESS, INC.,
Scholarly and Reference Division,
175 Fifth Avenue, New York, N.Y. 10010

ISBN 0-312-22545-8

Library of Congress Cataloging-in-Publication Data
Living with the European Union : the Northern Ireland experience /
edited by Dennis Kennedy.
p. cm.
Includes bibliographical references and index.
ISBN 0-312-22545-8 (cloth)
1. European Union—Northern Ireland. 2. Northern Ireland—
—Economic conditions.   I. Kennedy, Dennis, 1936–   .
HC240.25.N75S87   1999
330.9416'0824—dc21   99–25940
                                                                          CIP

Selection, editorial matter and Chapters 1 and 8 © Dennis Kennedy 2000
Chapters 2–7, 9 © Macmillan Press Ltd 2000

All rights reserved. No reproduction, copy or transmission of this publication may be made without written permission.

No paragraph of this publication may be reproduced, copied or transmitted save with written permission or in accordance with the provisions of the Copyright, Designs and Patents Act 1988, or under the terms of any licence permitting limited copying issued by the Copyright Licensing Agency, 90 Tottenham Court Road, London W1P 0LP.

Any person who does any unauthorised act in relation to this publication may be liable to criminal prosecution and civil claims for damages.

The authors have asserted their rights to be identified as the authors of this work in accordance with the Copyright, Designs and Patents Act 1988.

This book is printed on paper suitable for recycling and made from fully managed and sustained forest sources.

10 9 8 7 6 5 4 3 2 1
09 08 07 06 05 04 03 02 01 00

Printed and bound in Great Britain by
Antony Rowe Ltd, Chippenham, Wiltshire

Contents

List of Tables and Figures	vi
Preface	viii
Notes on the Contributors	ix
1 Introduction: Portrait of a Region *Dennis Kennedy*	1
2 A Region among Regions: the Wider View *Thomas Christiansen*	17
3 Europe and the Northern Ireland Economy *Graham Gudgin*	38
4 Changing Scene: EU Impact on the Rural Economy *John Davis*	71
5 Trading Partners: Northern Ireland's External Economic Links *Esmond Birnie*	94
6 For Richer or Poorer: the Social Impact *Quintin Oliver*	115
7 European Rules and a Changing Environment *J. S. Furphy*	128
8 Europe and the Northern Ireland Problem *Dennis Kennedy*	148
9 The European Connection and Public Opinion *M. L. Smith*	169
Index	197

List of Tables and Figures

TABLES

3.1	Average annual expenditure by EC Structural Funds in NI	48
3.2	UK net contribution to the budget of the EC	53
3.3	Operational programmes 1989–94 CSF	57
3.4	Sub programmes under Agricultural Development OP	59
3.5	Total impact of CSF expenditure in Northern Ireland	61
3.6	A comparison of the impact of individual CSF programmes	62
3.7	Share of EC12 in manufactured exports	68
5.1	Unemployment and GDP per capita in NI and the Republic of Ireland compared to the rest of the EU, 1994–5	96
5.2	Northern Ireland manufacturing sector	98
5.3	Northern Ireland manufacturing sales growth	99
5.4	Trade between NI and The Republic of Ireland	103
5.5	Relative importance of foreign owned manufacturing plants in NI and Great Britain	105
5.6	Development of large PLCs; NI compared to small European economies, 1997	106
5.7	Largest NI controlled manufacturing firms compared to the three largest Republic of Ireland companies	107
5.8	Ownership of the top 100 companies in NI and RoI	108
9.1a	How do you think of your country's membership of the EC?	173
9.1b	Would you say your country has benefited from the EC?	174
9.2	Respondents who think the UK should continue to be a member of the EC	175
9.3	GB respondents saying as a member state, the UK's relationship with the EC should be	175
9.4	GB respondents saying closer links with the EC would make the UK...	176
9.5	Respondents saying as a member state, the UK's relationship with the EC should be...	178

9.6	Would closer links with the EC make the UK…	179
9.7	How do you think of your country's membership of the EC?	181
9.8	Respondents' views on the future of the pound in the EC	186
9.9	Should the UK do all it can to unite fully with the EC?	188
9.10	Respondents' views on the future of the pound in the EC	190
9.11	Respondents' views on whether the UK should do all it can to unite fully with the EC	192
9.12	Attitudes to Europe among the 18–24, 45–54 and 65+ age groups	193
9.13	Political party identifiers' views that the UK should do all it can to unite fully with the EC, by age groups	194

FIGURES

3.1	GDP per person, Northern Ireland as per cent of the EC average (EC12)	40
3.2	Unemployment rates in NI, UK and EC12	42
3.3	Growth of GDP in Northern Ireland, UK and EC12	44
3.4	Growth in employment in Northern Ireland, UK and EC12	45
3.5	EC Structural Funds (£m 1996 prices)	48
3.6	EC Structural Funds as per cent of public expenditure in NI	50
3.7	The financing of public expenditure	50
3.8	EC Structural Funds as per cent of external funding of public expenditure in Northern Ireland	51
3.9	The components of EC subsidies to NI agriculture	65
3.10	EC agricultural payments as per cent of total farm income in NI	66
4.1	Agricultural land prices in the United Kingdom	83
9.1	Respondent's views on whether the UK should do all it can to unite fully with the EC	184
9.2	Respondents' views on increasing or reducing the powers of the EC	185
9.3	Respondents' view on the powers of the EC, by political party	189

Preface

Much of the material for this book originated in a conference held at Queen's University, Belfast, in February 1998, to consider Northern Ireland's experience over 25 years as a region within the European Union. In addition to the named contributors, the editor wishes to thank Mr John Simpson, of the European Economic and Social Committee, and Dr James Magowan, formerly of the Brussels office of the Northern Ireland Centre in Europe. Thanks are also due to Catherine Madden, Manager of the Resource Centre in the Institute of European Studies at Queen's University, for her help in organising the material and preparing the manuscript.

While the terms 'European Community' and 'European Union' are technically distinct they have become interchangeable in common usage. In this work the term European Union or EU is generally preferred, except where the context clearly indicates otherwise, or where the source quoted uses European Community or EC, as is the case with Eurobarometer and some other tables.

Belfast   DENNIS KENNEDY

Notes on the Contributors

Esmond Birnie is Lecturer in Economics, Queen's University, Belfast. He was elected in 1998 to the new Northern Ireland Assembly. Educated at Cambridge University, he worked as Research Assistant at the Northern Ireland Economic Research Centre, 1986–9. He is author of several comparative studies on Northern Ireland and other regions of the European Union.

Thomas Christiansen is Jean Monnet Lecturer in European Studies in the Department of International Politics at the University of Wales, Aberystwyth. He holds degrees in international relations and west European politics from the London School of Economics and did his doctoral research at the European University Institute in Florence. He has published on the European Commission, the role of subnational governments in the integration process and institutional reform of the European Union as well as on theoretical and normative questions of European governance.

John Davis is Director of the Centre for Rural Studies, Queen's University, Belfast, and Head of the Department of Agriculture and Food Economics. Director of Economic Research, Department of Agriculture for Northern Ireland. Educated at Queen's University, Belfast, and the University of Newcastle upon Tyne, he is former President of the Agricultural Economics Society of Ireland and current Honorary National Secretary of the British Agricultural Economics Society. He has published extensively on agriculture and rural affairs in Ireland and elsewhere. His most recent work dealt with the BSE crisis and its economic impact.

J. S. Furphy is former Chief Conservation Officer in the Department of the Environment for Northern Ireland (1965–97), in charge of all aspects of nature and countryside conservation, including the preparation of legislation. He was responsible for numerous surveys in Northern Ireland on behalf of the British Trust for Ornithology. He has an honours degree in geography from Queen's University, Belfast.

Graham Gudgin is Director of the Northern Ireland Economic Research Centre since its establishment in 1985. He was appointed, on secondment (1998), as special economic adviser to the First Minister of

Northern Ireland. Educated at the University of London (BA Hons, geography) and the University of Leicester (PhD), from 1978 to 1985 he was Senior Research Officer in the Department of Applied Economics at the University of Cambridge. An expert in econometric modelling, he is the author of numerous reports on the Northern Ireland economy. He has served as Adviser to the House of Commons Select Committee on Northern Ireland Affairs.

Dennis Kennedy is Lecturer, Institute of European Studies, Queen's University, Belfast. He has a degree in modern history from Queen's University, Belfast, and a doctorate in politics from Dublin University. He was formerly Deputy Editor, *The Irish Times*, Dublin, and Head of European Commission Office, Belfast, 1985–91. He has published on Irish affairs (*The Widening Gulf*, 1988), on Northern Ireland and the European Community, on European regional affairs, and on world trade politics.

Quintin Oliver served from 1985–1998 as Director of the Northern Ireland Council for Voluntary Action. He helped found the European Anti-Poverty Network and was its first President, 1991–5. From 1991 to 1997 he served on the Council of State of Ireland as the personal appointee of President Mary Robinson. He was educated at St Andrews University, and holds a Professional Diploma in Management from the Open University.

M. L. Smith is Director of the Institute of European Studies and Jean Monnet Professor in European Integration at Queen's University, Belfast. He has been Harkness Fellow at the Universities of Columbia and Stanford in the USA, and Lecturer at the Universities of Cambridge and Hull, where he was Head of the Department of European Studies. His research has covered west and east Europe and he has published on the politics of the Soviet Union and the problems of west European unity, especially in the period 1930–60. His work on public opinion about Europe in Northern Ireland is part of a long-term project using new survey data.

1
Introduction: Portrait of a Region

Dennis Kennedy

Northern Ireland is among the smaller and less prosperous regions of the European Union, with a population of 1.66 million, and an average GDP per capita below, but not spectacularly so, the average for the EU.

At the beginning of 1998, Northern Ireland along with the rest of the United Kingdom, Denmark and the Republic of Ireland, completed 25 years of EU membership. Those 25 years have also been, for Northern Ireland, 25 years of politcal unrest and violence. The outbreak of the latest and most sustained chapter in the 'troubles' of Northern Ireland coincided with the beginning of UK negotiations to enter the European Community in 1970. Since then, in Northern Ireland the European Union has had within its boundaries the most serious and sustained assault by political terrorism on democracy in Europe over the past quarter of a century.

Over the 25 years more than 3000 people died in terrorist-related violence, a massive death-toll in relation to the population of the province. The use of the car-bomb in urban areas meant that Belfast and many provincial towns were repeatedly devastated, imposing a burden of hundreds of millions of pounds on the public purse by way of compensation and reconstruction. The cost of security, of a police force trebled to its normal size, and of stationing large numbers of additional army personnel in Northern Ireland, was formidable over the period, though, ironically, it had the indirect result of bringing additional money from the United Kingdom exchequer into the province.

Twenty-five years is a period sufficiently long to prompt an assessment of the impact of EU membership on the economic and social life of the province, and on its own particular acute political problem. This collection of essays is an attempt to do that, but it is not just an account of how Northern Ireland has fared within the European Union. It is also a case-study of the experience of a small region of the European Union, and the significance, or otherwise, of the European context in the evolution of its problems and concerns over a substantial period of time.

Northern Ireland is not unique among the regions of the European Union, but it does have certain distinctions. It is a small but discrete region with a considerable degree of administrative autonomy within a large and still largely centralised member state. It is divided by sea from the landmass of the state of which it is a part, and by a currency difference from the other EU member state with which it shares the island of Ireland.

When the United Kingdom began negotiating entry into the EC in 1970, Northern Ireland enjoyed a considerable degree of devolution, with its own regional legislature and government, and its own civil service. By the time the UK entered the EC in January 1973, the Northern Ireland government had resigned, its Parliament had been suspended, and the province was being ruled directly from London. Though this was intended as a temporary measure, it continued, apart from a short return to devolution in 1974, for the whole of the period under review. Under direct rule however, the devolved administrative framework remained, with the Secretary of State for Northern Ireland, a member of the UK Cabinet, aided by a team of junior ministers, presiding over the provincial government departments in Northern Ireland. Devolved matters still required special Northern Ireland legislation enacted at Westminster.

As no elected representative from Northern Ireland was, or was ever likely to be, a member of the central government in this period – even today the governing party in the United Kingdom, Labour, bars anyone resident in Northern Ireland from membership – the province has continued in the very odd position of having a devolved administration and a team of ministers with all the appearance of a regional government, but who were, and are, in fact, members of the central government. In this regard, if no other, Northern Ireland has been a unique region.

It is among the poorer regions of the Union, ranking 44th (from the bottom) in terms of GDP per capita out of a total of 179 regions (in the EU of Twelve, before the latest enlargement), and 22nd (from the top) in terms of unemployment, in the European Commission's Fifth Periodic Report on the Regions.[1] More recent figures, on a modified regional basis, show that in 1996 Northern Ireland had a GDP per capita of 78 per cent of the EU regional average, placing it about 50th out of 76 regions.[2] Within the United Kingdom it is the poorest standard region, with a GDP per capita just 81.2 per cent of national average, unemployment of 8.2 per cent against a UK figure of 5.6 per cent, household weekly incomes well below the national average, and high levels of social deprivation. More than 40 per cent of those out of work are long-term unemployed, having been without a job for more than one year.[3]

In part these figures stem from the particular structure of the region's economy, much affected by the contraction of agriculture and the decline of traditional manufacturing industries. Northern Ireland is twice as dependent on agriculture as the rest of the UK – 4.5 per cent against 2 per cent in terms of contribution to GDP – while its agriculture is generally based on small farms on poorish land, with 70 per cent classed as less favoured. The decline of large, labour-intensive manufacturing industries has reduced the contribution of manufacturing industry to 29 per cent of Northern Ireland's GDP.[4]

Its GDP per capita, however, has been increasing as a percentage of the UK figure, and its regional growth rate for most of the 1990s has been well above the average for the United Kingdom as a whole.[5] Inward investment has picked up, and sales of manufactures outside the province have increased significantly. Unemployment has been dropping, the 1997 rate of 8.2 per cent being exactly half the 16.4 per cent recorded in 1987.[6]

Against good overall growth and declining unemployment in comparison to the UK average has to be set a lower than UK average growth in GDP per employee.[7] In the industrial sector the evidence is that competitiveness and productivity are not good. Average output per head in Northern Ireland has been put at 80 per cent of that in Great Britain, and substantially lower in relation to levels in some continental EU member states. Unsatisfactory levels of skills and training have been identified as part of the problem. The province, as a region of the European Union, is faced with a range of other disadvantages, including remoteness from markets, high cost of transportation and exceptionally high cost of energy.

It is unusual in other ways. It has a birth rate of 14.8 per 1000 of the population, which is among the highest of any EU region, and a population more than 47 per cent of whom are under the age of 30. This birth rate, however has been declining steadily; in 1990 it was 16.7 per 1000.[8]

For more than two decades Northern Ireland has benefited from aid for regional development from the European Community. Though at the latest count just above the threshold for classification as an Objective One region under the Structural Funds regime, (75 per cent of EC average GDP per capita) it has held Objective One status since that category was created. Public attention in the region has tended to focus upon the extent of this financial assistance, usually in the context of unfavourable comparisons with the considerably greater amounts that have flowed from Brussels to the Republic of Ireland.

Partly as a result of that perception, enthusiasm for European integration and for the European Union in Northern Ireland has never reached the intensity it has in the Republic. There is an often expressed feeling that Northern Ireland is 'less European' than its southern neighbour. Certainly its direct involvement in the institutions of the EU is almost nil in comparison with that of Dublin. Many of its citizens share the Euroscepticism displayed so vigorously by sections of the wider British public, as do some of its politicians.

Much of this is the inevitable result of being a small region of a large member state of a European Union which is still essentially a union of states, rather than of people or regions. What happens in London is still more important for Northern Ireland than what happens in Brussels, particularly where funding is concerned. But that does not make what happens in Brussels unimportant, and Northern Ireland has shared with other small regions in large states the challenge of ensuring that its particular regional concerns are properly taken on board by the member state in the presentation of national policy in Brussels, and, beyond that, of seeking to make its own regional voice heard directly in and by the institutions of the European Union.

The political and security situation in Northern Ireland has been a tragic distraction. The politics of the region as well as its media and public dialogue have been, and remain, concentrated on its own immediate problems, to the neglect of national or international issues. The recent more direct involvement of the European Union through the Special Support Programme for Peace and Reconciliation (SSPPR) has done something to change that situation; in any event, lack of interest in and knowledge of European Union matters is not restricted to Northern Ireland among the regions of Europe.

While a quarter of a century is an appropriate period on which to seek to base some assessment of the overall impact of EU membership on a region, these studies show there are particular difficulties related to this quarter century, and to the exercise as a whole when considering a small region of a large state. The first enlargement of the European Community in 1973 coincided with a fundamental change in the post-war European economic scene. Rapid growth and full employment quite suddenly gave way to much slower growth and rising and high unemployment, caused in the main by global factors outside the then European Economic Community.

In other areas too, such as concern for the environment, the developing EC interest reflected, and followed, concern at a global level. It was the United Nations Convention on the Human Environment in Stockholm in June 1972 which stimulated the European summit meeting in Paris in October 1972 to call on the European Commission to produce an action programme on the environment. It was not until 1973 that the Commission created a unit within its own services to deal with the environment, and even then it was combined with consumer protection.

So it would be rash to ascribe to European influence alone various developments over the years which might well have come about anyway as the result of broader trends and wider influences. It is, of course, impossible to say what would have happened to Northern Ireland had it not been within the European Community, and such hypothetical, if tempting, exercises are largely pointless. There is a problem too in any consideration of what is termed the 'Northern Ireland economy'. As Esmond Birnie warns us in Chapter 5, it would be a mistake to analyse the economy of Northern Ireland as if it were a quasi-independent state. Its degree of openness to, and integration with, the rest of the United Kingdom weakens the case for considering it a separate economic region. It is possible to measure at the provincial level many of the elements of economic performance, but in a highly centralised state none of the instruments of economic control is available at that level, and it can be unrealistic at times to talk about the Northern Ireland economy as distinct from that of the United Kingdom as a whole. In that sense the economic impact of EU membership on Northern Ireland as a region might be little more than the knock-on effect at regional level of the impact of EU membership on the overall United Kingdom economy.

With those reservations in mind, how, in fact, has Northern Ireland survived 25 years in the European Union? And what lessons does its experience have to offer to other regions, and to the whole question of regionalisation in Europe?

One rather surprising answer that might be drawn from the contributions to this book is that it has made very little difference. This is not to say that it has not had a considerable impact, as it obviously has had, notably in areas like agriculture, but even that impact has not resulted in a region dramatically different, in comparative terms, from the one that existed in 1972. For instance the GDP per person in Northern Ireland, as a percentage of the average in the EC, has remained fairly constant. Certainly there has been no dramatic improvement in the relative position of Northern Ireland over the quarter of a century. On the other hand Northern Ireland, over the same period, has been one of the fastest growing regions of the United Kingdom, in terms of both output and employment creation.

The unemployment rate has fluctuated, as it has everywhere else, but until very recently remained well above the European average. Its recent drop to below that level reflects improvement in the UK unemployment position, leaving Northern Ireland only marginally better off in relation to the UK. The sceptic might draw the conclusion that it is UK Government policy, and economic performance, not EU membership, which has helped reduce unemployment levels in Northern Ireland.

One area where membership clearly had an effect is in Northern Ireland's external trade, which has seen a significant increase both in exports as a percentage of output, and in the percentage of exports going to the rest of the Community. But even here some caution may be necessary. As Graham Gudgin points out in Chapter 3, the liberalisation of world trade has brought all tariffs down, greatly reducing the significance of free trade within the Community itself, and also reducing the particular attractions of the EC to inward investors in manufacturing.

There is little clear evidence that the inflow of money from the EU's Structural Funds has had a significant effect on Northern Ireland. The province has, from almost the start, enjoyed a modestly privileged position as a priority region. Initially this was of little significance as transfers from centre to region in the Community, outside the Common Agricultural Policy, were small indeed. From 1989 the flow of funds increased, and from 1989 to 1994 Northern Ireland was the only UK region to enjoy Objective One, or top priority, status – a privilege it now shares with Merseyside and the Highlands and Islands.

This has meant significantly increased allocations for Northern Ireland, but several factors have made difficult any accurate assessment of the impact of these funds on economic performance. One is that even the increased allocation to Northern Ireland still amounts to a very small percentage of total public expenditure in the province, currently about 3 per cent. Second is the question as to whether the amounts allocated in Brussels to EU programmes in Northern Ireland actually result in increased expenditure in the province.

Some commentators point out that the 3 per cent of total public expenditure figure is somewhat misleading. A more accurate indication of the significance of EU financial aid would be to assess it as a percentage of *relevant* public expenditure in the province – that is of public expenditure in the areas covered by EU programmes, which would exclude social security, health, education and policing. Moreover, the 3 per cent does not include transfer of resources into the province for farm price support under the guarantee section of the Agricultural Fund. Even so, the total inflow of financial aid to Northern Ireland remains small in comparison to the transfer of public money for similar purposes coming from the UK exchequer.

Assessing the impact of EU transfers is not made easy by the widespread dispersion of these funds across Government departments and programmes. The estimates for 1997–8 for the Department of Finance and Personnel listed more than 100 departmental budget headings through which EU funds were being disbursed in Northern Ireland.[9]

This in turn raises two further issues – efficiency and additionality. If European funding is scattered so widely, is it being used efficiently? And if it is going to so many existing departmental budget lines, is it infringing the principle of additionality? Under additionality, upon which the Commission insists, and which member states undertake to observe, funding from Brussels to member states must result in a corresponding increase in related public expenditure in the member state. As a great deal of Structural Funds money coming to Northern Ireland has been spent through existing and continuing government programmes, in vocational training for example, it is extremely difficult to determine whether, or to what extent, EU money is simply replacing what the government would have spent anyway. In a period of rigorous cutting back of public expenditure as part of government policy, this becomes even more opaque. As the transfer of money is from Brussels to central government in London, there is the further question of the extent to which genuine additionality at national level results in equally genuine additionality at the level of the region to which the money has been allocated.

This is not just a problem for Northern Ireland, but for many other regions of medium-sized or large member states which are net contributors to the EU budget. It also raises a question that is, in European terms, perhaps more theological than financial. Some advocates of additionality argue that not just should the actual expenditure be additional, but so too should be the types of action upon which the European aid is spent. In other words, Structural Funds aid should make a qualitative as well as a quantitative difference – it should not be spent to top up or expand existing national schemes and programmes, but should go to finance new, innovative actions, or actions with an identifiable European, as distinct from a national dimension.

To some this has a touch of 'Brussels knows best', a suggestion that a small group of functionnaires in the Commission's DG XVI or DGV know better than national or regional administrators what types of activity should be aided. It also implies that there is an ample supply of highly imaginative but practical schemes lying waiting to be implemented, needing only additional funding from Brussels to bring them on stream. Should EU regional policy be concentrated on aspects other than the transfer of money from Brussels – on coordination and control of state aids to regions, on ensuring a regional dimension to other policies, and restricting financial aid to states, not regions, which really need it, as under the Cohesion Fund?

It is easy to see that there is potential here for tension between national government and provincial administration, with the regional authority seeing Brussels as an ally eager to give financial aid to the region, while the central government of the member state resents interference from Brussels, and, certainly if it is a net contributor to the EU budget, may wish to keep public expenditure within its own jurisdiction under tight control. (In the case of the United Kingdom, the rebate mechanism applied to the British budget contribution has made this particularly so.)

As the regional government in Northern Ireland has been, for all of this period, also part of central government, such tension is unlikely to be manifested publicly at government level. But it is expressed by commentators, elected representatives of the region and lobby groups, and has led to a perception in the region of the European Commission as a benevolent authority, anxious to help the region, and indeed more anxious to do so than central government.

This embryonic alliance between region and Commission against member state central government came close to reality in the BSE crisis, when it was soon clear that the Commission was more willing to respond to Northern Ireland's claim for its exemption from the ban on United Kingdom beef exports than was the UK Government.

On agriculture in general, no one could argue that the impact of the CAP on Northern Ireland has been other than formidable. Agriculture is arguably the region's largest industry, and since 1973 has, for the most part, been controlled by policy set at European level. Graham Gudgin produces the startling information that in some years the value of EC assistance to agriculture in the region, through the CAP, has been the equivalent of total farm incomes, and that over the period it has averaged 70 per cent of farm incomes. Yet, as John Davis notes in Chapter 4 the rural scene in 1998 may have radically changed in some aspects, but remains dogged by some very familiar problems. Farm incomes are low, now descending to crisis levels, farms remain small by UK standards, and food processing is weak and heavily dependent on subsidies.

On the broad economic front then, it could be argued that while Northern Ireland has changed greatly during the 25 years of EU membership, that membership has not been a major catalyst for change, and has not contributed significantly to any dramatic improvement in the fortunes of the region. Nor has it promoted the degree of economic integration on the island of Ireland that many both predicted and hoped it would. Under the impact of the Single European Market, north–south trade has increased comparatively rapidly, as has economic inter-penetration, particularly in the form of larger southern companies buying into northern enterprises. Business organisations on both sides of the border have been actively pursuing closer relations and joint economic activity. But almost all of this dates only from the beginning of the 1990s and the completion of the Single Market. Before that, as discussed in Chapter 8, the two governments, while cooperating ever more closely on the political question, showed surprisingly little interest in their shared membership of the EU as a vehicle for promoting economic integration.

Opinion remains sharply divided on the importance of the all-island dimension to economic activity. As Esmond Birnie writes, much of the recent attention paid to it may owe more to a desire to promote cross-border co-operation as part of a political settlement, than to its real economic significance. He also questions the more optimistic assumptions that have been made as to the potential for further greatly expanded cross-border trade, given the very small markets on either side of the border, and the vastly greater markets elsewhere in the EU. Perhaps the most striking indication of the lack of commitment at government level to commercial and economic integration on the island, at least until very recently, is the state of the road between Belfast and Dublin. Even after 25 years of EU membership, and much expenditure of European money on infrastructural development on the island, this key route remains woefully inadequate.

But the European Union is not all about economics and money. Its founders were also concerned with peace and reconciliation, with the prevention of conflict in Europe. When Northern Ireland came within the boundaries of the EC in 1973, its own internal conflict was at its height, and there was much expectation that under the European umbrella, now sheltering the United Kingdom and the Republic of Ireland, and therefore the whole island of Ireland, it would be easier to find a political solution to the division underlying the violence.

Just over twenty-five years on, a comprehensive agreement has been signed, bombings and killings have almost stopped, and a new system of devolved government is being put in place in Northern Ireland, accompanied by new institutional links between the United Kingdom and the Republic. Has the European dimension been an element in this?

Chapter 8 argues comprehensively that the EC has played little or no role. While its institutions and member states have been consistently supportive of any moves by the UK and Irish Governments to deal with the problem, the Community itself has explicitly ruled out political intervention on its part, and has never put together the massive package of financial aid to tackle economic and social problems in the province that some have, from time to time, advocated as the only real means of help open to the Community.

Awareness of the violent political situation there may have, over the years, ensured that Northern Ireland received marginally more generous treatment under the Structural Funds than its economic condition, strictly speaking, would have merited, but exceptional aid had to wait until the Special Support Programme for Peace and Reconciliation was authorised in 1995. This was more than 20 years after Northern Ireland and its violence came within the boundaries of the Community, and was explicitly in support of moves towards a solution being taken in the Anglo–Irish context and within Northern Ireland itself.

Did the general context of EU membership help towards a solution, as many had anticipated? Almost certainly not, as division worsened and terrorism continued for more than two decades after entry. It is probably true that the ever-present violence and persistent crisis obscured for many any consideration of the European dimension, and in any event the impact of EU membership on attitudes grounded in local divisions and animosities was bound to be extremely gradual, taking decades rather than years. The fact that EU membership did not dramatically change the economic and social landscape of Northern Ireland for the better did nothing to accelerate any such awareness.

The background to this, as M. L. Smith outlines in Chapter 9, is the long-standing division within Northern Ireland on attitudes towards the European Union along political, that is unionist/nationalist, lines.

As he puts it, both nationalists and unionists have thought of the process of European integration as primarily offering a mechanism that might help achieve, or hinder, their own political aspirations. Frequent nationalist assertions that a united Ireland is a logical side-product of a united Europe have helped bolster an instinctive British Euroscepticism on the unionist side. To an extent, therefore, the European dimension has been a divisive, not a cohesive factor.

But what is generally true for society in Northern Ireland is not true for all parts. As Quintin Oliver argues in Chapter 6, involvement in European Union policies, funding and networking, has helped transform the voluntary sector, and this in turn has helped improve the quality of life for many. Action in the voluntary and social sector, greatly stimulated by European funding, has been largely cross-community, providing opportunities for both sides of the political division to work together for common ends outside the narrow confines of local politics. The significance of the European impact on the voluntary sector in Northern Ireland, not just through funding, is illustrated by the disproportionately large role played by individuals from the region in related European bodies. Similarly many of those prominent in voluntary organisations in Northern Ireland are now sitting alongside politicians in new forums being created as part of the emerging settlement.

Overall, Northern Ireland remains noticeably less Eurosceptic than the rest of the United Kingdom. While nationalist enthusiasm for things European partly explains this, even young unionist supporters, in the 18–24 age group, clearly favour the current European Union and the UK's membership of it. Moreover, the stated anti-European postures of many unionist political groups are combined with increased involvement in EU bodies and programmes, and unionists perhaps as much as others are inclined to look on the European Commission as a friend and potential ally in any dispute with national government over help for the region.

The violence and the associated political impasse in Northern Ireland, plus the strongly centralised nature of the United Kingdom state, have, for most of the period, tended to isolate Northern Ireland from the continuing debate on regionalism in Europe. As Thomas Christiansen recounts in Chapter 2, the past 25 years have seen the emergence of a formidable third level of governance in Europe – not reflected in the institutions and mechanisms of the European Union itself, but progressing radically in many of the member states, and now manifesting itself to some degree in all of those states.

Progress at European level has been slow. Twenty-five years ago the EC had no Regional Development Fund and no comprehensive regional development policy. Today, while the dream of a Europe of the Regions which flourished a decade ago has faded in the harsh light of reality, the idea of regionalism in Europe has strengthened. In many member states, including now the United Kingdom, there are moves towards administrative and representative devolution based on established regions. At European level, a significant percentage of the EU's budget is going to regional development through the Structural Funds. The creation of the Committee of the Regions, even though the committee falls well short of the expectations of regional enthusiasts, can be seen as formal recognition by the EU of sub-national authorities with democratic mandates. The principle of subsidiarity is enshrined in the European Treaties, and may yet be seen as significant in relations between national governments and regions as it is between the Union and member states.

As in many others areas, the experience of Northern Ireland in this regard is distinct. Twenty-five years ago it had just lost its regional parliament and government after half a century of administrative and parliamentary devolution. Since then it has lived in a regional twilight, retaining the full framework of a devolved administration, but governed by ministers of the central government, and legislated for by a United Kingdom Parliament in which its representation amounted to less than three per cent.

But even if special circumstances meant it did not share in what Thomas Christiansen calls the regional mobilisation in Europe – it was not demanding a return to devolution or autonomy, in fact the root of its problem was that it could not agree on what it wanted – Northern Ireland still experienced, in the European context, many of the problems confronting those regions which were indeed mobilised.

The winning of Objective One status under the reformed Structural Funds at the end of the 1980s prompted much concern about representation of Northern Ireland in Brussels. The energetic role being played at European level by the Republic of Ireland, the high-profile theatricals associated with European summits and other events in Dublin, plus the markedly more generous treatment of the Republic than almost anywhere else in allocation of European funding, combined to prompt questioning in Belfast as to whether Northern Ireland was doing as well as it might out of Europe, and as to how it was represented there.

In the European Parliament, Northern Ireland's three MEPs are unusual in that they together represent one unit, elected by proportional representation in a single multi-member constituency. But they also reflect the deep divisions within Northern Ireland, two of them being party leaders, and they all belong to different political groupings in the parliament. Only one of them, John Hume, belongs to a major political grouping (the Socialists) in the Parliament. Much media attention has focused on their joint actions, as in support of the Special Support Programme for Peace and Reconciliation, or on agriculture or other special issues, but they remain fundamentally divided. Northern Ireland currently has two members on the Committee of the Regions, and two on the Economic and Social Committee.

In principle, of course, Northern Ireland is represented by UK Ministers in the Council, and by the UK Permanent Representation in Brussels. As its own regional government is also part of the member state government, it has, in a sense, a uniquely direct input into UK policy. But as the members of the regional government are also members of the central government, and belong to parties with no base in the region, and represent constituencies outside the region, they are not thought likely to argue a Northern Ireland case against a UK national one.

The fixation with Dublin and its vastly superior access, as a member state in its own right, to the EU institutions was such that UK Government Ministers felt obliged, on more than one occasion in the inter-party talks in 1991–2, to remind Northern Ireland political parties that it was simply not possible to give the region a seat in the Council of Ministers.[10] Attention had also focused on the need for a Northern Ireland office in Brussels, and at one time at least three, if not four, separate initiatives were under way to establish such an office. In the end they all combined – political parties, local authorities, chamber of commerce and other special interest groups – to found the Northern Ireland Centre in Europe in 1991.

This began as a service point in Brussels for its founder organanisations, and was not a regional representation, as it had no official mandate to represent the region in any formal way, not being answerable to a regional assembly or administration. But as it has grown it has attracted financial support from government departments in Belfast and has taken its place as part of an expanding network of direct contacts between Northern Ireland and the institutions of the European Union. Such contacts have served Northern Ireland well, but in their diversity, lack of definition and low visibility they have also increased general uncertainty as to how, precisely, a region like Northern Ireland relates to the institutions of the European Union, and whether or not it is deriving full benefit from membership of that Union.

On the experience to date, it would seem that the European Union has not been able to solve Northern Ireland's problems – economic, social or political. Some expectations in this regard have been clearly unrealistic, and it would be unfair to blame the EU unduly. The idea put forward at the end of the 1980s, when a Europe of the Regions was much in vogue, that the solution to Northern Ireland was to make it a self-governing region within such a Europe assumed that a Europe of the Regions was imminent, and that the factions in Northern Ireland could agree on a form of self-government.[11] Similarly divorced from reality were the suggestions that giving the European Commission an institutional role in the administration of Northern Ireland would enable both sides to give allegiance to such an administration.[12]

In other regards the experience of Northern Ireland illustrates more routine shortcomings of the EU structure when it comes to dealing with regions and regional concerns. Thomas Christiansen describes the widespread mobilisation of regional interests throughout the member states over the period, and the substantial progress made within member states in meeting those concerns, and contrasts it with the inability of the EU itself to reflect this changed situation in its institutional structure.

At a more mundane level, in Chapter 7, which deals with the environment, J. S. Furphy points to the difficulties that can arise when a member state has to implement EC Directives not just at member state level, but also specifically by legislation at regional level. This can take time, and can result in the member state failing to meet the timetable in the Directive. Even though the Directive mechanism is designed to give flexibility to member states in implementing EC policy, it cannot always cope with the particular requirements of a region. This indicates a greater need for regional input into national policy formation towards pending European legislation, and also for more direct contact between region and European Commission in drafting legislation.

Up to now the EU's weakness in relating to and catering for the regions has been compounded as regards Northern Ireland by the province's lack of a devolved government elected by and responsible to the region. This may be about to change. In the context of broader devolution within the UK, the existence of devolved regional governments in Scotland and Northern Ireland, and possibly in Wales, with responsibility for a range of policy areas which come within the EU's mandate, will greatly increase pressure for change, both as regards the regional input into formulation of UK policy, and as to how regional interests can best be presented to the institutions of the EU.

In this the United Kingdom is catching up with other member states who have been wrestling with such problems for some time – notably Germany, Belgium, Austria and Spain. Pressure for change has come from below, from 'regional mobilisation', and the states of Europe have had to embark on programmes of reform and change to take account of these pressures within their own borders and within their constitutional arrangements. They may now have to make similar accommodation at European level – not by dissolving the member states in a Europe of the regions, but by finding mechanisms to reflect adequately the new regional reality within the institutions and mechanisms of the European Union.

The circumstances of the past 25 years have not been the best for a small, relatively poor and peripheral region to make its way in the European world. As these essays suggest, it is not easy to measure with any degree of accuracy the precise impact of European Union membership. Neither the economic and social, nor the political problems of Northern Ireland have faded away within a benign European embrace. In neither instance does this mean that European membership has had no impact, positive or negative, on Northern Ireland, for it is not possible to say what would have happened if the European dimension had not been there. But it does suggest that the European Union, as it operates now and has done over the past 25 years, offers no simple panacea for the problems of the regions.

Notes

1. *Fifth Periodic Report of the Social and Economic Situation and Development of the Regions of the Community,* (1994) Office of Official Publications, Luxembourg. (GDP data is based on 1989–91, unemployment on 1991–3).
2. *Regional Trends 33,* Office for National Statistics, London, 1998.
3. Figures for 1997 from *Northern Ireland Abstract of Statistics,* No 15 [NI Statistics and Research Agency] 1998.
4. *Regional Trends,* op. cit.
5. G. Gudgin (1998) 'The Economic Outlook and Medium Term Forecasts 1997–2001'. Paper given at NI Economic Conference, Galgorm Manor, Ballynena.
6. *NI Abstract of Statistics,* op. cit.
7. Gudgin, op. cit.
8. *NI Abstract of Statistics,* op. cit.
9. *Northern Ireland Estimates, 1997–8,* (1997) Department of Finance and Personnel, Stationery Office, Belfast.

10. Intervention by UK Government in Inter-Party Talks, June 1991. See transcript of Brooke-Mayhew talks published unofficially by Cadogan Group on Internet at *www.cadogan.org* 1997.
11. See, for instance, Richard Kearney (ed.), *Across the Frontiers: Ireland in the 1990s*, (1988) Wolfhound Press, Dublin.
12. SDLP proposal to Mayhew Talks, 7 May 1992, *Irish Times*, 13 May 1992.

2
A Region among Regions: the Wider View

Thomas Christiansen

The past 25 years have witnessed the emergence of a formidable third level of governance in Europe. 'Regionalisation', 'devolution', 'decentralisation', 'federation' – in different ways, such processes of territorial reform have made an active impact on the politics of each of the member states of the European Union. Given the gradual nature and often slow pace of this fundamental transformation in Europe, one might be tempted to speak of a silent revolution. But debates about territorial reform have usually been anything but quiet. Indeed, they are often marked by political conflict, which at times degenerates into politically motivated violence. But, considering the emotional charge and potentially centrifugal nature of conflict over territory and/or identity, it is rather remarkable that regionalisation in western Europe has progressed this far without a greater degree of fragmentation.

Regionalisation is usually a balancing act between the demands of the periphery for greater autonomy, if not independence, and the concern of the centre about the integrity of the state. Against this background, reforms can only be a compromise after lengthy negotiation, and often neither side will be entirely happy with the result. At the same time, any such territorial reform requires universal support and legitimation for its ultimate success. Against these odds, the developments of the past 25 years ought to be judged positively, even though there have been numerous problems and occasional reversals. In most states, the situation is anything but settled and further reforms are on the cards, but this merely testifies to the procedural nature of the phenomenon of regionalisation: rather than a single event, the reform of territorial politics is a process which implies the continuous re-negotiation of the balance of power between centre and periphery.

What is often seen as a zero-sum game in which the gains of one side are the losses of the other, has been made much more complex by the emergence of an influential further layer of governance – the European Union. In what is regarded as a system of multi-level governance,[1] power-sharing extends across a number of territorial levels and requires an increasing amount of co-ordination and co-operation, but also opens up new avenues of competition between regions and localities.[2] As part of this process, European integration has also created new paradoxes: on the one hand it has bound political actors on all levels more closely into policy-networks, but on the other, it has increased the credibility of calls for independence – the old goal of separatists – as such demands have become more viable within the framework of an integrated Europe.

In assessing these developments, this chapter first discusses mobilisation of the regions, looking at the variety of goals and means which have characterised such movements. The second section then moves on to study the growth of regional government – and growth here refers to both the number and the powers of regional authorities across Europe. The third section deals with the impact of European integration on the regional level. By way of conclusion, the chapter discusses the new opportunities for transnational relations which have arisen as a result of these developments.

Dynamics of regionalism

The mobilisation of regional awareness or identity has become a regular feature in European politics. But noting this does not say much about the sources, strategies and goals of regionalist movements, and it is with respect to these parameters that we see a wide variety of activism. The political terrorism of a group like the Basque ETA is worlds apart from the conservative politics of the Bavarian CSU, an established party which has governed its region since 1949. Both fall under the rubric of 'regional mobilisation' in that they draw their political support from the distinctiveness of their region, but differ fundamentally in terms of both the aims and the methods applied in order to achieve them. Naming two further regionalist movements – the PDS in Germany and the Lega Nord in Italy – appears to confuse the matter further: these are parties based less on a distinctive identity in a given region, but rather on the economic disparities in the state as a whole. And while the PDS campaigns for greater subsidies to support an East German population that largely sees itself as 'second class' in a united Germany, the success of the Italian Lega Nord is based in part on its opposition to the – allegedly too generous – redistribution from north to south.

Even these few examples demonstrate the diversity of regional protest in Europe. In categorising these movements, a distinction can first be made as to origins: on the one hand, there are movements based on a distinct ethnic or cultural identity in a particular region and, on the other hand, there are groups which seek to exploit economic disparity or geographic distance within states. At a time of revival of ethnic identities, and of a high incidence of territorial fragmentation in eastern Europe, it is tempting to view such mobilisation as the most important one. In western Europe, while protest based on distinct ethnic identities was at the heart of the first wave of new regionalist movements, arguments about economics were never far away.

In the late 1960s and the early 1970s, when there was widespread disenchantment with the bureaucratic and unresponsive nature of the modern state, those in ethnically diverse regions combined their protest against the nature of the state with the defence of the interest of particular communities or nations. As a result, political movements became noticeable in places such as Alsace, Brittany, Corsica, Flanders, Sardinia, Scotland and Wales.[3] In most cases, groups had been active in these regions for decades, but it was only during the 1970s that their growing membership and political significance propelled them into the limelight.

This indicative list contains a number of clues about the potential for mobilising regionalism. On the one hand, all the above regions contain people who regard themselves as distinct from the majority population in their respective state. In most cases, a separate language, its survival threatened, became the rallying point. But all of these regions are also peripheral – they are located not only geographically but also politically on the edge of their state. Critics will argue that they had been deliberately excluded from power. And, at a time when the economic fortunes of the continent were turning, these were also regions whose economic development was substantially below the national average. Cultural distinctiveness, political exclusion and economic deprivation combined in a powerful mix which helped to sustain regionalist protest movements and thus disturbed established party politics.

But ethnic identity as a catalyst also proved to be a double-edged sword for many regionalists. Language or religion may have provided clear markers of inclusion and exclusion for regional movements, but they also ensured antagonism with a state's majority population. In most cases, that majority population would also be present, as minority or even majority, in the region, and in such cases regional mobilisation turned out to be highly divisive. It also made it very difficult to gain overall legitimacy and support within the region, and indeed we see that in regions where nationalism is based on what has become a minority language – for example in Wales, Sardinia or Brittany – regionalist movements find it impossible to gain majority support.

However, in regions where a distinct language continues to be spoken by the vast majority of the population, we frequently have not only one successful regionalist party, but a number of them – as in Catalonia, the Basque Country, Wallonia and Flanders. In such cases, the competition between parties shifts to other issues, often reproducing the traditional Left–Right division in the party system. In such two-dimensional party systems the interesting question then is along which lines – identity or ideology – allegiance is stronger, but not one that can be answered conclusively.

The remarks about internal divisions already hint at the fact that regional mobilisation is often less a conflict between centre and periphery than a contest within the region. While there might clearly be a distinct identity, what that identity is will be open to debate. Deep-rooted divisions within the region might then lead to division and conflict, perhaps violence. In such cases – Northern Ireland is the prime example – the centre will be in a very difficult position: on the one hand faced with the need to intervene and pacify, on the other, trying to avoid charges of partisan support and oppression.

Matters are not made easier by regional conflicts with a cross-border element. In such cases, the already complex equation between opposed regional camps and the centre is further complicated by the 'foreign state'/'home country' to which a minority appeals for allegiance. But it has to be said that in post-war western Europe states have acted in a very balanced manner in this respect: moral support for minority rights has been combined with opposition to the use of force and co-operation between states rather than intervention in the politics of the regions. This is true for Ulster/Ireland, South Tyrol/Austria, South Slesvig/Denmark and North-Schleswig/Germany. As we witness the opposite of responsibility when it comes to the involvement of states in the minority issues in eastern Europe, this restraint by governments when faced with potentially explosive situations across their borders ought to be considered as one of the hidden successes of post-war conflict resolution in western Europe.

Moving from identity politics to economic issues, we can note again how one is frequently mixed with the other. Just as the protest of national minorities works best when coinciding with below-average (Scotland) or above average economic performance (Basque Country), so the mobilisation on the grounds of economic disparity is often usefully infused with identity. Thus the Lega Nord, which started out as the Lega Lombarda, made a very calculated attempt to combine its protest about corruption and 'unfair' redistribution in Italy with the purposeful construction of a 'Lombard' identity.[4] While such a construction might have failed, it has done the Lega's cause no harm to emphasise the difference between northerners and people from the south. Similarly, we can see how the PDS – not formally, but certainly *de facto* a regionalist party – gains public support in East Germany against a background of cultural alienation between East Germans and West Germans.

In terms of strategies, we should note the distinction already implicit in the reference to parties, movements and groups. Each of these terms implies the use of different strategies in support of the regionalist cause.[5] In most cases under review here, the presence of one or more regionalist parties indicates that the contest is essentially an electoral one. But in most cases, even what are now effective and well-organised political parties originally started out as political movements. Until the 1970s, only a small group of regionalist parties actually existed. The concern for a single issue – against the dominant trend of catch-all politics – meant that regionalist movements were largely absent from parliamentary life. In any case, electoral laws with their minimum thresholds and first past the post constituencies made it tremendously difficult for these movements to establish themselves.

But in many cases electoral isolation was turned into a virtue by making use of non-parliamentary means of opposition. This involved, on the one hand, demonstrations and civil disobedience, which for some turned out to be a slippery slope towards violence. But, on the other hand, there was greater concern for winning the moral argument, for framing the public's perception of various issues and, indeed, for maintaining the regional identity through language and symbolic action. One has to concede that, in this, regionalist movements were largely successful, as evidenced not only by the growth of government on the sub-state level, but also by the very survival of regional cultures and identities.

Once the dam of electoral isolation broke in the 1970s and 1980s, regionalist parties quickly gained representation at the centre on the basis of their previous symbolic, moral and discursive advances outside the parliamentary arena. From then on the major dilemma they faced was whether they ought to co-operate with parties committed to the continuity of the territorial arrangements of the state, or whether they ought to maintain a policy of principled opposition. Responses to this question have been varied, but one can say that involvement in parliamentary affairs often moderated regionalist demands.[6] Thus we can see how regionalist parties, while continuing a discourse hostile to the centre, frequently co-operate with regional or national governments. Examples here include the Lega Nord, Catalan and Basque nationalists, Plaid Cymru, and the PDS.

Though falling short of settling regional grievances, such co-operation was often vital in moving the process of regionalisation forward. Regionalist parties tend to be small players in the national arena (even if they are dominant in the region itself), but occasionally have had disproportionate influence when state-wide parties required minority support. The blackmail potential of such opportunities, together with their hold over the discourse on regional identity, has given regionalist parties a much stronger position than their electoral returns would lead one to expect.

The crucial question for regional mobilisation has mostly been the existence and the significance of a regional arena for political contest. Even under the most favourable conditions, regionalist movements and parties are, by definition, minority groups in the politics of the state. Thus, even if not hampered by restrictive electoral laws protective of the status quo, they remain structurally disadvantaged against the majority and thus have no hope of winning a 'democratic' contest. Ultimately, if fought at the centre, the regional cause remains condemned to defeat. Consequently, the following section looks at the emergence and the growth of regional government in order to understand the process of regionalisation in Europe.

The growth of regional government

Central and local government are fairly generic attributes of a functioning state. By contrast, regional government has not generally been seen as an absolute requirement of statehood, unless the state is constituted along federal lines. Instead, regional government is inherently contested, and it is this debate that much of the mobilisation discussed above has addressed. But it would be too simplistic to view the establishment of regional government merely as a response to demands from below. Central governments have had a variety of reasons to favour the creation of an additional tier of government between the local and the central. Apart from the need to respond to peripheral disenchantment with the distant centre, these reasons included efficiency gains expected from a decentralisation of welfare state administration, and social and economic regulation at that level.

While this might sound mundane, it raises a number of important observations. The first and foremost of these is that the emergence of regional government is as much, if not more, in the interests of the centre as it is in the interests of the periphery. Indeed, it is important to recognise that while regionalist mobilisation often aims at some loosely defined grey area between autonomy and independence, the establishment of regional government usually follows the blueprints of central decision-makers. The simple but fundamental point is that regional government, most of the time, works in the service of the centre, not in opposition to it. The frequent image of a regional level of government pitched against the centre in the defence of regional or local interests is a myth. A more useful image is that of central, regional and local government working as complementary institutions of the state, which are sometimes in conflict, but which are also co-operating on a regular basis.

More than simply common interests, central and regional levels of government are usually tied together by institutional interdependencies, through networks of policy-makers and by the intricacies of fiscal arrangements. Initially, this interdependence was often fairly asymmetrical, with the centre controlling most resources. But the history of the past 25 years has also seen the emancipation of regional government from the tutelage of the centre, and the achievement of a role in its own right in public policy-making. While the central decision-makers may have acceded to the creation of regional authorities in the anticipation that it would provide the framework for off-loading some of the more cumbersome and increasingly unpopular business of welfare statism, the history of regionalisation is also full of examples of unintended consequences. In some ways, the region in this process can be likened to Goethe's apprentice who has escaped the reins of his master.

Pressure from below, dependence on central government and the habit of institutions to develop a life of their own all combine to ensure that regional reform had progressed within a context of fairly continuous tension. Thus it is important to recognise, at the outset of the discussion of regional government, that this is not a question of 'a reform' in terms of a single event, even if decisive referendums, election results or the passage of crucial legislation might give that impression. Regionalisation is a process, both in terms of the development of regional mobilisation and in terms of the evolution of regional institutions.

Looking across western Europe, some patterns provide insights into the nature of this process. The first of these is that reform has often progressed through a number of stages: the decentralisation of central administrative services to regional institutions (which is also referred to as 'deconcentration'), the creation of consultative regional chambers (often consisting of local government representatives in the region), the direct election of regional assemblies, the transfer of competences to regional executives, and the assumption of legislative and fiscal responsibilities by regional governments. These stages do not necessarily occur in this order, nor is there any guarantee that there are no reversals – regionalisation cannot be seen as teleological exercise leading to a specific outcome. The premise of unintended consequences cuts both ways.

Having said that, the process of regionalisation in France, Italy and, now, the United Kingdom did follow roughly this pattern. In Italy, regional authorities were created in the 1970s, fulfilling a promise made in the Italian constitution some 30 years earlier. In France, the watershed came in 1982, when the incoming Socialist government of François Mitterrand passed the legislation for elections to regional assemblies. These had been in existence for about a decade in a purely consultative role. In both cases, the emphasis was on the deliberative aspect of regionalisation, and direct elections to regional assemblies were crucial in conferring legitimacy on the new level of government.

Executive functions were only gradually transferred to the new regions, and even then remained under the oversight of central administrative control. Most crucially, central governments in both Italy and France did not grant regional authorities fiscal autonomy in any meaningful way. In both countries the regional level's share of public expenditure has remained below 10 per cent of total governmental spending, and in both cases local government continues to be much more significant in fiscal terms.

Therefore, once the dust had settled on the apparently momentous reform of their intergovernmental relations, a hangover mood became discernible in both countries. The initial impact of regional reform turned out to be rather limited (Keating, 1988). With parliaments that were free to deliberate but unable to decide, and with regional executives which had to manage public policies, but were unable to raise the funds for any change in policy, regional reform came to be seen as a hollow promise. Responsibility without power meant that leading politicians refrained from competing for regional seat or office, and the wider public, in turn, demonstrated its lack of allegiance to this new level of government.[7]

As these reforms progressed during the 1970s and 1980s it became evident that regional government needed to engage two key aspects of post-war European politics: control over public finance and party political competition. The lack of either of these in the process of regionalisation explains to a large extent the limitations of reform in France and Italy.[8] At the same time, the importance of public finance and party politics goes a long way to explain the fundamental changes in Spain and in Belgium in the same period.

Belgium and Spain – both countries marked by linguistic and cultural diversity, and both facing political turmoil and the threat of violence during the 1970s – embarked on much more wide-ranging projects of reform than either Italy or France. In different ways, there were attempts to develop new solutions in order to square the necessities of expansive welfare state administrations with the demands of fragmenting societies. In both cases, the development of quasi-federal systems appears to have achieved a remarkable degree of stability against unfavourable odds. But, in both countries the price has been highly fragmented party systems and spiralling public debt.

But there are important differences. Spain was a special case in terms of its emergence from 40 years of Francoist rule. Franco's bloody suppression of minorities in Catalonia and especially in the Basque Country, and the violent backlash against it, made it imperative for the success of the entire project of democratic transition to pay special attention to the question of regional autonomy. But difficult choices were raised in the process: Basque and Catalan demands for a high degree of autonomy, even independence, had to be squared with calls from other regions, such as Andalucia, to maintain a strong link between centre and periphery in order to facilitate effective territorial redistribution.

The new Spanish constitution responded to these conflicting demands by offering regions – the newly created autonomous communities – differing degrees of autonomy and different speeds of getting there.[9] The resultant asymmetrical federalism which has developed in Spain is not without its problems, and throughout the 1980s and the 1990s the constitutional court has had a busy time resolving disputes arising from this uncharted territory. And while there has been a great deal of politically motivated violence in and beyond the Basque Country, the vast majority of people there, as well as in Catalonia, Navarro and Galicia, do support the current constitutional arrangements.

These minority regions have been governed by moderate regionalist parties which combine the defence of regional interests with a general support for the integrity of the Spanish state.[10] Therefore, despite the devolution of substantial chunks of governmental responsibility and fiscal authority to the regions, the survival of the Spanish state is not seen to be in danger. Indeed, in the second half of the 1990s, the reliance of governments in Madrid on the parliamentary support of Basque and Catalan parties has heralded an alliance between the centre and periphery. The challenge for decision-makers here is to manage the complexity of what has become a system of continuous bargaining, something which at the time of budgetary austerity in preparation for the European single currency has also become a threat to balanced public finances.

As in Spain, federal reform has turned out to be costly in Belgium. Here the breakdown of the traditional party system has been complete. There is now no party competing for votes across the country. Instead, practically all public authority and spending power has been handed to regional governments. Only foreign relations and defence remain as exclusive central responsibilities, and even these are largely in the hands of EU and NATO, respectively. Belgian territorial reform attempted to distinguish between people-related governmental functions (especially cultural and education policies) and territorial functions (such as infrastructure or regional planning). The former were entrusted to three 'cultural communities' (for the Flemish, Walloon and German-speaking groups), while for the latter, regional authorities were created in Flanders, Wallonia and the Brussels Capital region.[11] But the Flemish community, which had been the driving force in demanding a move away from the highly centralised Belgian state, had little patience for such distinctions, and territorial and communal functions were immediately fused in the creation of the Flanders region.

For most of the 1980s and 1990s, the UK stood out against the general trend towards regionalisation. Though much rocked by peripheral protest in the 1970s, which famously conjured up images of the 'break-up of Britain', referendums in Wales and Scotland in 1979 failed to win the required support – something which laid the issue of devolution to rest for a generation. Yet it did not go away: British politics combines a constituency, and therefore highly territorial electoral system with a very hierarchical administrative system, and as a result tension is rather pre-programmed. Scotland, especially, proved to be restless, and the way in which ostensibly unpopular policies were imposed on it under Margaret Thatcher did much to delegitimise central government.

Scotland and Wales, like Northern Ireland earlier, developed a party political landscape quite different from that of England, and many in this Celtic fringe identified less and less with Great Britain governed by the Conservative party. Institutional change was heralded by the 1997 general election, when the Tories not only lost their hold on power in the UK, but also all their seats in Wales and Scotland. Labour had promised to hold referendums in both regions (and in London) to decide whether parliamentary assemblies should be created there. The votes were affirmative – in Wales narrowly, in Scotland massively so. But the next step of setting up the assemblies and conducting the inaugural elections to them has not been very smooth, and much uncertainty surrounds the actual operation of the new bodies.

The Labour Party manifesto had also mentioned assemblies for the English regions, but the Blair government took no quick action in this respect. Local authorities in some regions in England had already established consultative 'assemblies',[12] and the Conservative government had started a process of deconcentration by creating regional offices in order to co-ordinate the activities of a number of Whitehall ministries. As in the Celtic fringe, the challenge in England is not the creation of a regional level of government, but the establishment of accountable and efficient institutions on that level. Replacing unelected quangos – quasi-non-governmental agencies – which had taken over much of the territorial management, with transparent and accountable regional government had dominated much of the campaign for Welsh and Scottish assemblies. Even though the English regions (with the exception of London which will elect a Mayor in 1999) have much further to go down that route, the direction suggests that also in England regionalisation is on the way.

The uneven pattern of regionalisation shows parallels with much of what happened elsewhere in the previous decades. The gradual and tentative establishment of, first, consultative councils in England (as in Italy and France), the much greater speed with which the periphery is moving towards autonomy in Scotland and Wales mirrors Spain's asymmetrical federalism and, in at least the Scottish part of the country, the eventual devolution of most government powers to the regional level follows Belgium. Against this picture of a country in the full flow of potentially far-reaching reform, it is little surprising that the talk of the break-up of Britain is back. What is more, opinion polls in Scotland suggest that there might actually be a popular majority in favour of independence.

Though operating to different timetables, all the larger countries are therefore in the process of regionalisation. Germany, a federal state since 1949, is a special case here. Clearly, the regional level of government – the *Länder* – is traditionally much more significant here than even the more powerful regions are in any of the other west European states. And yet, there have been secular trends in Germany indicating that an element of centralisation is built into the German federal system. Critics have gone as far as alleging that we are witnessing the emergence of a 'unitary federal state'.

The increase in the numbers and economic diversity of the *Länder* which came with unification might have been regarded as an endorsement of German federalism. Meanwhile, it has become evident that it is more difficult to reach agreement among 16 states than 11. The aftermath of unification also makes it more difficult for regional leaders to appear in a united fashion *vis-à-vis* the federal government.[13] On balance, there is actually little to suggest that the federal system as such is in danger, but there has been a distinct power shift from the *Länder* level to that of the federal government.[14]

Finally, a brief look at some of the smaller and/or less populated states shows that, there also, the creation and subsequent strengthening of intermediate, regional structures has taken place. The Scandinavian countries as well as Greece and Portugal have all developed some sort of regional government which was weak or previously missing from their political systems. In practically all these cases, reform has had a strong emphasis on administrative decentralisation, and there has been the familiar pattern of a new level of government competing with local authorities for media attention, public finance, policy competence and legislative authority. As in the case of England, it remains to be seen how much further these steps will be taken towards the creation of more powerful regional governments.

The unique conditions of each society and state structure demand specific answers in terms of public policy or institutional reform. But beyond these domestic pressures, European integration has challenged national systems across western Europe, even though the impact has been diverse. What has become evident in the past two decades is that

Europe matters for the territorial politics of its member states, which is why, in the following section, we take a closer look at the interaction between the two levels.

Territorial politics in the European Union

A useful distinction to be made in discussing the impact of European integration on processes of regionalisation is that between negative and positive integration. The former describes the removal of trade and other barriers between member states, while the latter concerns the development of common policies within a European framework. The EU has always pursued both these tracks of integration, but is generally seen as having been more successful in the negative than the positive integration process. The most important example of negative integration has been the Single Market programme, which was at the core of the Single European Act and aimed at establishing 'four freedoms' of movement for capital, goods, services and persons in the European Community. Through the 1992 programme of re-regulation at the European level, the competitiveness of European industry was to be enhanced, and massive changes in the economic structures of the member states were the result.

Though this process has mostly been discussed in terms of the implications it has had for national systems,[15] the impact on the regional level has been no less significant.[16] Where regional authorities had a role in economic and social regulation, they quickly became aware of the opportunities and the challenges ahead. Regions lost much of the protective layer of national non-tariff barriers, as much more flexible European Directives replaced national regulations and standards. In what has since been seen as the development of regulatory competition,[17] they had to engage directly with business and labour in order to maintain or enhance the competitive advantage of local economies.[18]

This development had a number of dynamic effects. First, regional actors, who since then had been fairly far removed from the decision-making centres in Brussels, began to realise the implications of European legislation and policy-making. The establishment of direct contacts, culminating in the opening of hundreds of regional lobbying offices in Brussels, was the result. Second, there were bound to be at least relative winners and losers in this process,[19] and regional actors discovered, sometimes painfully, the need to be responsive to market forces. This put the spotlight on the resources of regional authorities, something which includes not only their ability to provide potential investors with financial and infrastructural support, but also the networking capacity of regions.[20] By this is meant the co-operation of a variety of actors from the public and private sphere – local and regional government, investment agencies, trade unions, training organisations, chambers of commerce – with the aim of creating a favourable business environment.

Regulatory competition had a third dynamic effect, which was to generate a rethink in national capitals about the degree to which far-reaching powers needed to be devolved to regional governments. Given the uneven and asymmetrical development of regional structures across Europe, and often *within* states, the fairly sudden arrival of market-led re-regulation meant that regions with weak administrative structures, limited budgets and restricted regulatory capacity were bound to lose out in the process. As business was quick to exploit the opportunities of this new environment, national and regional governments had to follow suit in order to maintain the competitive edge.[21]

The result of these developments was a further push for territorial reform in Europe. In addition to the previous pressures of regional mobilisation and administrative decentralisation, regions were now also developing an important function in the sphere of social and economic regulation. But more than territorial competition, it was a question of transnational learning and inter-regional co-operation (of which more in the following section). In the process, the German *Länder*, whatever critical view of their capacity for action was taken at home, became the reference point for regional actors across the EU.

But regulatory competition in the Single Market was only one way in which the quickening pace of European integration impacted on regionalisation. Another, and perhaps better known aspect of the new relevance of Europe for regional politics was in the area of positive integration. In this respect, the EU's attention to economic disparity among regions was one of the major reforms of the past decade. The Structural Funds – combining the economic assistance of regional, social and agricultural funds – were fundamentally reformed in 1988, something which had a significant effect on a large number of regions.[22]

Part of the nature of this reform was to concentrate European assistance on the less developed regions, which meant that much higher amounts of money began to flow into areas designated as Objective One. Much of this area, which includes Southern Italy, Greece, Spain, Portugal and Ireland, had very weak, if any, regional structures, and a major effect of the Structural Fund reform was to act as a catalyst in the evolution of regional levels of government. The deliberative process preceding the adoption of Community Support Frameworks, the participation of regional and local actors in the implementation phase, and the need to absorb and co-finance the EU inflow of money all combined to generate a willingness and a capacity among regional actors to become much more responsible for public policy-making.[23]

It would be going too far to regard Structural Fund reform as the only cause of territorial reform, or the consideration of it, in Portugal, Greece and Ireland, but it certainly was one of the main driving forces. Together with the institutional requirements of EU funding, there was also new thinking in regional policy-making. This identified the ability of regions to generate endogenous growth, rather than the simple transfer of funds from the centre, as the key to successful regional development, and, under the concept of partnership, local, regional and national decision-makers as well as Commission officials worked together towards the necessary change in administrative culture.[24]

Given the massive impact of both negative and positive integration on the regional level in Europe during the 1980s and 1990s, it comes as little surprise that regional actors – with a greater degree of responsibility and self-confidence – also sought a greater role in the decision-making system of the European Union. Their demands, carried both to Brussels and to national capitals, succeeded in the creation, in 1995, of a new European institution, the Committee of Regions. Though in advance hailed as a future third chamber in the EU's legislative process, it is, in fact, a purely consultative body which provides the Commission, Council and Parliament with opinions on legislative proposals.

Given the high expectations, the role the Committee has actually played was bound to come as a disappointment to some. The Committee's 'opinions' proved to be a blunt tool in shaping new policy or legislation,[25] but, more importantly, the 222 Committee members discovered that the image of a broad alliance of regional and local governments, pitched against the European institutions and member state governments, had little semblance to the true state of affairs.[26] There was actually substantial disagreement among regions about a range of EU policies, in part due to the structurally different interests of regions, in part due to the underlying process of territorial competition, and in part simply due to the high number and diversity of regions in Europe.

Through their active and sustained engagement with the EU policy-making machinery, regional actors saw the potential for conflict as well as co-operation. There has been a growing recognition – for many a sobering experience – that in their nature regional interests are not fundamentally different from national interests, and that political survival for regional officeholders might require them staunchly to defend those interests within the EU context. Direct contacts between regional actors and EU officials, and the reliance on national clout in Brussels, both form part of the patchwork of strategies for regional interest representation. The overall result has been a complex picture of administrative and political interaction at a number of levels, blurring the traditional distinctions both between private and public and between inside and outside.

New perspectives for transnational relations

One of the more intriguing consequences of this process of Europeanisation of regional politics has been the growth of opportunities for horizontal co-operation. Negative integration, through the removal of barriers to trade, and positive integration, by funding cross-border co-operation between regions in different member states, have opened up a whole host of new possibilities. Regions in border areas have been quick to pick up these opportunities, and in the process have transformed the nature of transnational relations in western Europe.[27]

In the immediate post-war period, any direct contact between territorial units of neighbouring states was bound to be suspect, given the legacy of minority conflicts in the inter-war years. Whatever progress was being made with respect to customs barriers and the like, the physical divisions between states remained largely untouched. If anything, the process of European integration was also a way of restoring the territorial integrity of member states. There continued to be ethnic minorities seeking closer ties with another state – prime examples included the Irish nationalist minority in Northern Ireland and the German-speaking community in South Tyrol – but, as mentioned above, these had little currency with national governments, and concerned the European project even less.

Notwithstanding the general sensitivity about national borders, where regional authorities had a relevant administrative role, and where national governments were willing to contemplate bilateral contacts on the sub-state level, limited experiments in cross-border co-operation came about. These tended to concern very specific border issues such as environmental regulation of rivers or the facilitation of cross-border infrastructure. During the 1950s and 1960s, such projects mushroomed in the Benelux area and along the Franco-German border.[28] In the Alpine area, too, regional governments reached across borders, even the Iron Curtain, to deal with specific issues arising from transport, tourism and environmental protection.[29]

Whatever these early examples of cross-border co-operation achieved, they made precious little impact on the overall situation of regions in Europe. Over time, regions would gain more importance, first as arenas for ethnic mobilisation and electoral competition, and subsequently also as the locus of substantial governmental functions. But the development of external relations or private foreign policies remained very limited. Even between two countries as closely allied as Germany and France, and even after more than a decade of regionalisation in France, regional decision-makers have found the possibilities for cross-border co-operation across the Rhine to be very narrowly circumscribed by national officials.[30]

Against this background of the considerable limitations placed on any such moves the developments of the past ten years ought to be judged as significant achievements. Positive and negative integration in the European Union have opened up numerous possibilities for regions to co-operate directly with one another. The emphasis here is on *possibilities*, for it required regional actors to take up the challenge and use the opportunities which presented themselves. On the whole they have done so, and the result has been a very different map of territorial politics in Europe.

A massive rise in the number and size of cross-border co-operation initiatives is only one aspect of this. Funded through the EU's Interreg and Interreg II programmes, hundreds of regional and local authorities are now in the process of working within mutually agreed frameworks. Crucially, the rules of these programmes require not only co-operation, but the establishment of 'lasting institutional structures' in order to improve planning and public policy-making across the border. These initiatives have generated a strong response at regional level, indicating the need felt for this kind of work.

But the growth in transnational relations has not been limited to those regions sharing a common border. In what is more generally called inter-regional co-operation, regions with overlapping interests, even if located in different parts of the Union, have begun to work together. One obvious area for synergy here is the combined lobbying for specific EU policies, whether this is in the agricultural, technology or industrial field. But another aim of alliances such as the 'Four Motors', which brings together Lombardy, Rhône–Alpes,

Baden-Württemberg and Catalonia, is to enhance industrial co-operation, trade and investment among the private companies and public agencies in the respective regions.[31]

When it comes to facilitating opportunities for small and medium-sized enterprises or for technology transfer initiatives to gain a foothold in a foreign market, such examples of inter-regional co-operation are clearly valuable. At the same time, they remain liable to the limitations placed on regional co-operation, not only by national governments, but also by the structural differences and particular interests of regions themselves.[32] Much of what is done in terms of cross-border and inter-regional co-operation is therefore essentially symbolic in nature. Regional governments rarely have the tools, or the same tools, to enter meaningfully into making public policy jointly.

All this is only the beginning of a process which will require frequent rethinking, but which does open promising opportunities for most European regions. With the gradual expansion of regional powers within states, and with the frequent meeting of regional decision-makers in the European arena – first in the Assembly of European Regions and now also in the Committee of the Regions – there can be little doubt the future has in store more sophisticated co-operation, as well as more sustained competition between regions.

Even if co-operation on this level is often mainly symbolic, it still is a powerful testament to the way in which regions have come of age in Europe. Old sensitivities about the territorial integrity of nation-states might not have been forgotten, but they have taken second place to the grasping of economic and political opportunities in this new environment. The third level of government in Europe has been established, and the new dynamics of this system of multilevel governance are now being explored in greater depth.

Conclusion

Serious challenges are ahead for Europe's regions. In the economic field, monetary union and the eastward enlargement of the Union will both have a strong, though uneven, impact on regional economies. These processes will renew questions about the capacity of regions to compete in the context of European and global competition. Regions will need the right regulatory tools and resources to succeed in this future, but national and European institutions will also need to ensure that positive integration, the provision of support for weaker regions, keeps pace with negative integration, if the European project is not to alienate a large section of the third level.

Regional mobilisation shows no sign of diminishing, and in part this is related to the exposure felt in peripheral regions when confronted with the negative effects of liberalisation and competition. On the other hand, regions have developed the political structures to contain and respond to demands made, and regional mobilisation in Europe now is less a question of extracting favours from the centre, but of gaining majority support in the region itself, something surprisingly often more difficult to achieve.

While European integration and territorial reform have fundamentally altered the context of regional politics, regionalisation remains a process of tension. What has changed in the past 25 years is the way in which regional government has not only become accepted, but in fact has become an entrenched feature in the states of the European Union. After decades of sometimes noisy, sometimes quiet, reform there can be no doubt that regionalisation has changed the political landscape in western Europe. A brief look at the situation in central and eastern Europe, not to mention the Balkans, shows that it is in fact a decidedly western development.[33] Given the prospect of enlargement, the challenge for the next 25 years lies in the transfer of lessons from regionalisation in western Europe to the wider area, *without* ignoring the much more pronounced problems there of ethnic diversity, administrative culture and economic performance.

Notes

1. G. Marks (1993) 'Structural Policy & Multilevel Governance in the EC' in A. Cafruny and G. Rosenthal (eds), *The State of the European Community*, Lynne Rienner, Bonek Co, 1993.
2. M. Keating (1998) *Territorial Politics in Europe – A Zero-Sum Game? The New Regionalism. Territorial Competition and Political Restructuring in Western Europe*, EUI Working Paper RSC No. 98/39, European University Institute, Florence.
3. S. Rokkan and D. Urwin (1982) *The Politics of Territorial Identity*, Sage, London.
4. C. Ruzza and O. Schmidtke (1982) 'The Roots and Success of the Lega Lombarda: Dynamic Mobilisation and the Media', *West European Politics*, Vol. 16, No. 2, pp. 1–23.
5. L. De Winter and H. Tursan (eds) (1998) *Regionalist Parties in Western Europe*. Routledge, London.
6. J. Rasmussen (1990) 'They Also Serve: Small Parties in the British Political System', in F. Müller-Rommel and G. Pridhan (eds), *Small Parties in Western Europe*, Sage, London, pp. 152–173.
7. N. Kogan (1975) 'The Impact of the New Italian Regional Governments on the Structure of Power within the Parties', *Comparative Politics*, Vol. 4, pp. 383–406.

8. Y. Mény (1988) 'Radical Reform and Marginal Change' in B. Dente and F. Kjellberg (eds). *The Dynamics of Institutional Change – Local Government Reorganization in Western Democracies*, Sage, London, pp. 130–149. See also R. Leonardi *et al.*, 'Italy – Territorial Politics in the Post-War Years: The Case of Regional Reform', *West European Politics*, Vol. 10, No. 4, 1987, pp. 88–107.
9. J. Valles and M. Foix (1988) 'Decentralisation in Spain: a review', *European Journal of Political Research*, Vol. 16, No. 3, pp. 395–407.
10. F. Pallarés *et al.* (1994) *Non State-Wide Parties in Spain: An Attitudinal Study of Nationalisms and Regionalisms*, paper prepared for the ECPR joint sessions of workshops, Madrid.
11. E. Witte (1992) 'Belgian Federalism: Towards Complexity and Asymmetry', *West European Politics*, Vol. 15, No. 4, pp. 95–117.
12. A. Robinson (1992) 'Regional Identity in Tomorrow's EC and the Case of the North of England', *Economist Intelligence Unit European Trends*, Vol. 2, pp. 68–76.
13. C. Jeffery (1997) 'Farewell the Third Level? The German Länder and the European Policy Process' in C. Jeffery (ed) *The Regional Dimension of the European Union*, Frank Cass, London.
14. R. Sturm and C. Jeffery (1993) 'German Unity, European Integration and the Future of the Federal System: Revival or Permanent Loss of Substance' in C. Jeffery and R. Sturm (eds), *Federalism, Unification and European integration*, Frank Cass, London, pp. 164–177.
15. W. Streeck and P. Schmitter (1991) 'From National Corporatism to Transnational Pluralism: Organized Interests in the Single European Market', *Politics and Society*, Vol. 19, No. 2, pp. 133–164.
16. D. Mitchell (1992) 'Wales and the Political Impact of "1992"', *Contemporary Wales*, Vol. 5, pp. 7–23.
17. G. Majone (1993) *Deregulation or Reregulation? Policymaking in the European Community Since the Single Act*, EUI Working Paper SPS No. 93/2, European University Institute, Florence.
18. P. Cooke (1992) 'Regional Innovation Systems: Competitive Regulation in the New Europe', *Geoforum*, Vol. 23, No. 3, pp. 365–382.
19. D. Thomas (1996) 'Winner or Loser in the New Europe? Regional Funding, Inward Investment and Prospects for the Welsh Economy', *European Urban and Regional Studies*, Vol. 3, No. 3, pp. 225–240.
20. P. Cooke and K. Morgan (1993) 'The Network Paradigm: new departures in corporate and regional development', *Environment and Planning D: Society and Space*, Vol. 11, No. 3, pp. 543–564.
21. A. Amin and N. Thrift (1995) 'Institutional issues for the European regions: from markets and plans to socioeconomics and powers of association', *Economy and Society*, Vol. 24, No. 1, pp. 41–66.
22. G. Marks (1992) 'Structural Policy in the European Community', in A. Sbragia (ed.), *Euro-Politics*, The Brookings Institution, Washington, D.C., pp. 191–224.
23. R. Leonardi and S. Garmise (1992) 'Sub-National Elites and the European Community', *Regional Politics and Policy*, Vol. 2, Nos. 1–2, pp. 247–274.

24. P. Cooke, T. Christiansen and C. Schienstock (1996) 'Regional Policy and a Europe of the Regions' in P. Heywood, R. A. W. Rhude and V. Wright (eds), *Developments in West European Politics*, Macmillan, London.
25. M. Farrows and R. McCarthy (1997) 'Opinion Formulation and Impact in the Committee of the Regions', *Regional and Federal Studies*, Vol. 7, No. 1, pp. 23–49.
26. T. Christiansen (1996) 'Second Thoughts on Europe's Third Level: The European Union's Committee of the Regions', *Public Journal of Federalism*, Vol. 26, No. 1, pp. 93–116.
27. T. Christiansen (1998) 'Borders and Territorial Governance in Europe', in R. Kicker, J. Marke and M. Steiner (eds), *'Changing Borders: Legal and Economic Aspects of European Enlargement*, Frankfurt/M, Peter Lang Verlag, pp. 78–106.
28. M. Woltess (1994) 'Euregios along the German Border', in U. Bullman (ed.), *Die Politik der Dritten Ebene*, Normos, Baden-Baden, pp. 407–418.
29. J. Perulli (1992) 'The Political Economy of a "Mid–European Region": The Alpe Adria Community' in C. Crouch and D. Marguard (eds), *Towards creater Europe? A Continent without an Iron Curtain*, Blackwell, Oxford, pp. 154–169.
30. J. Scott (1989) 'Transborder Co-operation, Regional initiatives and Sovereignty conflicts in Western Europe: the Case of the Upper Rhine Valley', *Publius*, Vol. 19, No. 1, pp. 139–158.
31. S. Borras Alomar (1995) 'Inter-regional Co-operation in Europe during the 1980s and 1990s', in N. Soerensen (ed.), *European Identities*, Odense University Press. Odense.
32. F. Morata (1997) 'The Euro-region and the C-6 Network: the New Politics of Subnational Co-operation in the West Mediterranean Area', in M. Keating and J. Loughlin (eds), *The Political Economy of Regionalism*, Frank Cass, London, pp. 292–306.
33. E. Kirchner and T. Christiansen (1998) 'The Importance of Local and Regional Reform for Democratisation and Marketisation' in E. Kirchner (ed.), *Decentralisation and Transition: The Visigrad Countries*, Macmillan, London.

3
EU Membership and the Northern Ireland Economy

Graham Gudgin

Accession to what was then the European Economic Community in 1973 marked a turning point in the economic management of the United Kingdom, even though the changes were relatively small in the early years of membership. The same was also true of Northern Ireland as part of the UK, although in Northern Ireland the impact of Europe has been overshadowed by more dramatic changes for much of the subsequent period. While the last 25 years of economic development have occurred within an EU context, they have been in many ways more heavily influenced by the change from the semi-autonomous status of the Stormont years to direct rule from Westminster since 1972. Also over the last 25 years the economy has been influenced in important ways by the almost continuous history of political violence. By coincidence 1973 also proved to be the watershed in post-war growth. Rapid economic growth and full employment prior to 1973 changed with the OPEC oil price rise to a new period of slower growth and high unemployment. There has also been a series of fundamental changes in economic policy within the UK and Northern Ireland. The policy of privatisation has, for instance, changed the balance between public and private sectors, and new government agencies have been formed, in the case of LEDU (Local Entereprise Development Unit) with a lifetime matching that of EU membership.

This chapter reviews some of the key changes in Northern Ireland economy since 1973 and assesses the extent to which these changes might be ascribed to the impact of membership of the EU. This is a complex task, in part because economic change usually results from a wide range of influences. It is also complex because the impact of EU membership has occurred through a range of channels. The most important of these are:

(i)   European spending in Northern Ireland through the so-called Structural Funds and related European initiatives to promote economic and social development.
(ii) The influence of the Common Agricultural Policy, working through control of agricultural prices as well as direct expenditure on Northern Ireland farming.
(iii) The removal of barriers to trade, initially within the nine members of the Common Market in 1973, subsequently widened to its present fifteen members, and the completion of the 'Single Market' through a combination of standardised regulation and removal of unnecessary controls.
(iv) The indirect influence of membership of a large free trade area on the attraction of inward investment.

An assessment of the ways in which these changes have affected Northern Ireland is of intrinsic interest in understanding the development of a regional economy. While majority opinion in Northern Ireland has usually not viewed membership of the EU as a good thing, there is a widespread view among business, local administration and other areas of Northern Ireland life that European membership has brought substantial economic benefits, not least in direct financial inputs.

This chapter describes the development of EU regional policies and their application to Northern Ireland through the Structural Funds. The issues of scale and additionality are discussed in detail, and the nature of the policy interventions are illustrated along with a 'bottom up' attempt to measure their economic impact in one period, that of the Community Support Framework 1989–93. The chapter also briefly introduces some of the main issues in an assessment of the CAP, and briefly considers the impact of trade liberalisation.

The Northern Ireland economy in a European context

Northern Ireland is one of the most economically disadvantaged regions of the UK and ranks among the least prosperous in the EU. This disadvantage is usually measured by two key economic indicators, the level of GDP per head, and the unemployment rate.

GDP per person

GDP per head in Northern Ireland has varied between 80 and 87 per cent of the European (EC12) average, that is the EU average prior to the accession of Austria, Finland and Sweden (Figure 3.1). This figure is a little higher than the conventional European Commission measure which excludes Northern Ireland's share of UK output from the Continental Shelf (North Sea Oil). The European Commission figure in its latest Periodic Report on the Regions, for instance, is 75.1 per cent of the EC12 average in 1990.[1] On this latter measure Northern Ireland came 135th in the league table of GDP per head out of 176 EC12 regions.[2] Regions poorer than Northern Ireland were almost all in Greece, Spain, Portugal, the Republic of Ireland and especially East Germany. If these areas were excluded, Northern Ireland would have been the eighth poorest region of the 136 regions in the nine member states which constituted the EC when the UK joined. The poorer regions among this EC9 group of states were all in southern Italy and the Republic of Ireland.

The relative position of Northern Ireland's per capita GDP has hardly changed since pre-accession days. In 1970 for instance, Northern Ireland's per capita GDP as measured by the European Commission was 76.3 per cent of the EC9 average. At that date there were 13 poorer regions out of 105 regions in total. Of these ten were in southern Italy and two in France. The other was the Republic of Ireland.

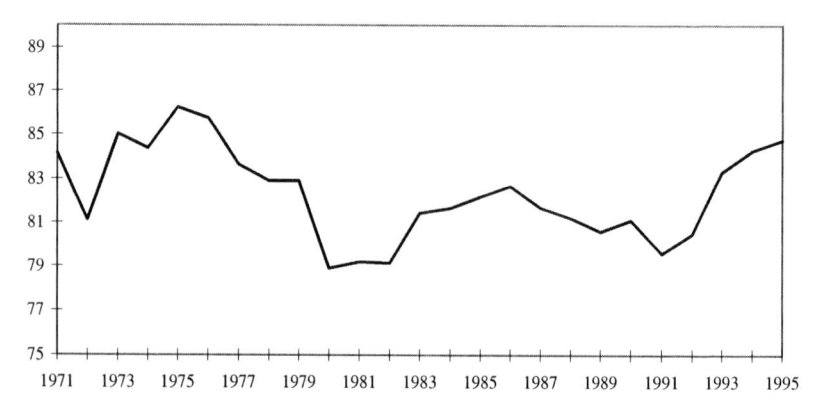

Figure 3.1 GDP per person, Northern Ireland, as percentage of the EC average (EC 12)
Sources: European Commission, *European Economy*, November 1989; *OECD Economic Outlook*, July 1997.

Although Northern Ireland's prosperity has grown substantially over the last 25 years, it has remained in much the same position relative to the rest of the European Community. What this tells us is that the per capita value of goods and services produced in Northern Ireland has remained steadily around 20 per cent lower than the EC12 average. This is not the same however as saying that standards of living are similarly lower. Fiscal transfers within the UK result in living standards in Northern Ireland which are higher than would be suggested by comparisons of per capita GDP. In 1995 for example, per capita GDP in Northern Ireland was 83 per cent of the UK average. However personal income was closer to the UK (and hence EC) average at 93 per cent. In addition, expenditure per head on most public services which contribute to living standards (for example, health, education, housing) was significantly higher in Northern Ireland than in Great Britain. Taking both of these aspects together implies that living standards in Northern Ireland are around 97 per cent of the UK average and hence close to the European (EC12) average.

The unusually large gap between per capita GDP and living standards as measured above reflects the very large financial inflow into Northern Ireland in the form of the so-called subvention from the UK exchequer, which finances around a third of the province's public expenditure. This is sufficient to finance high expenditure on public services, while taxes remain at UK average levels and incomes are boosted by social security and other transfers from Great Britain. (We might note in passing that Northern Ireland differs considerably in this respect from the Republic of Ireland where living standards are *lower* than indicated by per capita GDP because financial outflows in the form of repatriated profits are greater than the inflows, which come mainly from EU subsidies.)

There are many reasons for the relatively low level of GDP per head, but most important have been low productivity and high unemployment. Low productivity itself is due partly to a mix of industrial activities dominated by sectors which have relatively low levels of output per employee wherever they are located. These include agriculture, food processing and textiles and clothing. A second factor in low productivity is a tendency for individual industries to have relatively lower levels of output per employee compared to the same industries elsewhere in the UK or Europe. In agriculture and industry productivity is reduced by reliance on small producers. In the manufacturing sector prices and wages are reduced by the need to compensate for transport costs which are higher by around two per cent of output due to the Irish sea crossing.[3] High unemployment contributes to low GDP per head because of the larger number of people not contributing to output.

Unemployment

The second conventional measure of regional economic performance is the unemployment rate. Northern Ireland has had an extremely high rate of unemployment until 1997. In the era of virtual full employment in Europe prior to 1975 unemployment rates in Northern Ireland were close to six per cent of the workforce. Unemployment rose steadily after 1973 to reach a peak of almost 18 per cent in 1986, since when it has fallen equally persistently to a 20-year low of under eight per cent at the start of 1998 (Figure 3.2).

Unemployment was well above the European average in every year after accession until 1997 (Figure 3.2). Northern Ireland's unemployment rate averaged two percentage points above the European (EC12) average in the 1970s, but worryingly widened to seven percentage points by 1986. Since then the gap has narrowed, slowly at first, but rapidly since 1992, until in 1997 a historic cross-over occurred with Northern Ireland's unemployment rate falling below the EC12 average for the first time.

As Figure 3.2 indicates Northern Ireland has reflected the national UK trend for unemployment to fall during the economic recovery phase since 1992 (when the UK left the European Exchange Rate

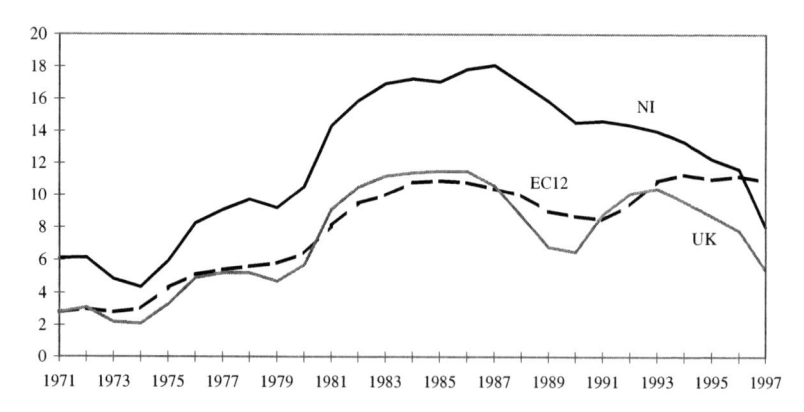

Figure 3.2 Unemployment rates in NI, UK and EC12 (percentage of labour force)
Note: NI Rates Standard to OECD Definition.
Source: *OECD Economic Outlook* Standardised Unemployment Rates.

Mechanism and sterling was devalued by 14 per cent). Unemployment in the rest of the European Community has, in contrast, remained at the historically high level of 12 per cent. One contributory factor has been the budgetary restraint necessary to meet the Maastricht criteria for entering the European Single Currency.

In the 1970s Northern Ireland had the twelfth highest unemployment of the 110 regions of the then member states (EC9).[4] By the early 1990s this position had changed little. Northern Ireland still had the eighteenth highest unemployment rate even though the number of regions had increased to 177 with the accession of Greece, Spain and Portugal.[5] Of the regions of the EC9 countries Northern Ireland was still the seventh worst, with the list of the high unemployment regions little changed in 20 years. Of the traditionally high unemployment regions (in southern Italy and Ireland with the addition in the 1980s of much of Spain and Greece) only Northern Ireland has made the transition to a low unemployment region. By 1997, Northern Ireland's unemployment rate was three percentage points below the EC12 average.

Since August 1996, unemployment in Northern Ireland has fallen particularly rapidly, faster than in Great Britain, with the number of jobless falling by a third in 12 months. During this year 28 000 left the unemployment register while only 9000 jobs were created. The main reason appears to have been the administrative reforms associated with the introduction of the UK Jobseekers Allowance (JSA) in mid-1996. It is likely that a substantial proportion of those leaving the register may have been fraudulent claimants, and if so, it suggests that real unemployment may not have been as high in some earlier years as reported at the time. Even so it seems likely that unemployment rates were nevertheless above the European average in every year prior to 1997.

Offsetting this over-reporting of claimant unemployment is a probably more extensive under-recording due to a high degree of concealed or unreported unemployment. One of the main reasons has been a major growth of those on Incapacity Benefit. Numbers were stable at 40 000 until the mid 1980s but have since increased to almost 100 000 over a period in which health standards are generally believed to have improved (although problems of drug abuse, and the closure of mental hospitals may have led to rising numbers). This tendency is noted throughout the UK especially in areas of high unemployment.[6] In Northern Ireland it seems possible that 40–50 000 people, who 15 years ago may have been viewed as fit for work, are on this benefit and are consequently excluded from the official unemployment count. If so, the real rate of unemployment in Northern Ireland might be over

12 per cent and still above the European average. However it is not known whether similar under-recording also occurs in other member states.

Growth in GDP and jobs

The reasons for Northern Ireland's tradition of high unemployment are not those usually suggested. Although Northern Ireland is a low income region, it is not a low growth region. Indeed its low wage level contributes to rapid growth as might be expected. Northern Ireland's GDP has usually expanded at a rate similar to or slightly faster than the European average (Figure 3.3). This is true since the early 1980s, but is especially true of the 1990s, when Northern Ireland has grown almost twice as fast as the EC12 average.

The superior growth of Northern Ireland is even more evident measured in employment (including the self-employed). Employment in Northern Ireland expanded at close to the European average until the late 1980s. Since then it has grown very much faster (Figure 3.4). This growth advantage, which has been most obvious over the 1990s amounts to an extra 75 000 jobs in Northern Ireland. Although Northern Ireland's employment growth was underpinned by the expansion of the public sector in the 1970s, in the 1980s it is clearly the private sector which has led the way. Relatively low wages and a generous regime of government grants and subsidies have made the manufacturing

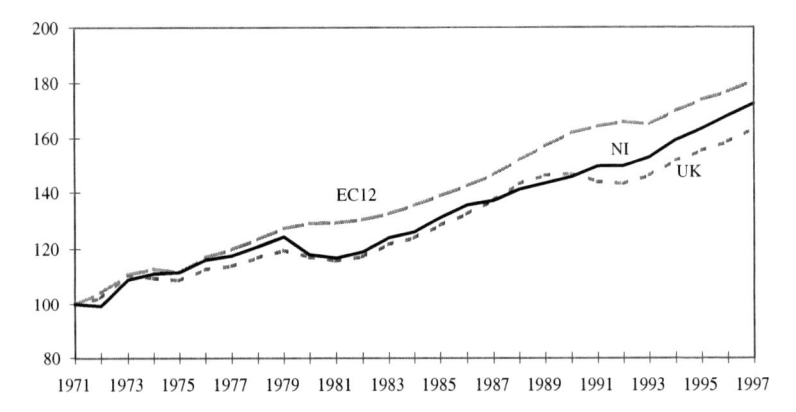

Figure 3.3 Growth of GDP in Northern Ireland, UK and EC12 (1971 = 100)
Sources: European Commission, *European Economy* November 1989, Table 10; *OECD Economic Outlook*, July 1997.

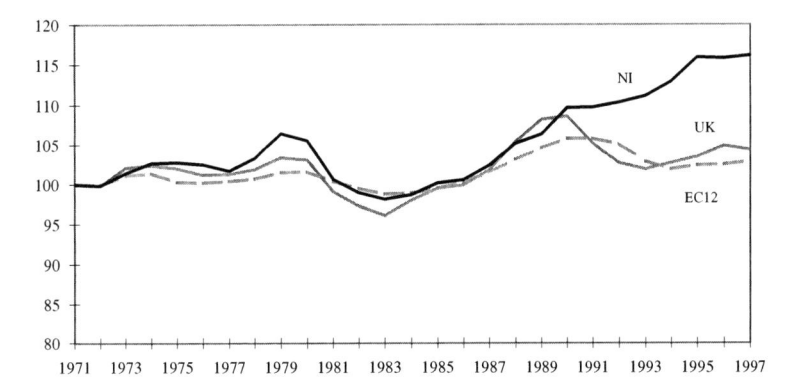

Figure 3.4 Growth in employment in Northern Ireland, UK and EC12 (1971 = 100)
Sources: European Commission *European Economy*, November 1989, Table 1 (1971–87); *OECD Employment Outlook*, July 1995.

sector highly competitive and exports have grown rapidly in recent years.[7]

Since Northern Ireland's record of job creation has been generally better than the European average, it might have been expected that unemployment would have been relatively low through much of the period of membership. In this case Northern Ireland might have been like parts of Portugal where unemployment is low even though per capita GDP is also well below the European average. However Northern Ireland has a particularly high rate of natural increase in population with the highest birth rates in Europe. In this respect it is similar to the Republic of Ireland, but not to the predominantly Catholic countries of southern Europe which have low birth rates. The Republic's birth rate was formerly Europe's highest, but has been falling rapidly, and since 1986 has been below that of Northern Ireland.

Even with a relatively good record on job creation by European (although not world) standards, the growth of employment has not been sufficiently rapid to employ all of the natural increase in population of working age. The result has been that net out-migration has been necessary to prevent unemployment from rising to ever high levels. The statistical evidence is that the rate of out-migration is heavily influenced by the extent to which the local unemployment rate exceeds that in Great Britain. When this unemployment gap narrows the level of out-migration tends to diminish and population begins to rise rapidly. As a consequence there appears to be a long-term equilibrium in which Northern Ireland's unemployment rate remains at least three percentage points above that in Great Britain.[8]

European Structural Funds

The accession of the UK in 1973 along with its close trading partners Denmark and Ireland, led to only small changes to the established structure of the EEC, the main innovation being the introduction in 1975 of an explicit regional policy instrument, the European Regional Development Fund (ERDF), charged with assisting the development and restructuring of poorer regions. Previous adjustment funds, the Social and Agricultural Guidance funds, had not been strongly targeted at poorer regions, and indeed only the Mezzogiorno and the French overseas territories constituted severely disadvantaged areas. The accession of the UK, with a number of lagging regions (especially Northern Ireland), and the Republic of Ireland increased the rationale for a specifically regional fund. At the same time, the dominance of the CAP in EC expenditure meant that the UK needed to insist on alternative support funds to reduce its net financial contribution to the EC.

Since 1975 EU expenditure has continued to be dominated by the CAP although its share in total spending has fallen from 70 per cent in 1975 to 50 per cent in the 1990s. Together with the CAP Guidance fund, the European Social Fund (ESF) and the ERDF constitute what are generally known as the Structural Funds.

Northern Ireland has always been a priority region for EU Structural Funds spending. This was true in the period prior to the Single European Act when Structural Funds were largely allocated to member nations on a quota basis. The UK quota reflected the extent of the UK's regional problems, most prominent of which were those of Northern Ireland. As a result Northern Ireland received 9.6 per cent of the UK's ERDF funds in the period 1973–87, and 17.0 per cent of its ESF funding.[9]

Since 1988 Northern Ireland has been an 'Objective One' region along with Greece, Portugal, most of Spain, the Republic of Ireland and Southern Italy. Although Northern Ireland was above the 75 per cent of GDP threshold for inclusion in the Objective One category throughout the period, it was nonetheless included, pushing Northern Ireland's share of UK Structural Fund receipts up to 16.4 per cent and its share of the EU total up to 1.2 per cent.[10]

Although 'Objective One' status qualifies a region for the highest rate of EU spending, it does not result in a uniform per capita rate of support. Northern Ireland's allocation of Structural Funds has been around 70 per cent of the EU per capita average for Objective One regions since 1989:[11] Northern Ireland's allocation has also contrasted sharply with that of the Republic of Ireland which was three times larger per capita for 1989–94 and twice as large subsequently.

Since 1988 there have been two multi-annual programmes, the first for 1989–94 and the current programme covering the period 1994–9. In addition to the main Structural Funds, the ERDF, ESF and EAGGF (Guidance), Northern Ireland has also received finance from most of the Community Initiatives. The amounts of money for these initiatives have generally been relatively small, with larger allocations going to INTERREG and STAR, which financed the installation of an optic fibre cable ring by BT in Northern Ireland.

The province has also benefited from two exceptional schemes. In 1979 Belfast was selected, along with Naples, as one of two beneficiaries of an Integrated Operations programme, a scheme designed to tackle the Community's most severe urban problems in a more integrated and intensive fashion than had occurred hitherto. This led indirectly to special funding for Belfast under an Urban Renewal Regulation of 1983, providing £62m (£101m at 1996 prices) to finance physical infrastructure schemes.

In August 1995 the European Commission approved expenditure of 300m ecus (£190m) for the period 1995–8 with a possible extension for two further years under a Special Support Programme for Peace and Reconciliation (SSPPR), launched to support the paramilitary cease-fires of August and November 1994. This is augmented by an additional 146m ecus (£90m) from the UK and Irish governments, with 80 per cent of total resources going to Northern Ireland and 20 per cent to the border counties of the Republic. The SSPPR continued despite the breakdown of the IRA cease-fire in February 1996, and in 1997 was extended to the year 2000.

Levels of expenditure

Total EU expenditure on Structural Funds in Northern Ireland rose steadily in real terms through the 1970s to reach £100m pa in 1996 prices by 1980 (Figure 3.5). Real expenditure doubled in the early 1980s in part due to special aid for urban renewal in Belfast. Since then total spending has fluctuated between £100–200m per annum (in 1996 prices) and has averaged £170m. These rather large fluctuations in part reflect the timing of programmes with lower spending at the start of new programmes, as in 1990 and 1994, with a build up once the programme becomes fully operational.

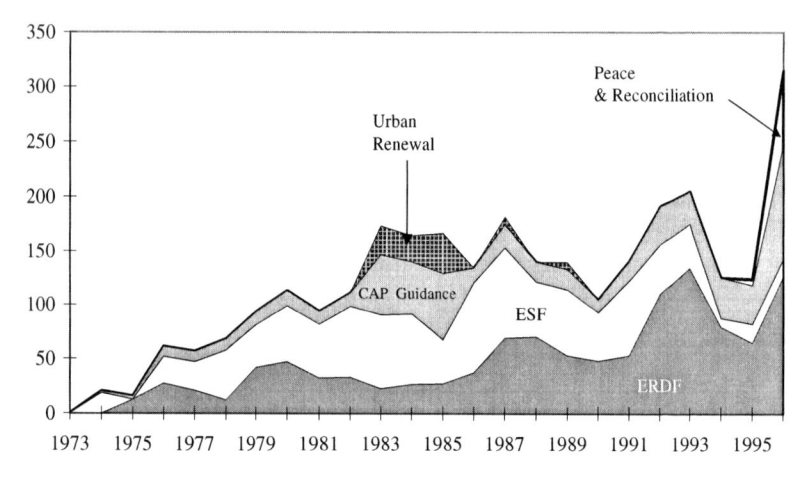

Figure 3.5 EC Structural Funds (£m 1996 prices)
Source: NI Appropriation Estimates, DFP.

Table 3.1 Average annual expenditure by EC Structural Funds in NI (£m 1996 prices)

	1973–80	1980–89	1989–94	1994–96
ERDF	19.1	40.5	79.7	90.0
ESF	25.6	62.0	52.5	14.1
EAGGF Guidance	7.6	18.1	21.1	32.6
Urban Renewal	–	10.6	1.3	–
Peace & Reconciliation	–	–	–	24.6
Total	52.4	131.6	155.1	163.7

Note: ERDF includes Community Initiatives. Figures are for financial years starting at 1973/74.
Sources: NI Appropriation Accounts (1987–97), DFP; Trimble (1990).

The 1994–9 programme received an allocation of 247m ecus per annum (£185m in 1996 prices) plus an estimated £21m for Community Initiatives. This was almost double the 1989–94 programme allocation, and by 1996 actual receipts had reached almost £250m (Figure 3.5). On top of this £68m was received from the Special Support Programme for Peace and Reconciliation in 1996, taking total structural fund receipts above £300m for the first time. This level is likely to be maintained throughout the remainder of the 1994–9 programme and the 1994–9 Peace and Reconciliation programme. It is unlikely that the Peace and Reconciliation programme will be extended for a further period. Moreover the Agenda 2000 decision to interpret the 'Objective One' qualifying criteria strictly means that Northern Ireland is unlikely to qualify. The promise of generous transitional funding will prevent a sudden fall in funds, but the decline from a level of £300m per annum is likely to be steep.

It is a complex matter to assess the economic impact of almost any aspect of public expenditure, and this is true of EU Structural Funds. The magnitude of the expenditure in relation to the size of the economy must be taken into account, as well as the nature of the expenditure, and there are issues of secondary or 'knock on' effects. Additionality is also an important issue when considering any EU funding. In fact there are two separate aspects to the additionality problem. Firstly, we must consider macro-economic additionality – whether EU funds are additional to Northern Ireland, or whether instead the same spending would have been carried out by the UK Government in the absence of EU support. Secondly, whenever spending involves grants or subsidies for private companies or individuals it is necessary to assess whether the expenditure is likely to have been financed by some alternative source in the absence of the EU assistance. This can be termed microeconomic additionality. Finally, there are issues of displacement, when for instance the grant aided expansion of a company in Northern Ireland displaces activity from another local company, leading to a diminution in the total impact.

Magnitude of Structural Fund spending

EU spending on Structural Funds in Northern Ireland averaged around £150m pa (in 1996 prices) through much of the 1980s and 1990s, although it has risen to £250m pa since 1996 with the addition of the Peace and Reconciliation programme. These sums represent a significant but small addition to total spending in Northern Ireland. They amount to £100–170 per annum for each person in the province, but constitute only 1.7 per cent of GDP even in 1996. Perhaps the most informative comparison is with the totality of public expenditure in Northern Ireland. This is shown in Figure 3.6 where it can be seen that EU Structural Funds comprised around 2 per cent of Northern Ireland's public expenditure through the 1980s and 1990s rising to 3 per cent in 1996.

This comparison is carried one step further in Figure 3.7, which compares EU Structural Funds spending with the main sources of finance for public expenditure. Estimated tax revenues raised within Northern

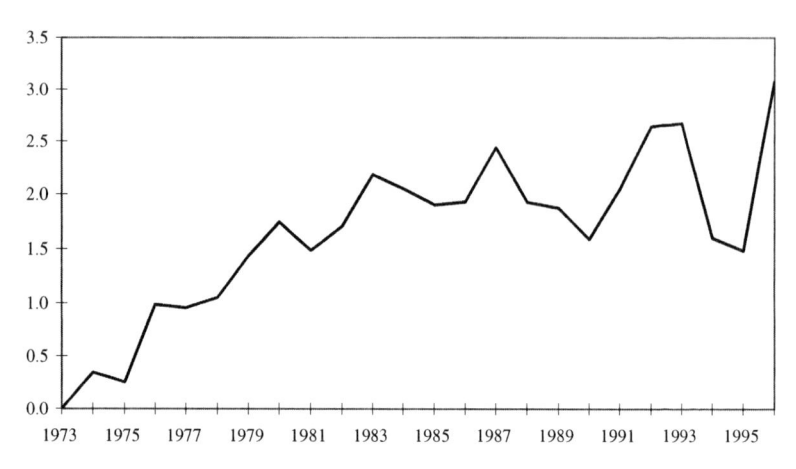

Figure 3.6 EC Structural Funds as percentage of public expenditure in Northern Ireland
Sources: NI Estimates, DFP; NI *Annual Abstract of Statistics*.

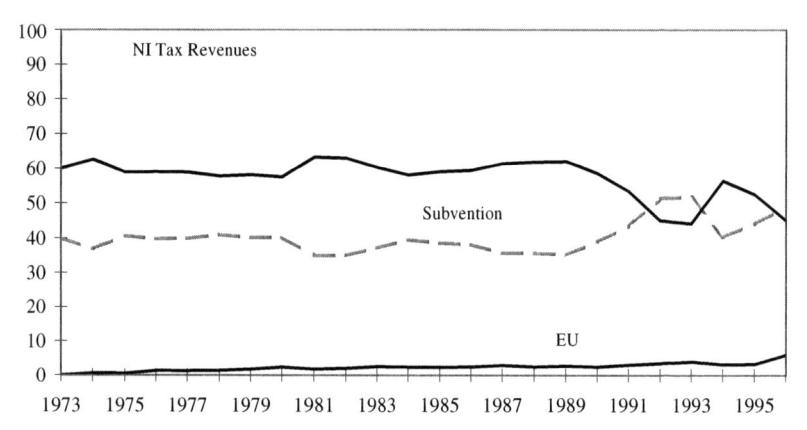

Figure 3.7 The financing of public expenditure (percentage of public expenditure)
Sources: NI *Annual Abstract of Statistics*; NI Estimates 1987/88; Parliamentary Questions on NI Subvention; Trimble.

Ireland have usually supplied 60 per cent of total public income, falling to 50 per cent through much of the 1990s. The subvention from the UK exchequer has contributed most of the rest of government income in Northern Ireland, running at around 40 per cent, until the 1990s when it temporarily exceeded locally raised revenue as a source of funds and has averaged closer to 50 per cent. In fact the subvention itself can be considered to consist of two sources of finance. Most of the subvention consists of a transfer of tax revenues from Great Britain to Northern Ireland, the remainder is Northern Ireland's share of UK Government borrowing. The tax transfer has been relatively stable for 25 years at close to £2bn per annum (in 1996 prices). Northern Ireland's share of the UK deficit has usually been much smaller, at around £0.3bn per annum (in 1996 prices). In the late 1980s it was temporarily negative as the UK budget went into surplus, but in the early 1990s it rose to an unprecedented degree, and in 1993 was over £1.5bn (in 1996 prices).

The important comparisons for current purposes are that the UK tax transfer has on average been 15 times as large as EU Structural Funds, while Northern Ireland's share of the UK public deficit has usually been at least twice as large. The Structural Funds share of all *external* sources of finance for public expenditure in Northern Ireland was close to 7 per cent in most years since 1980, rising to 12 per cent in 1996 (Figure 3.8).

Although EU Structural Funds spending represents only a small proportion of total public spending in Northern Ireland, it can be argued that its impact on economic growth is much larger than this because most structural funding is spent on investment for growth whether in physical infrastructure, in company development (including R&D), or in the enhancement of human capital. A more accurate comparison in line with this approach would be to compare Structural Funds spending with the total expenditure of the main Northern Ireland spending

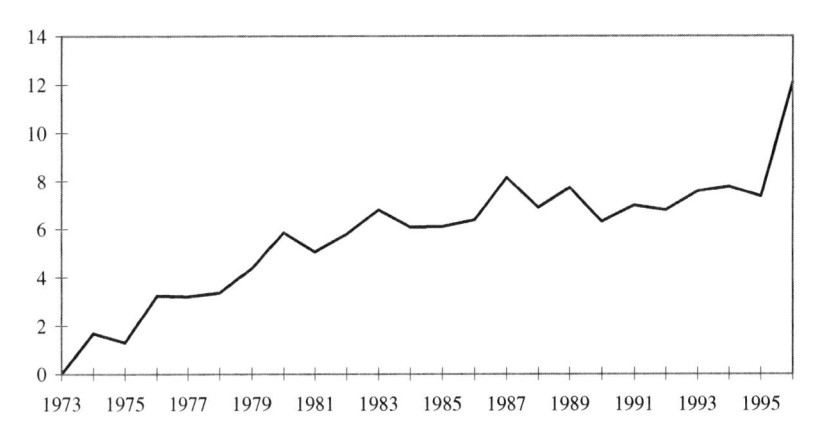

Figure 3.8 EC Structural Funds as percentage of external funding of public expediture in Northern Ireland
Sources: Northern Ireland Estimates, DFP; NI *Abstract of Statistics*.

programmes concerned with this economic development, including the development of transport and other physical infrastructure. If we take the relevant programmes to be Agriculture, Fisheries and Forestry, Industry Energy Trade and Employment, and Environment, the EU Structural Funds contribute a quarter of this spending.

Since spending on these programmes collectively is currently £1.0bn and much higher per capita than in Great Britain, the EU contribution can be viewed as substantial and important. However the fact that Structural Funds comprise only 2 per cent of total public spending suggests that this might relatively easily be replaced by alternative sources of revenue, or by a reallocation of priorities within the public sector budget total.

The question of the additionality of EU Structural Funds over UK Government expenditure has been a matter of continuing controversy. This has been true both for relations between the European Commission and UK Government, and internally within Northern Ireland as a difference between those who view EU intervention as an important factor in local economic development and those who do not.

The principle of additionality is an important part of EU regional policy. The EU requires a commitment from member state governments to ensure that Structural Funds supplement rather than replace national expenditure (Council Regulation 724/75). This is, in essence, an issue of sovereignty or at least political control, with the EU insisting that the Structural Funds should be spent as additions to national expenditure plans and in a way which meets the approval of the Commission.

The official UK approach has been that anticipated EU contributions are taken into account in the process of determining the level of expenditure on the various government programmes, and in consequence public spending is higher than it would otherwise be.[12] In the case of Northern Ireland, the UK Government assertion is that it anticipates the level of Objective One funding from the EU in setting its expenditure plans for Northern Ireland as part of the normal annual planning cycles for the following three years.

The question of additionality then comes down to whether the UK assertion, outlined above, is more than a fiction to circumvent EU rules. This is a matter which cannot be definitively proven either way. The UK Government's assertion of additionality at the level of the UK as a whole is credible in one sense and is accepted by the European Commission in its annual assessment of compliance with Structural Funds regulations. This sense is that UK Government expenditure plans are made in the light of expected revenue (and hence the need to borrow) and anticipated receipts from the EU are part of these revenue expectations. However this is not the same as saying that the Structural Funds are additional to Northern Ireland. As far as government in Northern Ireland is concerned, expenditure plans are published (and revised annually) with local Departments subsequently charged with offsetting as much as possible of the planned UK expenditure through applications under the various EU Structural Funds rules. Since 1988 this has involved Northern Ireland Departments preparing budget programmes for EU funding in five year cycles. As far as Northern Ireland is concerned the task is to recoup from Brussels as much as possible of public expenditure already planned by the national authorities.

The question of the additionality of EU funds to Northern Ireland should also be seen in the context of the UK's net contribution to the EU Budget. The UK has been a net contributor to the budget in virtually every year since accession. Although the UK net contribution is very small as proportion of GDP (Table 3.2), there is a strong national advantage in maximising receipts to offset the contributions established under treaty obligations at just over one per cent of GDP. Since the UK Government's paramount aims have been to reduce public expenditure in total, this means that not only must receipts from the EU be maximised but they must also not be permitted to add to existing expenditure plans except in the sense described above. This principle of reducing public expenditure has been strongly adhered to throughout the period of Conservative Government in the UK from 1979–97. There are no signs yet that the principle is to change under a Labour administration.

Table 3.2 UK net contribution to the budget of the EC (£m 1996 prices)

	1976	1981	1986	1991	1996
UK Payment	1807	4312	4396	3786	6722
(% of GDP)	(0.4)	(0.9)	(0.7)	(0.6)	(0.9)
UK Receipts	964	3568	3342	3182	4390
(% of GDP)	(0.2)	(0.5)	(0.6)	(0.5)	(0.6)
Net Payments	845	1044	1054	536	2332
(% of GDP)	(0.2)	(0.3)	(0.1)	(0.1)	(0.3)

Note: UK Receipts include the Fontainebleau Rebate negotiated in 1984.
Source: UK National Income and Expenditure.

It can be argued that the current arrangements do not maximise receipts from the EU, either for Northern Ireland or for the UK as a whole. A gross rather than net approach from HM Treasury could result in larger receipts from the EU. In this case Northern Ireland expenditure plans would incorporate an expected level of EU receipts. Northern Ireland Departments would then be free to bid for whatever EU funds they could, and would be allowed to retain any excess over and above the level anticipated by the Treasury. Since there would now be a genuine incentive to raise the level of receipts, we might expect that the actual level would be higher. The difference in the degree of local self-interest in maximising EU receipts may help to explain why per capita receipts in the Republic of Ireland have been two or three times higher than in Northern Ireland even when both were Objective One regions, and before the Republic began to benefit from the Cohesion Fund.

The policy of non-additionality was dented in 1992 by the Kerr–Millan Agreement on additionality which followed a refusal by the European Commission's Directorate General for Regional Affairs to release agreed UK funds for the RECHAR Scheme to restructure declining coalfield areas. Previously, the UK Government had accepted the funds (like all other Structural Funds receipts), but not increased the budgets of the GB local authorities for which the funds were intended. Following the Kerr–Millan Agreement the UK Government agreed to increase local authority spending in total although not necessarily in the target areas.

There is little sign that the Kerr–Millan Agreement made any substantive change to additionality in Northern Ireland. However, one result has been that the government in Northern Ireland now calculates its own contribution to projects assisted by EU funds (the so-called 'PE cover') and publishes these calculations in a table in its annual Public Expenditure Report. These figures are not informative to most commentators (including the House of Commons Select Committee on Northern Ireland Affairs) and can be viewed as essentially cosmetic.

The non-additionality of EU funds applies to the majority of EU Structural Funds receipts in Northern Ireland, including Community Initiatives. However it appeared not to apply also to most of the spending for Urban Renewal in Belfast in the early 1980s. The other major exceptions to the rule of non-additionality are the following:

(i) The Special Support Programme for Peace and Reconciliation – An undertaking was given by Prime Minister John Major from the inception of this programme in 1994 that funds for this programme would be additional to existing government plans.

This included not only the 240m ecus allocated from the Structural Funds for Northern Ireland, but also the UK Government's matching funding of 81m ecus. Incidentally, the firm undertaking of additionality implies that this is an exception to the normal treatment of EU funds in Northern Ireland. This treatment was a clear exception to previous practice including the refusal to relax the non-additionality policy in 1986 in respect of special EU measures proposed to support the Anglo–Irish Agreement.

(ii) Expenditure for charities and industrial training boards and certain public corporations.

With these exceptions it seems clear that the policy of non-additionality implies that EU Structural Funds spending in Northern Ireland does not result in an increase in public spending. In as far as this is true there is no direct economic benefit to the province from receipts from the Structural Funds. This conclusion would apply to the ERDF, ESF and EAGGF (Guidance). As explained below, it does not apply to CAP spending outside the Structural Funds, for example EAGGF (Guarantee). However the final test of additionality would come if EU funding were to be withdrawn from Northern Ireland. This is likely to begin to happen from 2000 onwards. The Peace and Reconciliation programme will almost certainly not be continued, and the Structural Funds will begin to be phased out.

Even though EU Structural Funds spending in Northern Ireland should be regarded as largely non-additional as *EU funds*, the spending itself clearly has an impact on the economy irrespective of the source of finance. One of the administrative innovations which has accompanied EU Structural Funds since the 1988 reforms has been an intensive set of evaluations. Each operational programme (1989–93) or sectoral programme (1994–9) within the successive structural plans is now evaluated at the planning stage, at mid-term and after completion. These evaluations are usually independent of government, and are more comprehensive than undertaken by the UK government for equivalent programmes. They provide a basis for the evaluation of the impact of Structural Funds spending ignoring the question of whether this spending would or would not have taken place in the absence of EU intervention.

The various evaluations of the 1989–93 Northern Ireland Community Support Framework Programme (CSF) are summarised in Gudgin.[13] This study uses the individual evaluations of the operating programmes to estimate an aggregate or macro-economic impact on the Northern

Ireland economy as a whole using the NIERC Econometric Model of the Northern Ireland economy, adjusted to include an estimated nine sector input–output framework.

The 1989–93 programme was negotiated during 1989, resulting in the Community Support Framework document agreed jointly by Government in Northern Ireland and the European Commission. The document identified five broad priorities or themes which subsequently became the Operational Programmes (OP) within the overall CSF Programme.

1. Improvement of the Social and Economic Environment (Physical and Social Environment OP)
2. Reducing the Effects of Peripherality (Transportation OP)
3. Strengthening and Diversifying the Industrial and Tradable Services Sectors (Industrial Development OP)
4. Development of Agriculture and Tourism (Agricultural Development OP, Tourism OP)
5. Human Resources Development (Human Resources OP)

These priorities reflected existing policy concerns in Northern Ireland and the existing policy framework. In many ways the 1989–93 CSF was a continuation of existing policy and EU assistance was mostly channelled through existing government agencies which changed neither their organisation nor their policy aims as a consequence of EU support (much of which had existed in previous years without forming part of any over-arching framework programme).

There is little evidence that EU officials played any role in the formulation of the plan other than to decide on the eligibility of its elements for assistance. The final allocation of expenditure over the five years was 702m ecus (£522m) including uprating for inflation. The allocation across the six Operational Programmes is shown in Table 3.3.

In addition to these Operational Programmes were a series of nine Community Initiatives. Of these, eight were relatively small with a joint cost of £41m. The other was the INTERREG Programme for economic development along the border (£57m).

Full evaluations were undertaken for Industrial Development (NIERC) and Agricultural Development (QUB, Centre for Rural Studies). Partial evaluations were also available for Transportation (DOE Economics Branch) and Physical and Social Environment (UU, Centre for Public Policy Research). The detailed impact is reviewed here by examining the first two of these Operational Programmes.

Table 3.3 Operational programmes 1989–1993 CSF

Operational Programme	EC Contribution	
	£m	(per cent)
Industrial Development	78.4	(15.5)
Agricultural Development	70.4	(13.9)
Human Resources	163.3	(32.2)
Tourism	33.4	(6.5)
Transportation	123.0	(24.3)
Physical and Social Environment	38.3	(7.6)
Total	506.8	(100.0)

Source: Community Support Framework 1989–93 United Kingdom (Northern Ireland) European Commission, Luxembourg.

Industrial Development Operational Programme (IDOP)

The industrial development programme consisted of £271m of projects and measures mostly within the aegis of the Department of Economic Development and its agencies, the IDB, LEDU, T&EA and IRTU, plus a number of projects concerned with industrial infrastructure and energy. The EU contribution to these measures was one third, with funds drawn from both the ERDF and ESF.

Two thirds of the IDOP programme involved assistance to industry for investment in capital equipment, R&D and marketing including exports. These were the routine activities of IDB, LEDU and IRTU and most of the funds were disbursed through these agencies. The remainder of the programme was split evenly between T&EA training schemes, and infrastructural developments including industrial estates, improved electricity supplies and a pipeline bringing North Sea gas to Northern Ireland.

The programme part financed an impressive list of achievements including 3000 projects in small firms associated with the creation of 2000 jobs, training for 54 000 people, and 18 infrastructure projects.[14] In their assessment of the programme, Scott and McEldowney use assumptions for additionality varying from virtually zero for electricity improvement through 50 per cent for capital investment to 100 per cent for the completion of local enterprise agencies. These assumptions were based on a series of previous evaluations of related government programmes.

Scott and McEldowney calculated a direct impact of the EU share of spending on this programme assuming only partial additionality as outlined above, taking each of the 17 measures separately. Using a range of further assumptions, these estimates were fed into the NIERC model of the Northern Ireland economy to calculate a wider economic impact including secondary impacts on other sectors through such things as the purchase of inputs and the spending of incomes generated in the assisted projects.[15] The aggregate impact estimated in this way was an increase in total GDP in Northern Ireland of 2.7 per cent by the end of the programme with the creation of 6300 jobs of which two-thirds were outside the target sector of manufacturing. The average cost per job, across all sectors, was estimated at £14 000.

Agricultural Development Operational Programme (ADOP)

Similar methods were used to assess the aggregate impact of the Agricultural Development Operational Programme (ADOP). The estimates on which the direct impact calculations were based were those of Moss and Lewis–Bowen.[16] The aims of the ADOP were to advance the development of agriculture in Northern Ireland to protect the social and physical environments of rural areas. The instruments of this policy were capital grants, agricultural training schemes and livestock improvement schemes, mostly aimed at smaller farms. Over 80 per cent of all claims for assistance were made from small farms with two or fewer people working on them. Two-thirds of the assistance went to the less favoured areas which cover 70 per cent of Northern Ireland, mainly in the south and west. In total there were 19 285 claims for over 40 000 individual projects and total grant expenditure of £61m (1996 prices).

The programme consisted of four sub-programmes with financial support as in the table below. As can be seen from the diverse and small-scale nature of the projects supported, it would be extremely difficult to produce a rigorous estimate of the direct impact of the assisted projects. In some cases farmers were obtaining grants for improvements which they viewed as mainly enhancements to the value of their property. In other cases the spending would normally count as routine maintenance for most viable small businesses. In most cases it was judged that at least some of the expenditure would have taken place even in the absence of ADOP grant assistance. The degree of additionality of the projects was assessed for individual projects but was generally in the range 50–60 per cent.

Using the Moss and Lewis–Bowen estimates, the calculation of the macro-economic impact of the ADOP spending was an increase in total Northern Ireland GDP of less than 0.3 per cent with the creation of

Table 3.4 Sub-programmes under Agricultural Development OP

	No. of Claims	Grant Expenditure £m (per cent)
1. Efficiency and Competitiveness • Concreting farmyards, roads • Fencing, drainage, re-seeding • Silos (new and repairs)	29 648	23.7 (39)
2. Quality and Marketing • Winter Housing for livestock • Stock handling facilities • Equipment for handling fruit & vegetables	7 238	17.0 (28)
3. Rural Environment • Painting and repairing farm buildings • Removal, screening of eyesores, etc. • Storm drainage • Waste disposal	5 724	6.8 (11)
4. Farm Diversification • Capital equipment • Feasibility studies • Marketing costs	667	13.8 (23)
Total	43 277	61.3 (100)

Source: Community Support Framework 1989–93 United Kingdom (Northern Ireland) European Commission, Luxembourg.

1200 jobs, at an estimated cost per job of £49 000. However it should be borne in mind that the main aim of most agricultural development schemes is raising farm incomes rather than job creation.

Aggregate impact of the CSF programme

The NIERC estimates for the aggregate impact of all six operational programmes of the 1989–93 CSF Programme are given in Table 3.5. These estimates make allowance for loss of additionality at project level. In other words the calculations attempt to measure the economic impact of the CSF assistance, *over and above what is likely to have occurred in the absence of that assistance*. There is however no attempt to account for macro-economic additionality, and it is assumed that in the absence of CSF assistance the same levels of expenditure would have been incurred by the UK Government. The impact of the CSF is measured relative to a base forecast, and Table 3.5 shows a difference in output, expenditure or employment above this base level. This difference is shown as a percentage of the base except in the case of employment and unemployment when it is in thousands of jobs or thousands of unemployed people.

The result of aggregate CSF spending of £500m over the five-year period 1989–93 is estimated to be a rise in GDP in Northern Ireland of 3.6 per cent by 1993 (Table 3.5). The year of peak impact is 1993, both because most expenditure was concentrated at that time and because the supply-side impact tends to increase over the period as productive capacity is accumulated. After 1993, the estimated level of expenditure declines sharply and the impact of the CSF on demand becomes small. Most of the productive capacity however remains in place. It is assumed in most cases that the level of productive capacity depreciates by 5 per cent per annum after its inception. As a consequence the impact of CSF spending is estimated to decline after 1993. To indicate the estimated rate of decline, the impact is shown for 1999. As can be seen, GDP remains above its base level by 2.9 per cent in 1999, six years after the end of the CSF programme.

Similarly, the levels of exports and consumer spending are permanently raised by the CSF programme. Exports remain 3.3 per cent above their base level in 1999 and consumer spending is 2.1 per cent higher than it would otherwise have been. Investment is raised chiefly during the years of actual programme expenditure, but falls below base level after 1993. The capital stock however remains permanently raised.

Estimates of employment created by the CSF programme are that 10 300 new jobs are created by the peak year of 1993. Thereafter the total falls gently, and 7400 additional jobs are estimated to be still available by the end of the decade. This level of job creation leads to reduction in the number of unemployed. By 1994, unemployment is estimated to have been 6700 lower than it would have been in the absence of the CSF.

The sectoral pattern of job creation depends to some extent on assumptions made about the direct impact of CSF-funded projects. New employment is estimated to be widely spread across sectors with around one-quarter in manufacturing and one-fifth in construction. As expected, both of these sectors are estimated to have gained a share of new jobs which is disproportionately greater than their existing share of employment. Most new jobs are, however, estimated to have been created in the private services sectors including distribution, transport and communication, finance and business services, and other services. A number of jobs are also supported within the public sector, many of them in organisations providing vocational training.

Table 3.5 Total impact of CSF expenditure in Northern Ireland (allowing for additionality)

	1989	1990	1991	1992	1993	1994	1999
GDP (per cent)	0.7	1.4	2.0	2.9	3.6	3.5	2.9
Exports (per cent)	0.4	0.9	2.0	3.0	4.1	4.8	3.3
Investment (per cent)	2.1	4.1	4.2	6.3	6.1	2.7	−0.6
Consumer Spending (per cent)	0.2	0.5	0.8	1.2	1.7	2.0	2.1
Output							
Manufacturing (per cent)	0.7	1.3	2.4	3.8	5.0	5.9	4.1
Construction (per cent)	1.7	3.0	3.9	6.2	7.0	5.8	3.3
Private Services (per cent)	1.0	1.5	2.3	3.3	4.0	4.2	3.1
Employment (thous)	2.1	4.9	6.2	8.4	10.3	9.3	7.4
Unemployed (thous)	−0.4	−1.0	−1.7	−3.5	−5.6	−6.7	−5.1

Source: Gudgin (1996).

Not all of the CSF programmes are judged to have been equally effective in creating new jobs or in reducing the numbers of the unemployed. The estimation of the effectiveness of individual programmes depends partly on existing micro-economic studies, but also on a number of assumptions.

Estimates of the contribution of individual CSF programmes are shown in Table 3.6. These estimates need to be interpreted carefully. Several of the programmes had primary objectives other than employment creation and in such cases employment was only a side-effect of the programme. Except for the economic development programmes the job creation and cost per job created are inappropriate or insufficient indicators of effectiveness and value for money.

Easily the most effective programme in terms of job creation is Industrial Development (IDOP). This is estimated to account for over half of all new jobs in existence by 1993. In later years this proportion rises further due to the importance of the productive capacity (in terms of plant equipment and skills) brought into existence through CSF assistance. By 1991, it is estimated that 70 per cent of the additional jobs would be within projects assisted within the IDOP.

Table 3.6 A comparison of the impact of individual CSF programmes

	1993	1999
Employment (no. of jobs in thousands)		
IDOP	6.3	5.1
ADOP	1.0	0.9
Human Resources	3.3	1.7
Tourism	0.2	0.1
Transportation	0.4	0.3
PSEP	0.1	0.0
CSF	11.1	7.2

Source: Gudgin (1992).
Note: Individual Programme estimates do not necessarily sum to totals due to interaction effects.

Most of the remaining jobs are estimated to have been created within the Human Resources Programmes. These include both employment of staff within organisations providing vocational training, and additional jobs created in the private sector as the result of the enhanced availability of skilled labour. Many of the new jobs created by the Agricultural Development Operational Programme are due to diversification projects in food production. Other programmes, Tourism, Transportation and Physical and Social Environment have their main impact via the boost to demand provided by new construction work. The supply-side impacts are judged to be low.

The estimated cost per job is obtained by dividing the total cost in grants by the number of jobs generated. The grant cost in this case includes both £507m of CSF expenditure plus £57.9m of associated UK public expenditure provided chiefly for industrial development projects and for public amenities in tourism. The total cost per job in 1993, of expenditure under the 1989–93 CSF, was £55 000. This would not seem unduly high given the proportion of expenditure on infrastructure and community projects.

Many of these jobs will be long-lasting and a more meaningful measure may be the cost per job-year. Since the longevity of some jobs is almost infinite there is no clear cut definition of the lifetime of a job. In this study a 30 year period is adopted for the purposes of calculating costs per job-year. In most cases the number of jobs created is assumed to decline by 5 per cent per annum from the date of creation.

This assumption provides an estimate of 170 000 job-years over a 30 year period of 5700 jobs on average in each year. The grant cost per job-year is thus £3300. Since this is below the cost of unemployment benefit, the cost effectiveness of the programme might be viewed as favourable.

The cost per job of most programmes is below this average level. The average is however boosted by a very high estimated cost per job in the Transportation Programme. This programme consisted largely of projects to improve harbour facilities mainly at Belfast but also at Londonderry, Larne and Warrenpoint. Large expenditures were also made at the province's airports, mainly at Aldergrove and Eglinton. The remainder of the programme consisted of railway extensions and a series of by-pass roads.

Although all of these developments led to significant improvements in Northern Ireland's infrastructure, it was difficult in many cases to see that they made an impact on economic growth in the province commensurate with the expenditure involved. If the main impact on the aim of reducing peripherality was a reduction in transport costs it was difficult to see that such reductions would either be large or that they would play any substantial role in reducing the costs of exporters.

The Common Agricultural Policy

The Common Agricultural Policy (CAP) was one of the twin legs on which the original Economic Community was founded, with a German and Dutch desire for free trade bartered for protection for French and Italian (and to some extent also German) farmers.

In practice prices were set from the beginning close to those of the high price countries. Consequently prices rose from a level of around 17 per cent above world price levels in the mid 1950s to over 50 per cent by 1966.[17] Commission figures for 1967/68 show that prices were 75 per cent above world levels for beef and 397 per cent for butter.

This then was the regime which the UK joined in 1973. The UK accepted an overly protective regime of high agricultural protection in return for access to European markets for industrial goods. This position was not however fully shared by Northern Ireland where agriculture was both more important in the wider economy and less efficient (being based on smaller farms and poorer land compared with Great Britain). In these respects Northern Ireland had a closer resemblance to the peasant agriculture of southern Europe than to the larger and more efficient farms of Great Britain formed by a process of enclosure and a century of free trade.

The CAP continued to maintain its high price regime until the late 1980s when burgeoning product surpluses drove the costs of price support to unsustainable levels, stimulating demand for reform. This began in 1988 with a move away from price support. A new set of reforms under Commissioner MacSharry in 1992 cut price support, especially for cereals, and reduced production through set-aside. Instead of price support farmers were to be compensated through direct subsidies (e.g. headage payments) and the originally temporary milk quotas were in practice to become permanent. Further reforms are currently under discussion as part of the Agenda 2000 debate with proposals to reduce prices further towards world prices.

Agriculture is an important element of the Northern Ireland economy accounting for 4.7 per cent of GDP (down from 6.7 per cent in 1973), and also providing a basis for a food processing industry which contributes a further 3 per cent of GDP. However only 5.7 per cent of the workforce are in agriculture (compared with 10 per cent in 1973) with a further 2.8 per cent in food processing. The average size of farm is small at half the UK average and as noted above two-thirds of agricultural land is in the Less Favoured categories being largely upland and unsuitable for most agriculture under free market conditions.

Farmers have not fared particularly well under the CAP regime. Farm incomes in real terms have remained lower throughout the last 25 years than they were at accession in 1973, although incomes in 1973 were at a high level due to world shortages of agricultural products. Incomes have also been extremely volatile. Most striking has been the rise in the public support element of farm incomes. EU support for Northern Ireland agriculture comes through three financial mechanisms:

(i) Northern Ireland's share of intervention payments and other agricultural price support undertaken through the UK Intervention Board of the Ministry of Agriculture Fishing and Forestry (MAFF)
(ii) Direct subsidies to farmers (i.e. Suckler Cow Premium, Sheep Annual Premium, Beef Special Premium and Hill Livestock Compensatory Allowances)
(iii) Support for farm improvements, product quality and product diversification through the Guidance section of the EAGGF.

The real value of these payments is given in Figure 3.9 which shows the decline in importance of price support in the 1990s, at least until the special measures taken in 1996 as a result of BSE. Also shown is the growing importance of direct subsidies in the 1990s. EAGGF Guidance support is a relatively small part of the total. The value of total spending was close to £150m per annum in 1996 prices through most of the 1980s and 1990s but rose to £250m in 1996 as a result of the BSE crisis.

In addition to the EU subsidies listed above Northern Ireland agriculture is also affected by quota restrictions on milk, which again support prices, and have a capital value as assets. On top of EU financial support are UK domestic subsidies and assistance paid directly by the Department of Agriculture in Northern Ireland (DANI). This includes contributions to such payments as Hill Livestock Compensatory Allowances as well as support for veterinary and scientific services.

The value of EU assistance to Northern Ireland agriculture has averaged around 70 per cent of total farm incomes since the late 1970s and in several years of low incomes has been 100 per cent (Figure 3.10). CAP support, together with domestic DANI support for agriculture, has averaged around 100 per cent of farm incomes and in several years has been over 100 per cent (Figure 3.10). This is possible because a substantial part of price support goes to pay storage and administration costs as well as export subsidies which constitute a payment from taxpayers to foreign consumers. In addition some of the payments including veterinary costs and research are indirect.

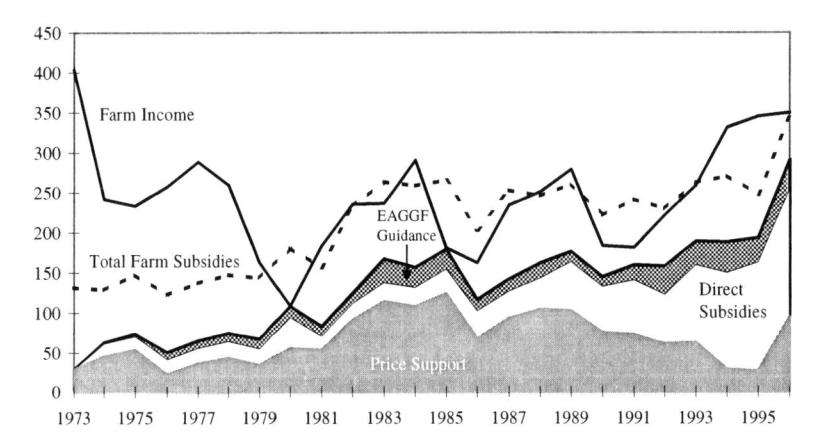

Figure 3.9 The components of EC subsidies to Northern Ireland agriculture (£m 1996 prices)
Sources: NI Estimates, Government Expenditure Plans (Northern Ireland, MAFF).

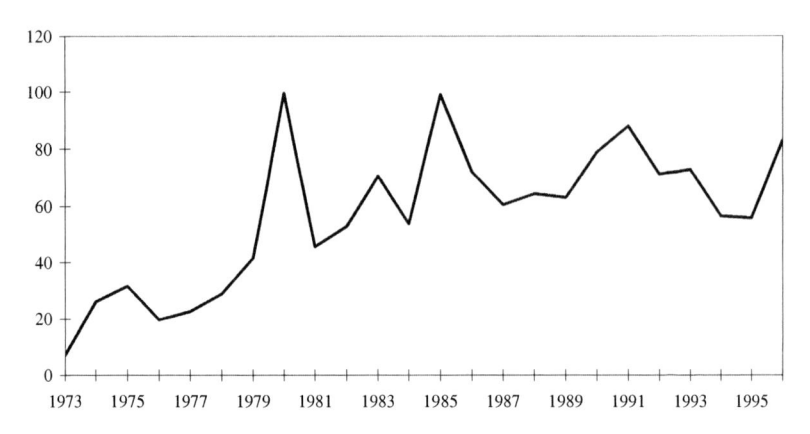

66 *Europe and the Economy*

Figure 3.10 EC agricultural payments as percentage of total farm income in Northern Ireland
Sources: NI Estimates, Government Expenditure Plans (NI, MAFF); NI *Abstract of Statistics*.

Nonetheless it is sobering to realise that subsidies to agriculture are equivalent to all of farm income.[18] It is even more bizarre to record that the subsidies from taxpayers described in Figure 3.9 amount to only part of the overall value of support, since the cost to consumers of high administered prices is estimated at close to £120 per person each year.[19] This constitutes a total annual payment of £180m by Northern Ireland consumers. Hence the total cost of agricultural support for Northern Ireland agriculture, including that borne by Northern Ireland consumers, is one and a half times the total value of farm incomes in Northern Ireland. It is thus close to three-quarters of the aggregate value of total farm income plus total GDP (wages and profits) from food processing in Northern Ireland.

Assessment

It is clear that the CAP regime of support to agriculture underpins much if not most of the financial viability of agricultural production in Northern Ireland. Without this support it seems doubtful that most of agriculture in Northern Ireland could survive. The exceptions might be the larger and more efficient beef and dairy farms on the minority of low land, mainly in the east of the province.

The question for policy is whether this level of support is either sensible or equitable. The answer for Northern Ireland would depend on the alternative uses of the subsidies saved from a dismantling of the CAP. The saving to consumers in lower food costs would lead to greater consumer spending on other goods and services, and much of this would increase demand for non-agricultural producers within Northern Ireland. If the £300m of taxpayers subsidies to agriculture were used to reduce personal taxation a similar outcome would result. Alternatively an equivalent increase in public expenditure in Northern Ireland would expand incomes and jobs and could be directed to activities such as tertiary or vocational education or other measures to strengthen the competitiveness of the wider economy.

Whether such transfers would compensate Northern Ireland for the loss of much of its agriculture and food processing industry would be a matter for careful calculation. However we can note that some of the province's most successful food producers, for example those in poultry meat, are in sectors least supported by the CAP and would gain further from lower feed prices.

Finally, it seems almost certain that any diminution of agricultural subsidies would increase equity since much of the subsidy is a transfer from poor urban dwellers to relatively affluent farmers, whether these are large grain farmers in East Anglia gaining millions from set-aside payments or moderate-sized farmers in Northern Ireland with assets worth over a million pounds.

A note on trade

The chief reason for the UK's joining the EEC in 1973 was a desire to gain access to the large European market for industrial goods on a free trade basis. Although the post-war trend towards trade liberalisation had begun by 1973 industrial tariffs were still relatively high, and the abandonment of tariffs between the UK and the rest of the EEC had a significant impact on the volume and direction of UK trade. The share of the EU in UK export markets for all goods rose from 36 per cent in 1973 to 53 per cent in 1995.

The rise in the importance of EU markets for Northern Ireland manufactured goods (including processed food) is shown in Table 3.5. In the 1970s exports accounted for only 13 per cent of manufactured production in Northern Ireland, although 43 per cent of this went to EC12 markets (Table 3.5). Since 1977, the proportion of exports has increased more than three fold to 43 per cent in 1995 with almost 60 per cent of these exports accounted for by EC12 markets including the Republic of Ireland.

68 Europe and the Economy

Table 3.7 Share of EC12 in manufactured exports

	Exports as per cent of Output		EC12 as per cent of Exports	
	1977	1995	1997	1995
Northern Ireland	13.4	43.7	43.3	59.7
UK	21.0	35.7	37.6	57.0

Sources: CSO *Annual Abstract of Statistics*; O'Reilly (1977).

There is little doubt that the liberalisation of trade with the EU has had a positive impact on levels of both output and exports in Northern Ireland. Much of this impact is likely to have occurred in the early years of membership when tariffs were first reduced.

The general reduction of tariffs since 1973 as part of the GATT process has diminished the impact of free trade with EU partners. Hindley estimates that the tariff on EU imports now averages only 5 per cent for most goods, although it is higher for textiles (at close to 20 per cent) and for food. It thus seems likely that much, although not all of the growth in trade with EC12 states would have occurred due to GATT liberalisation, although it would have occurred later than it actually did.

Conclusion

It is difficult to escape the conclusion that membership of the EU is no longer an especially important issue for Northern Ireland. The considerable initial value of free trade with the large and prosperous markets of Europe has been undermined by the general reduction in tariffs under GATT liberalisation. It is not obvious what proportion of inward investment is influenced by access to EU markets, but in any case the unfavourable external image of Northern Ireland has meant that the volume of inward investment has been relatively small over the last 25 years. Again, since general tariffs are now low the advantage of actual EU membership to potential inward investors is no longer very large.

Although the advantage of Structural Funds receipts from the EU is hardly mentioned by Hindley and Howe[20] in their assessment of the benefits of EU membership to the UK, it might be expected that these benefits would loom much larger in any advantage gained from membership by Northern Ireland. In fact Structural Funds comprise a small proportion of public spending (3 per cent) even with the temporary boost from the Special Support Programme for Peace and Reconciliation. Since most of these funds have been treated by the UK authorities as non-additional to Northern Ireland (even if they are additional to the UK) they make relatively little practical difference to the size, composition or performance of the Northern Ireland economy.

The Northern Ireland economy has grown faster than the EU average over the last 25 years as might be expected for a low wage, highly subisdised region with a rapid natural increase in population. However its productivity and standards of living have remained in a similar position relative to the European average throughout the period. What changes there have been are much more easily accounted for by UK policy than by membership of the EU.

The sectors which are clearly dependent on EU policy are agriculture and food processing which together account for about one twelfth of total GDP in Northern Ireland. The entire income of these sectors appears to be comprised either of direct subsidy from taxpayers or from high prices paid by European (mainly UK) consumers. Since the UK is consistently a net contributor to the EU budget, these costs are essentially borne by UK taxpayers and consumers. This level of support has delayed the inevitable contraction and rationalisation of this industry and has hindered the development of replacement activities. Large and important questions of how to manage the countryside have also been put on ice. The real losers here have been poorer urban dwellers who have paid high food prices and high taxes while being denied access to the countryside for both recreation and housing.

Notes

1. European Commission (1994) GDP per head in PPS, average for 1989-91.
2. Excluding French Overseas Dependencies.
3. PEIDA (1984) *Transport Costs in Peripheral Regions*, Occasional Paper No. 7, Belfast, Policy Planning and Research Unit, Department of Finance and Personnel.
4. European Commission (1981) *The Regions of Europe*, First periodic report on the social and economic situation of the regions of the Community, Com (80) 816 Final, Brussels.
5. Excluding French overseas dependencies.
6. C. B. Beatty, S. Fothergill, T. Gore and P. Herrington (1997) *The Real Level of Unemployment*, Centre for Regional Economic and Social Research, Sheffield Hallam University.

7. M. O'Reilly (1997) *Made in Northern Ireland. Sold to the World*, NIERC, DED, IDB, Belfast.
8. G. Gudgin (1998) 'The Northern Ireland Labour Market' in A. Heath (ed.), *Ireland North and South*, British Academy, London.
9. M. Trimble (1990) 'The Impact of the European Community' in R. Harris, C. Johnson and J. Spencer (eds), *The Northern Ireland Economy: A Comparative Study in the Economic Development of a Peripheral Region*, Longman, London.
10. European Commission, 1996.
11. European Commission, Table 34, 1996.
12. See House of Commons Official Report, sixth series, Vol. 59, pp. 821–9, 8/5/84.
13. G. Gudgin (1996) *The Macro-Economic Impact of the European Community Structural Funds on Northern Ireland 1989–93*, NIERC, Belfast.
14. R. Scott and J. McEldowney (1994) *Evaluation of the Industrial Development Operational Programme for Northern Ireland 1989–94*, NIERC, Belfast.
15. Gudgin, op. cit.
16. J. E. Moss and J. Lewis–Bowen (1994) *Socio–Economic Evaluation of the Agricultural Development Operational Programme*, Queen's University Belfast, Department of Agriculture.
17. R. Howarth (1992) 'The Common Agricultural Policy' in P. Minford (ed.), *The Cost of Europe*, Manchester University Press.
18. Farm income is defined as 'total income for farming'. This includes income from employed family members but excludes incomes of hired labour. The latter would add about 10 per cent to total farm incomes.
19. B. Hindley and M. Howe (1996) *Better off Without: The Benefits or Costs of EU Membership*, IEA Occasional Paper No. 99, IEA, London.
20. Ibid.

4
Changing Scene: EU Impact on the Rural Economy

John Davis

Rural affairs have played a very prominent role in the economic and cultural life of Northern Ireland. With the exception of the Greater Belfast and Derry areas the region remains almost entirely rural. Within the European Union agricultural and rural policies have been a cornerstone (some might say a millstone) in the development of common policy frameworks. The Common Agricultural Policy (CAP), including Structural Funds measures to promote rural development, remains by far the largest common policy programme in the EU: expenditure under CAP accounted for about 55 per cent of the total EU budget in 1996.[1] Thus the CAP is a very important source of support for the region's agricultural sector and rural society. It remains very much an *agricultural* support mechanism, indeed its primary goal in practice is to redistribute income in favour of farmers; over 90 per cent of CAP spending is for this purpose. The CAP has been rightly criticised for, among other things, the narrowness of its support and adverse distributional effects within agriculture, the large costs it imposes on EU consumers and taxpayers and for the price depressing effects it has had on the traditional markets of agricultural exporting nations such as New Zealand and Argentina.

This chapter looks at some aspects of agricultural and rural change in Northern Ireland within the context of the EU's policy framework. Thus, the starting point is 1973, the year in which the UK became a member of the European Economic Community. Agriculture and rural development are treated as analytically distinct topics although obviously both are part of the same rural reality. This approach is used partly for ease of treatment but also to reflect the fact that the activities have tended to be compartmentalised from an EU policy standpoint. The chapter has three main aims. Firstly, to explore the role of agriculture and its ancillary industries in the region and some of the key changes since EEC accession. Secondly, to provide an overview of the consequences of EU membership for the farm sector, for farm households and wider rural society. Thirdly, to examine the emergence of EU promoted rural development policy and practice in Northern Ireland and to identify some issues related to the implementation of this policy in the region. After establishing the nature and role of the agri-food sector in Northern Ireland the chapter goes on to examine experiences within the main farm commodity sectors: included in this section is a look at agri-environmental issues, the agri-money system and the effects of the CAP on agricultural land prices. It then provides an overview of some of the consequences of 25 years of EU membership for the farm sector. The chapter goes on to look at some of the changes and issues associated with rural development initiatives in the region and finishes by speculating on future directions in EU rural policies from a regional perspective.

Agri-food in Northern Ireland

Agriculture and its ancillary industries, increasingly referred to as the agri-food sector, makes a significant contribution to the economy of Northern Ireland: in terms of its importance to the economy the sector lies somewhere between its counterparts in the Republic of Ireland and Great Britain. At the time of accession in 1973 agriculture on its own contributed about eight per cent of GDP (Gross Domestic Product) in Northern Ireland. By 1996 its contribution had fallen to five per cent; this latter figure may be compared with eight per cent in the Republic of Ireland and about two per cent in Great Britain. The agricultural workforce at accession represented about 11 per cent of the total regional workforce; by 1996 this had fallen to six per cent. Again, we can compare the latter with about 13 per cent in the Republic and just over two per cent in Great Britain. Taking agri-food in the region as a whole, the contributions to GDP and employment declined from 12 and 15 per cent respectively at accession to eight and ten per cent in 1996.[2]

It is frequently argued by the farming lobby that agri-food constitutes the single most important sector of the economy of Northern Ireland. There is some justification for this assertion, even though its relative importance has diminished over time. For example in the 'countryside' it contributes between 20 and 30 per cent of the rural economy.[3] Moreover, it remains an important source of exports from the region: about two-thirds of its output is currently 'exported' (sold outside the region) and this represents about one quarter of total external sales of the region's manufacturing sector.[4]

Farms in Northern Ireland are largely owner-occupied family businesses. Since 1973 there has been consolidation of farm holdings: the total number declined from 42 000 to 28 000 between 1973 and 1998 and the average size of holding increased from 25 to 36 hectares. Of course, it may be questioned whether, over a 25 year period, this degree of structural change has been adequate to develop international competitiveness in the region's agriculture and thus to maintain the livelihoods of those remaining in the industry. Evidence presented later in the chapter will suggest that structural improvements have not progressed sufficiently fast. The highly protectionist nature of EU farm policy embedded in the CAP must be viewed as a very important if unquantified factor contributing to such a modest rate of structural adjustment – well under two per cent per year.

The average size of agricultural holding in 1998 was above that in the Republic (29 hectares) but only about one-half the size of farms in Great Britain (70 hectares). It is sometimes said that the scale of agriculture in Northern Ireland is very close to the EU average but this is somewhat misleading. It is true that the contribution to employment is broadly similar: but agriculture in the EU as a whole contributes less than three per cent of GDP and the average size of holding (about 15 hectares) is much smaller.[5] Indeed, dairy enterprises in Northern Ireland are larger on average than in any other EU state.

However, it is worth emphasising the structural differences and weaknesses of agriculture in the region compared with the rest of the UK. For example, about 61 per cent of cattle and sheep farms are classified as 'very small' compared with about 40 per cent in Great Britain: dairy herds have about 47 cows on average compared with around 70 in Britain. These structural contrasts can create problems and dilemmas when it comes to representing the interests of Northern Ireland in policy formation within an EU/UK negotiating framework. For example, attempts by the EU to modulate CAP support towards smaller farms have, in the past, been resisted by the UK government. The much heavier dependence on food exports in the region can also create unique pressures not experienced to the same extent in the rest of the country, as the EU-imposed 1996 beef export ban illustrates.

The relatively mild and moist climate of the region creates strong comparative advantage for grazing livestock enterprises. These enterprises, especially dairying, have low opportunity costs relative to other regional and international competitors. Over 80 per cent of the value-added in agriculture is accounted for by dairying and beef and sheepmeat/wool production: dairying is the largest single element at the farm and processing levels. The intensive sector – pigs and poultry – has a relatively small share of on-farm value-added. However, the poultrymeat industry is the largest employer in food processing and in terms of product development and innovation is probably the most successful part of the food sector. Arguably, its success is due in no small measure to the fact that it has operated with minimum intervention and support under CAP over the last twenty-five years and has been forced to develop its international competitiveness in order to survive. Crops are relatively minor in Northern Ireland. Indeed, the potato, once synonymous with farming in Ireland, now contributes only two per cent of the industry's output.

In the search for future growth and development opportunities in the regional and rural economy the agri-food sector will continue to make an important contribution. These opportunities are most likely to occur in the post-farm processing industries as they continue to professionalise their operations, incorporate more advanced quality control measures and move towards the production of higher added-value products. However, it is questionable whether these industries will be able to make a significant contribution to future growth in rural employment. In the dairy processing industry, for example, Davis[6] identified substantial inefficiencies and the need for rationalisation; this could result in significant job losses in the medium to longer term. Moreover, the EU agricultural policy environment is probably entering an era of relatively constrained support for farm production and so further growth in farm output is likely to be severely restrained. In short, although the agri-food sector must continue to develop its international competitiveness, its contribution to future growth of the rural economy will be limited and its overall importance will probably decline in relative terms.

Finally, some brief comments about trends in rural society. In Northern Ireland about 41 per cent of total employment is located in rural areas: this is much higher than the UK average of 15 per cent and well above the figures of 31 per cent for Wales and 22 per cent for Scotland. There has also been a degree of 'urban to rural shift' of population and employment within the region. Of the 26 District Council areas, only Belfast has a declining population. During the 1970s and 1980s rural areas were the only parts of the UK to experience significant total employment gains. In Northern Ireland this amounted to over 15 per cent; compared with 8 per cent in Scotland and under 12 per cent in Wales. The structure of rural society has changed significantly: it is no longer linked directly or indirectly with agriculture to the extent it was in the pre-EEC accession era. These points are made simply to illustrate that rural change is a dynamic and complex process and that it is difficult to generalise about problems often associated with rural areas, such as depopulation and deprivation. A fuller discussion of some of these issues is included later in the chapter. The reader may also wish to refer to a House of Lords Report on the Future of Rural Society.[7]

Experiences under the CAP

Farm households in the region had quite high expectations at the time of EEC accession, as their farm businesses came gradually under the powerful influences of the CAP. Any attempt at evaluating whether these hopes were realised, and indeed the wider implications of the CAP for the region, raises some very difficult questions. There are inherent problems in trying to establish links in any precise way between the development of a sector of the economy and the operation of a particular policy framework, even one as powerful as the CAP. For example, we do not know the counterfactual position – the policy regime which would have existed in the absence of the CAP. Therefore, this section restricts itself to establishing some facts about changes in agriculture and the wider rural economy, some of which can be linked directly or indirectly to the CAP.

Dairy sector

At the time of accession in 1973 it was expected that agriculture in the region would benefit from the high price productivist policies of the EEC. This hope was probably fulfilled most clearly in the case of the dairy sector. Following generous increases in institutional support prices for milk, especially in the early 1980s, dairy cow numbers and milk output expanded rapidly; by 1983 milk production was about 90 per cent higher than the immediate pre-accession level.[8] In 1984, the European Commission imposed Community-wide milk production quotas in order to halt the very rapid growth in dairy support expenditure within CAP. Expansion of milk output in Northern Ireland was brought to a halt at just below the 1983 level of production. This was followed by various downward adjustments in quotas; although recent imports of quota to the region have returned production to about the 1983 level. Dairying remains by far the most competitive and profitable farming enterprise in Northern Ireland, as reflected partly in its ability to import production quotas from other regions of the UK.

One 'casualty' within the dairy sector which can be attributed more or less directly to the EU's policy framework was the Milk Marketing Scheme which provided the statutory powers under which the Milk Marketing Board operated. This Scheme had been established, as in other regions of the UK, in the 1930s: it enabled the producer dominated Boards to sell milk to processors on behalf of dairy farmers. The statutory powers of the Boards gave them almost complete monopoly powers in the first-hand milk market. Although their powers were increasingly circumscribed by government they were nevertheless regarded by milk producers as the bulwark of their industry. However, by the early 1990s the Boards found it increasingly difficult to defend those powers within an EU policy regime which was promoting trade and integration in the European Single Market, and which had a strong presumption against monopoly powers. There was a particular problem for the Board in Northern Ireland in that the land frontier with another member state facilitated increasing trade in milk, thus undermining the Scheme's regional administered pricing structures. These pressures inevitably led to the abolition of the Board in 1995 and to the creation of a voluntary marketing framework; about 70 per cent of producers remained loyal to the new producer organisation, United Dairy Farmers, whilst the remaining 30 per cent exercised their new freedom to sell milk directly to processors. Amongst other things the Milk Board was no longer able to operate as a monopoly and processors could no longer shelter behind the administered pricing and profit margins of the old regime. The change in the competitive environment in the region's milk sector was sudden and dramatic; producers and processors are still trying to come to terms with the new situation.

Beef sector

Experiences in the beef sector were disappointing, as this was the main area where expansion had been expected in anticipation of EEC membership. There had been a period of very rapid growth in production prior to 1974, and higher profitability. Accession unfortunately coincided with a depression in demand and prices following the 1973–74 oil crisis. The transitional arrangements to full adoption of the CAP support measures were not adequate to maintain farm returns and this precipitated a crisis in the industry and a decline in the beef herd which actually continued until 1983. Following reductions in the dairy herd in the years following milk quotas, the beef herd entered an expansionary phase in 1987 which lasted until 1994. However, because of a marked reduction in imports of store cattle from the Republic of Ireland the total number of finished cattle marketed in 1994 was about 15 per cent lower than a decade earlier. Beef enterprises are small scale compared with dairying and tend to be concentrated in the more remote and deprived areas. Their profitability is also weak by comparison with dairying and is highly sensitive to fluctuations in beef market prices.

In early 1996 a crisis in the beef sector was precipitated by a world-wide ban on UK beef exports imposed by the EU'S Council of Ministers. This followed the 20 March 1996 announcement by the British Minister for Health of a probable link between the consumption of beef products, prior to the 1989 ban on the use of specified bovine offal in foodstuffs, and the disease CJD (the human form of BSE). The ban was a very clear example of the power of the EU in regulating the trade of a member state. There was a sharp fall in consumer confidence in beef in both domestic and export markets and the ban meant that export demand for the region's beef was effectively reduced to zero. The impact was particularly detrimental to the beef industry in Northern Ireland as about 68 per cent of production was being sold outside the region and about 50 per cent by volume exported from the UK.

During 1997 a major study of the economic impact of the BSE crisis on the UK and its regional economies was undertaken on behalf of the Ministry of Agriculture, Fisheries and Food. The work in Northern Ireland by Caskie et al.[9] analysed the overall effects of the export ban on the regional economy. They concluded that the various measures introduced by the British government and the EU to compensate beef producers had been successful in stabilising the market in the short-term: direct payments under these measures in 1996 alone amounted to about £130 million. The results of their modelling exercise showed the very severe income and employment consequences for the regional economy of any sustained loss in export demand. About 20 per cent of the jobs supported by beef farming were predicted to be under threat. Moreover, the losses would be concentrated in those farming enterprises which were already generating relatively low incomes, often located in the more disadvantaged areas.

It is interesting to speculate about whether and how the BSE saga would have developed if the UK had been outside the EU. It could be argued that the high EU prices for milk compared to the world price provided incentives, in a region with very strong comparative advantage in dairying, for the feeding of dairy cows with relatively high levels of protein derived from animal offal. Indeed there was an increasing supply of this material due to the policy-induced build-up in sheep numbers in the region. Another important contributing factor seems to have been the UK government's decision in the early 1980s to deregulate the processing of this offal, thus allowing the infective material to enter the food chain. Would the world-wide ban on the UK beef exports have been imposed by the UK government? It is extremely unlikely, although a *de facto* ban may well have been imposed by a substantial number of export customers. Nevertheless, a region such as Northern Ireland, with a relatively low incidence of BSE and a highly developed animal traceability system, would probably have begun to re-establish export markets much faster than was possible within the EU/UK framework.

Sheepmeat sector

This is one area which clearly benefited from EEC accession. Although a common support regime was not introduced until 1980 the breeding flock increased in every year from 1975 to 1993. The attractiveness of the sheep enterprise increased substantially following the introduction of a sheepmeat support regime in 1980: production has now more or less stabilised. The limitations placed on dairy farmers by EU production quotas also gave a boost to sheep production as an alternative enterprise in the 1980s. The total volume of sheepmeat output almost doubled in the decade to 1997. The sector was one beneficiary of the BSE crisis as demand switched to alternative meats, with prices in 1996 about 24 per cent higher than in 1995.

Beef and sheep farming both benefited from the introduction in 1975 of Directive EC 268 which authorised member states to introduce special aids in so-called Less Favoured Areas (LFAs). These aids were intended mainly to compensate hill farmers for natural disadvantages suffered as a result of location and topography. The LFA areas were extended in 1984: in Northern Ireland about 70 per cent of the total land area is now designated LFA. The Hill Livestock Compensatory Allowances (HLCAs) payable to beef and sheep farmers in the LFAs help to maintain the unique character of farming in the hills and uplands. In 1996, about 17 000 holdings in the region benefited from HLCA payments which totalled over £14 million. At time of writing the scheme is under review by the UK government; see Davis *et al.*[10] It seems likely to be replaced by one which places greater emphasis on conserving the fragile ecosystems found in many hill areas.

Pigmeat and eggs

This sector arguably was the most adversely affected by EC entry. A major influence on its competitiveness is the cost of cereal-based feed inputs. Following entry, much greater reliance had to be placed on relatively high price cereals within the Community, as access to cheaper grains on the world market was cut off. There was also the problem for producers that the EC was self-sufficient in pigmeat and eggs and they were not well supported under the CAP: of significance also was the fact that their consumption was in long term decline at the time of accession. Although pigmeat output recovered from a dip immediately following accession it still remains well below the levels of the early 1970s. The BSE-induced switch to alternative meats also benefited this sector and producer prices in 1996 were 18 per cent higher than the previous year. Egg production declined more dramatically especially in the decade following accession, after which it stabilised: output is now only about 50 per cent of the level at time of entry.

Poultrymeat

This industry by contrast has been a remarkable success story within the intensive sector. It is one of the most interesting cases in the rural economy of Northern Ireland. Unlike pigmeat and egg producers, the industry has been operating in a favourable market environment as a result of rapidly expanding demand stimulated by a fall in the price of poultrymeat relative to red meat, and shifts in consumer preferences in favour of white meat. Output has increased almost four-fold since the time of EC entry. A key factor in this industry has been the relatively rapid improvement in technical efficiency in production, resulting in a 40 per cent real terms fall in poultrymeat prices in the decade to 1996. Coupled with this has been very effective vertical integration, quality control, product development and aggressive marketing: these features are in marked contrast to much of the remainder of agri-food which has been heavily protected under CAP. As with beef substitutes the poultry industry benefited from the BSE crisis with output value 18 per cent higher in 1996 than the previous year.

Agriculture and environment

The interaction between agriculture and the natural environment raises a number of complex questions. On the one hand agriculture may be seen as having a positive impact through providing a form of stewardship or conservation of the countryside. On the other hand, the intensification of agriculture brought about by the high price productivist policies of the EU has been associated with, amongst other things, increased pollution of waterways, destruction of plant and animal habitats and reductions in biodiversity. For example the HLCA payments to LFA farmers have been blamed for overgrazing of hill land and fundamental changes in certain moorland landscapes. It is difficult to generalise about these issues as there are quite different views in society, for example about the preferred types of natural landscape and the priorities to be given to different environmental enhancement measures. Moreover, it can be quite difficult to discern the preferences and priorities of the general public on these matters as distinct from the views of environmental elite groups.

The first important formal recognition by the EU of the potential environmental problems associated with the CAP was in the 1992 MacSharry reforms which introduced the so-called Accompanying Measures: Agri-Environment, Regulation (EEC) 2078/92, as well as stocking rate limits on eligibility for the new cattle and sheep headage-based direct compensation payments. The Agri-Environment programme provides support in member states for a range of measures designed to enhance the environmental impacts of agriculture. In Northern Ireland a notable example is the Environmentally Sensitive Area (ESA) Scheme. The ESAs are location specific schemes tailored to enhance the environmental features of defined geographic areas: there are now five of these in Northern Ireland. The reader is referred to a comprehensive evaluation by Moss and Chilton[11] of the original ESA in the Mourne Mountains and Slieve Croob. Their study showed that the ESA Scheme was one model of how farmers could be compensated for the delivery of environmental improvements, many of which had a public good value. The Scheme was shown to provide very good value for money especially when the non-market or public good benefits of the improvements were taken into account. It is likely that agri-environment schemes of this nature will play a much more significant role in the future CAP framework. This issue is discussed later in this chapter.

Agri-money

No review of the impact of EU membership on the agri-food sector in the region would be complete without reference to the notorious EU 'agri-money' or 'green money' system. The system itself is horrendously complex, especially as it has operated within the region, and so what follows is very much a simplified account. For more detailed explanations of the current system see Stainer,[12] and its earlier version.[13]

The 'green money' system was first devised as a means of countering the effects of currency instability within the EU on farm commodity and retail food prices. The reader should note that all internal EU support prices for farm commodities are set in ecus (or previously using an 'agricultural unit of account'). In the early days of the CAP (1960s) these prices were translated into national currency terms at the then prevailing fixed exchange rates. However, with the currency instability of the late 1960s and the 1970s this would have resulted in substantial fluctuations in farm and retail food prices. The reason for this is that EU support prices have typically been well above world market prices and therefore have effectively determined EU market prices.

The first manifestation of this problem was in 1969 when the French franc was devalued. This would automatically have increased French farm and retail food prices. Rather than allow this to happen, the French government retained the pre-devaluation rate of exchange for the purpose of determining farm prices: thus there appeared the notional 'green' currency rate. However, there would have been an immediate problem if accompanying trade measures had not been taken. French farmers and traders now had an incentive to sell their production in the German market, receive payment in Deutschmarks and convert these to francs at the new advantageous market exchange rate. This had the potential seriously to undermine the German agri-food market. In order to counter this a frontier tax was imposed on French exports which was related to the currency differential: equally other EC exporters to the French market were entitled to a refund or export subsidy. These taxes and refunds came to be known as Monetary Compensatory Amounts or MCAs. Although it was intended that the system would be phased out over a number of years, the currency instability of the 1970s meant that it became a permanent feature and applied to all member states.

During certain periods over the last 25 years the operation of the 'green money' system has had fairly profound effects on the agri-food sector in Northern Ireland. The problems arose mainly because of the different farm price policies pursued by the UK and Irish governments and, of course, because of the fact that the land frontier could not be adequately policed to prevent smuggling of farm commodities. The 'green money' problems in the region were probably at their height in the second half of the 1970s. Sterling had been substantially devalued against other major European currencies. However, in order to shield consumers from food price increases the UK government was unwilling to devalue the 'green' rate sufficiently to bridge the gap between it and the market rate of exchange. At times there were very large gaps between the market and the 'green' rates, of the order of 25 to 30 per cent. In Ireland, the government was much more farmer-oriented and did not allow such large monetary gaps to develop. This created huge incentives to smuggle farm products from Northern Ireland to the Republic, thus avoiding MCA payments. Allegedly, some of this produce was reimported legally, attracting a refund, and then smuggled out again. This practice became known as the 'carousel'. In one two-week period in 1976 virtually all of the cattle marketed in Northern Ireland 'disappeared': the competitiveness of the meat processing sector had been completely undermined. In order to counter the effects the UK government was forced to introduce costly rescue measures, the Meat Industry Employment Scheme. This amounted to payments to meat processors of about £35 million in 1977–8 and £40 million in 1978–9 in order to restore their competitiveness. These monetary problems continued throughout the 1980s but to a lesser extent than in the 1970s (although there was a serious smuggling problem in the mid- 1980s). The 'green money' system still exists but, with the completion of the Single European Market in 1992, strict limits were placed on the level of permissible divergence between the 'green' and market rates. This means that farm commodity prices now reflect currency movements much more directly. This was illustrated in the large windfall gains to farmers following the exit of sterling from the ERM (Exchange Rate Mechanism) and the subsequent reversals following the appreciation of sterling in 1996 and 1997. The 'green money' episodes illustrate in a very stark way the dire consequences which can arise from differential rates of implementation of common policies by member states.

The agricultural land market

Finally, one of the most interesting aspects of accession was the impact on the region's land market. The real prices of agricultural land in Northern Ireland from 1959 to 1995 are shown in Figure 4.1. It would be easy to over-simplify the factors underlying these price trends: for a more in-depth analysis the reader is referred to work which, at the time of writing, was being carried out by Myles Patton, Department of Agricultural and Food Economics, the Queen's University of Belfast.

It has always been assumed that rational behaviour on the part of farmers would result in the price of agricultural land being driven

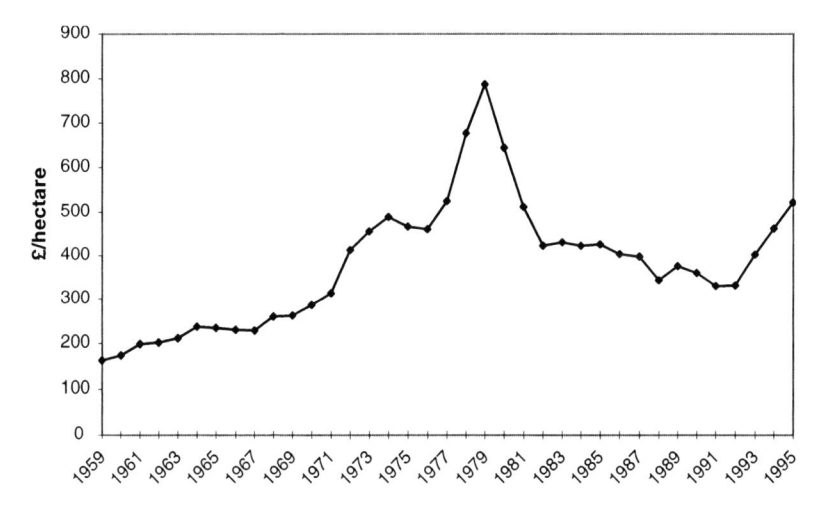

Figure 4.1 Real prices of owner-occupied agricultural land in Northern Ireland (1959 prices)
Source: M. Patton, Department of Agricultural and Food Economics, The Queen's University of Belfast.

mainly by its productive value, that is prices for different categories of land would reflect the profitability of farming enterprises carried out on that land. During the 1960s real land prices increased steadily, reflecting a steady upward trend in farming incomes. However, after 1970 the link between farm incomes and land prices was broken. It would seem that the immediate pre-accession period was one of optimism in agriculture as farmers expected to gain from the high levels of support under the CAP. This gave rise to increased demand for land both prior to and following accession. Land prices rose at unprecedented rates during the 1970s: by 1979 prices reached an all time high, an almost three-fold increase in real value compared with the pre-accession period. During this period we also witnessed a definite breaking of the link between land prices and farming incomes: indeed, following accession, incomes entered a downward trend which lasted until 1980, despite earlier expectations.

After 1979 the land price 'bubble' burst and prices fell sharply over the next three years. Although the rapid decline was halted in 1982, prices continued to decline throughout the 1980s. This trend was probably linked to a change in direction within the CAP, signalled by the introduction of milk production quotas in 1984. There was also an expectation that similar quotas would be introduced for the other major farm commodities, although this did not actually happen until the 1992 CAP reforms. Interestingly, the steady downward trend in land prices during the 1980s was associated with a definite upward trend in farming incomes during the same period. In short, it can be argued plausibly that behaviour in the land market in the 1980s was conditioned by sober reflection on the excesses of the 1970s, fuelled by the over-optimistic expectations of a CAP cornucopia.

The first half of the 1990s saw a return to what seemed to be more rational behaviour in the land market. This was a period of rapidly rising farming incomes which, in 1995, reached their highest level since accession. Land prices rose very rapidly during this period: indeed in 1993 the price of agricultural land in Northern Ireland moved significantly ahead of the price of owner-occupied land in England, thus reversing an historic price relativity. It remains to be seen whether this apparent return to rationality in the land market is sustained.

An overview

How should we view the overall impact of 25 years of EU membership on agri-food and the wider rural economy? It is very difficult to quantify this in any precise way. We have no way of knowing the counterfactual policy or how the sector would have responded to competitive pressures under such a regime. What we *can* say is that there have been very large financial transfers into the sector; yet partly because of the very unsophisticated nature of the CAP, significant economic and social problems persist in rural areas.

Subsidies, dependence and instability

It seems fairly clear that the differential effects of the CAP commodity regimes have resulted in an agri-food sector which now looks significantly different from what it might otherwise have been. The level of support to the sector has been high, probably considerably above what would have been paid if the UK had stayed outside the EU. For example, over the four years to 1995 transfer payments (farm subsidies) averaged about 50 per cent of total income from farming. In 1996, the additional payments to counter the BSE crisis meant that these transfers accounted for virtually the entire income from farming. During much of the first half of the 1990s farm incomes were buoyant; by 1995 they were at their highest level in real terms since 1973. This situation was due to a fortuitous coincidence of events, linked directly to

EU policies, rather than to any significant improvement in performance. Firstly, there was the devaluation of sterling against the ecu following its exit from the Exchange Rate Mechanism in 1992, thus giving farmers higher sterling returns for commodities with prices set in ecus. Secondly, world prices for agricultural commodities remained relatively high during much of the first half of the 1990s. Thirdly, the CAP reforms of 1992 introduced new direct headage payments to beef and sheep farmers. These were supposedly to compensate them for the reductions in institutional support prices introduced by the reform package. However, they continued to be paid despite the rise in world commodity prices and their value was enhanced by sterling's devaluation: in effect, farmers were over-compensated.

However, farm incomes are notoriously unstable and in 1996 and 1997 suffered dramatic turnarounds in virtually all farm types. These sharp reversals were due to a combination of factors: a total of six 'green' rate revaluations since mid-1996 which effectively reduced internal support prices by about 19 per cent; falls in world market prices for milk and cereals; and of course the BSE crisis. In 1995 a typical dairy farm's net income was around £23k but by 1997 this had fallen to about £8k. On cattle and sheep farms the already meagre net income of about £6.5k in 1995 had fallen to under £5k in 1997. These figures help to illustrate the very fragile nature and fluctuating fortunes of agriculture in the region. With the possible exception of some elements of dairying, much of agriculture, especially in the more marginal areas, would not be viable without subsidies. On many of the smaller cattle and sheep farms, usually located in the more disadvantaged areas, net farming income consists almost entirely of compensatory (subsidy) payments. This may come as a surprise to the reader. It is a fairly startling fact about the industry's competitive position when one considers the very high level of EU support over the last 25 years.

Farm households

Whilst the situation in the farm business sector is important in any overview, the author would argue that the position in farm households as a whole also needs to be considered: indeed in many ways this is the more appropriate unit of analysis. At the farm household level the picture becomes more complex and, due to data problems, somewhat less complete. It is widely known, for example, that farm households have been increasingly allocating their labour to a range of activities both on and off their farms and often at the same time retaining their land and some form of active involvement in agriculture.

This diversification of household labour is sometimes referred to as *pluriactivity*: it has brought about a quiet revolution in the nature of farming and the farm household, assisted by various EU farm diversification programmes.

Research by Davis *et al.*[14] has produced new perspectives on the incomes of farm households in the region. They analysed the sources and overall levels of incomes in a large sample of households engaged in agriculture in three peripheral regions of the EU – Northern Ireland, Republic of Ireland and Greece. Firstly, they established a Minimum Income Requirement (MIR) or 'poverty line' for each household in the sample which reflected household composition and stage in the household's reproductive cycle. Households were then allocated to one of six groups; three above MIR and three below. The groups above MIR were differentiated according to the relative importance of farm income to total household income. In the case of Northern Ireland they found that whilst farming provided the major source of income overall (54 per cent), only about one-third of households could be described as 'farm-based', that is they were above MIR and generated virtually all of their income from farming. The frequency of 'poor' households was high. About 35 per cent of active households in Northern Ireland were in this category, although this was much lower than the Republic of Ireland figure of 70 per cent. Interestingly, although farming was the single most important source of income for 'poor' households in Northern Ireland, it contributed less than 50 per cent of their total income: welfare payments were the second most important source. These findings highlight the wide variety of circumstances in households engaged in agriculture, and the fact that the CAP has certainly not eliminated the income problems of a large number of these households.

Many of the problems identified above are endemic in agri-food and rural areas of Northern Ireland. They are extremely intractable and may continue to prove fairly resistant to EU policy interventions. It is partly for these reasons that new thinking and approaches to the development problems of rural areas have gradually been taking shape during the 1990s. These have shifted the emphasis slightly within the traditional CAP framework from a mainly sectoral towards a more spatial approach to intervention in rural areas. The rationale for this shift was given initially in the Commission report 'The Future of Rural Society'.[15] These new policy strands have come to be known collectively as rural development.

The emergence of rural development

The growing prominence of rural development policies signals a desire on the part of the EU to move away from an almost exclusively sectoral policy (agriculture) towards a greater emphasis on a territorial or area-based (rural) approach to development. Rather than simply supporting a single industry or occupational group the new policies seek to bring together a wider range of people from an area to implement a more inclusive development plan for their area. The policies have a strong communitarian flavour and abound with terms such as 'partnership', 'community', 'empowerment' and 'participation'. These are what Anthony Cohen[16] has called 'feel good words'; they implicitly sound desirable and who can be against them? Yet when we examine more closely the stated aims and instruments of such policies we are left wondering about their theoretical or conceptual basis. For a more in-depth critique of the development of rural policies in Northern Ireland see Davis and Shortall,[17] on which this section relies heavily.

Institutional arrangements

The formal institutional responses within the region to the new EU rural policies have been significant. The first was the vesting of responsibility for rural development within the Department of Agriculture for Northern Ireland (DANI). It established a Rural Development Division (RDD) to develop and implement policy, administer EU rural development initiatives and promote awareness of needs in rural areas. The RDD then appointed three rural area co-ordinators, with responsibility for co-ordinating statutory measures, liaising with local groups and advising on regeneration plans: this represented the top-down element of policy. Another important step was the establishment of the Rural Development Council (RDC) in 1991. This body is managed by a council of fifteen members representing a broad spectrum of rural interests. The RDC was funded by DANI and given two main roles. Firstly to provide support to local groups; to help them form, organise, train, appraise needs and resources and formulate plans and project proposals. The RDC had a clear ethos of community development and had regional offices located in areas of disadvantage. The second role was to advise on all matters relating to rural development in Northern Ireland. This advice was seen as emanating from the RDC development officers' close contact with community groups in rural areas, and represented the bottom-up link. From the start there seemed to be overlap in the roles of the DANI area co-ordinators and the RDC development officers. The final formal response was the establishment, in 1991, of the Rural Community Network. It too was a part of the government's rural development initiative, part-funded by DANI, with further funding through voluntary trusts. It has operated as an umbrella network for community groups and represents the needs and aspirations of rural communities. The RDC and, to some extent, the RCN operate in ways which seek to bring together the top-down statutory responses and the bottom-up initiatives of community groups.

In addition to the formal structures there is quite complex set of more *informal* arrangements. For example, many partnership boards are also actively involved in implementing rural development programmes and projects. These include: District Council Partnership Boards which handle Peace and Reconciliation funding, Area Based Strategic Action Groups (ABSAGs) which administer DANI rural development funds, and Local Action Groups (LAGs) which are responsible for LEADER funding. It is not difficult to see the potential for overlap, duplication and even conflict between these various groups: there will almost certainly be a need for rationalisation and simplification of the rather complex apparatus which has emerged.

Rural development programmes

The plethora of complementary and overlapping programmes can also be somewhat bewildering. To begin with there is the Rural Development Strategy (1994–9) which is funded under the region's Single Programming Document: this is the rural strand of the Structural Funds.

Having been categorised as Objective one, the region also qualified for the LEADER Community Initiative, a pilot programme for integrated rural development, intended to serve as a model for future practice. LEADER is a partnership between the EU, national government and Local Action Groups. The LEADER I programme, 1990–4, provided funding of about £4 million. Unlike the rest of the EU, a formal organisation, the RDC, was the regional LAG for LEADER. It funded sixteen projects undertaken by non-profit, community-based companies in disadvantaged rural areas. The RDC itself questioned the efficacy of its role as the only LAG, given that one objective of LEADER was for local groups to formulate their own development plans. Under the LEADER II (1994–9) programme a total of 24 LAGs and other collective bodies have received funding through DANI. Funding is not restricted to non profit making bodies, and it can be used to finance activities outside disadvantaged areas. The LEADER II programme has modest funding of about £13 million but is probably the highest profile EU initiative in the sector.

Northern Ireland also qualified for the INTERREG I and II programmes. These aim to build up lagging regions along the border areas within the EU. INTERREG has considerably more funding than the LEADER programme; it is providing £125 million for both parts of Ireland; this covers all of the province except the Greater Belfast Area. It is channelled through the Department of Finance and Personnel, and as it deals with the border region, it has a particular impact on rural areas.

Alongside these EU rural programmes, Northern Ireland also receives substantial funding through the International Fund for Ireland (IFI), and more recently the Special Support Programme for Peace and Reconciliation (SSPPR). The IFI was set up in 1986, its objective being to promote economic and social advance in Northern Ireland, and to encourage reconciliation and contact between the two communities. The SSPPR seeks to pursue its aims through economic and social development. Both the IFI and the SSPPR have rural regeneration sub-programmes which provide greater funding than LEADER.

Issues in rural development

The emergence of EU-driven rural development initiatives in the region has been a fascinating experiment which has attracted widespread interest and attention. However, the level of financial support, although significant, has not been particularly large compared to agricultural spending or to mainstream programmes. For example, in the five years to 1996 annual average public expenditure on rural development was around £7 million; although on an increasing trend, with £13.7 million spent in 1996. This may be compared with the annual average level of direct subsidies to farmers over the same period of about £148 million (including the 1996 BSE aid). The rural development programme has been successful in promoting the formation of a large number of community development organisations. According to the Rural Development Council the number of these increased from 45 in 1991 to 150 in 1997. These groups are involved in a wide range of overlapping activities: local enterprise development, tourism, training, local service provision, environmental schemes; cross-community work. There is tremendous energy, quite high levels of voluntary activity in some groups and a palpable sense of enthusiasm and commitment at the local level.

It is not the purpose of this chapter to engage in a detailed critique of the region's rural development programmes and activities. However, it is worth mentioning a few issues which need to be debated for the future. Although these are not unique to rural development they are nevertheless relevant to the ongoing regional debate about future priorities and directions of EU rural policies. For a fuller discussion of these issues see Davis and Shortall[18] and Matthews.[19] Firstly, there is a question about the policy goals and priorities amongst the main themes of economic regeneration, social cohesion, environmental conservation and political stability. Secondly, there is the issue of the time needed for pre-development work, that is the stage that precedes development, sometimes referred to as capacity building.[20] It is not clear how long there needs to be a policy commitment to pre-development activities. This issue has particular significance when we consider, for example, the core aim of the Rural Regeneration strand of the SSPPR. Thirdly, there is the question of the legitimacy of development partnerships and local governance. The funding arrangements and pressures can mean that partnerships are assembled very quickly. Issues of legitimacy and representation then arise: Bryden[21] asks, 'what is "going on" when the state by-passes legitimate authorities (local elective authorities) in transferring power and responsibility to quasi-autonomous, or autonomous, bodies like Local Enterprise Companies, ad-hoc local groups, committees, and so on?'

A fourth question concerns the efficacy of the area-based approach to rural development. There may be a fairly compelling administrative logic in the selective channelling of relatively small amounts of funding to disadvantaged geographic areas. However, more empirical evidence is needed on the extent to which the benefits of financial injections can actually be captured by these areas: even if the benefits are retained there is also a question about how they are distributed. For evidence on some of these issues see the study of Mid Wales Development by Willis and Saunders.[22] Finally, there is the relationship between rural development and the mainstream programmes which dominate in expenditure terms. Without adequate co-ordination there is the scope for considerable dead-weight and displacement activity.[23]

Conclusion

This chapter has attemped to explore the effects of 25 years of EU membership on the agri-food sector and rural society in Northern Ireland. It has highlighted a number of fairly profound changes which were linked to EU agricultural and rural policies. The scale of EU intervention has been fairly massive yet many of the traditional problems remain. Much of the agri-food sector still suffers from serious structural weaknesses and would not be viable without the current high level of subsidies; this is especially true in the more remote disadvantaged areas. Poverty remains a problem in many farm households especially those associated with beef and sheep enterprises in areas where there are relatively few off-farm employment opportunities. In wider rural society there has been a tremendous amount of policy-driven development activity since the late 1980s. This has operated in a fairly segmented way from agricultural policy and has been quite successful in engaging with the non-farming rural community but less so with farmers. Evaluation of much of this activity is difficult. Substantial questions remain about the sustainability of some of these initiatives if the level of public support is stepped down.

One question which must be asked, from a regional perspective, is whither agri-food and rural development? Any forward look must be ever mindful of likely future directions in the EU policy framework, given that the sector will continue for the foreseeable future to be heavily dependent on policy transfer payments; a dependence begat by the CAP. In the period before the publication of Agenda 2000 a quite radical line of thinking about CAP reform was evident in the Commission. This was reflected in Buckwell's[24] proposals for a major restructuring of CAP towards a Common Agricultural and Rural Policy for Europe (CARPE). This envisaged a major shift away from farm commodity support towards Environmental and Cultural Landscape Payments and Rural Development Incentives. Although the Agenda 2000[25] and subsequent Commission proposals[26] are not inconsistent with this approach, they represent a limited and fairly conservative response; perhaps not surprising when one considers the political economy of rural policy formation in the EU.

The main thrust of the institutional proposals is for deepening of the 1992 reforms through further shifts from price supports to direct payments. However, it is proposed that support will be modulated through a ceiling covering all direct income payments which can be made to individual farms: member states will be able to introduce differentiation criteria in relation to the ceiling. Although the level of the ceiling will be a key concern for many larger UK farmers it is unlikely to pose a major threat to the level of support available to farmers in Northern Ireland.

An important strand of the proposals is the more prominent role envisaged for agri-environmental measures. These may be viewed as a more socially acceptable rationale for supporting farmers' incomes, whilst at the same time responding to society's needs for environmental services. The principle of cross-compliance will probably be much more prominent, for example making payments of direct income supports to farmers conditional upon their use of acceptable environmental practices.

The future role of rural development policy is not clear. There is a clear desire to streamline and rationalise procedures and structures. However, it is difficult to see how rural development measures in practice can become the so-called 'second pillar' of the CAP, with a budget allocation of around four per cent from 2000 to 2006 in the current EU–15.

There is quite a lot of uncertainty about how far and how fast the reforms will go. Arguably, by the end of 1998, the momentum was being lost; and as Matthews[27] had demonstrated, the EU budget constraint could cease to be the force for change that it was in the past.

Notes

1. Commission of the European Communities (1996), *The Agricultural Situation in the European Union*, Brussels/Luxembourg: Office for Official Publications.
2. Department of Agriculture for Northern Ireland, (1997) *Statistical Review of Northern Ireland Agriculture*, 1996, Economics and Statistics Division.
3. Department of Finance and Personnel (1997), *Quarterly Economic Report (June)*, Economics Division.
4. Department of Agriculture for Northern Ireland (1996), *Size and Performance of the Northern Ireland Food and Drinks Processing Sector, 1994*, Economics and Statistics Division.
5. Department of Agriculture for Northern Ireland (1997), *Statistical Review of Northern Ireland Agriculture, 1996*, Economics and Statistics Division.
6. J. Davis (1991) *The Competitiveness of the Northern Ireland Dairy Sector*, Department of Agricultural and Food Economics, The Queen's University of Belfast.
7. House of Lords Select Committee on the European Communities (1990), *The Future of Rural Society*, London, HMSO.
8. T. F. Stainer (1985) *An Analysis of Economic Trends in Northern Ireland Agriculture Since 1970*, Economic and Statistics Division, Department of Agriculture for Northern Ireland.
9. P. Caskie, J. Davis and C. Papadas, (1998), *The Impact of BSE on the Economy of Northern Ireland*, Centre for Rural Studies, The Queen's University of Belfast.
10. J. Davis, P. Caskie, G. Gilbreath and M. Wallace (1998), *A Socio-Economic Evaluation of the Hill Livestock Compensatory Allowances Scheme*, Centre for Rural Studies, The Queen's University of Belfast.
11. J. E. Moss and S. M. Chilton, (1997) *A Socio-Economic Evaluation of the Mourne Mountains and Slieve Croob Environmentally Sensitive Area Scheme*, Centre for Rural Studies, The Queen's University of Belfast.

12. T. F. Stainer (1997), 'The EU Agri-Monetary System', *First Trust Economic Outlook and Business Review*, Volume 12.2, June.
13. T. F. Stainer, (1988), 'The EC's Agri-Monetary System Illustrated in the Context of Cross-Border Trade in Ireland', Papers in Agricultural and Food Economics, 1, 54–81. DANI, Belfast.
14. J. Davis, N. Mack and A. Kirke, (1997), 'New Perspectives on Farm Household Incomes', *Journal of Rural Studies* 13, 57–64.
15. European Commission (1998), *The Future of Rural Society*, COM(88) 371, Office of Official Publications, Luxembourg.
16. A. Cohen (1985), *The Symbolic Construction of Community*, London, Routledge.
17. J. Davis, and S. Shortall, (1998), 'Rural Change in Northern Ireland: Experiences in the European Union', in Davis, J. (ed.), *Rural Change in Ireland*, Institute of Irish Studies, Queen's University Belfast.
18. Ibid.
19. A. Matthews, (1995), 'Agricultural Competitiveness and Rural Development', in J. W. O'Hagan (ed.), *The Economy of Ireland*, pp. 328–62. Dublin, Gill and Macmillan.
20. P. Commins, and M. Keane, (1994), 'Developing The Rural Economy – Problems, Programmes and Prospects', in *New Approaches To Rural Development*, NESC Report No. 97. Dublin, NESC.
21. J. Bryden, (1994), 'Towards Sustainable Rural Communities: From Theory to Action', in J. Bryden (ed.) *Towards Sustainable Rural Communities*, pp. 211–35. Guelph, University of Guelph.
22. K. G. Willis, and C. M. Saunders, (1988), 'The Impact of a Development Agency on Employment: Resurrection Discounted?', *Applied Economics*, 20, 81–96.
23. C. Curtin, T. Haase, and H. Tovey, (1997), *Poverty in Rural Ireland: A Political Economy Approach*, Dublin, Oak Tree Press.
24. A. Buckwell, (1997) 'Agricultural Economics in a Brave Liberal World', *European Review of Agricultural Economics*, 24, 339–58.
25. European Commission: (July 1997), 'Agenda 2000: for a stronger and wider Europe', Office of Official Publications, Luxembourg.
26. European Commission: (18 March 1998), 'Proposals for council regulations (EC) concerning the reform of the Common Agricultural Policy', Com. 1998/158/final.
27. A. Matthews, (1996), 'The Disappearing Budget Constraint on EU Agricultural Policy', *Food Policy*, 21, 497–508.

5
Trading Partners: Northern Ireland's External Economic Links
Esmond Birnie

Northern Ireland is a small region and it is almost self-evident that the links with the rest of the UK, other parts of the European Union (EU) and the rest of the world, will therefore have a profound effect on the performance of the regional economy. This chapter considers such connections. The focus is on the economic interconnections between Northern Ireland and other regions and countries. This is not in any way to deny the importance of the social and cultural interrelationships between Northern Ireland and the rest of the world.

A previous chapter in this book (that by Graham Gudgin) has assessed the performance of the Northern Ireland economy since 1973 and the extent to which EU membership has impacted on this. That chapter considered one of the major economic links between Northern Ireland and the rest of the world: the net transfer of funds from Brussels along with the much larger subvention from London. In contrast, this chapter will give attention to Northern Ireland's trading links.

Although trade data are far from perfect (their coverage is often limited to recent years only and restricted to manufacturing) it is usually possible to produce a fuller picture of Northern Ireland's interregional trading than would be the case for other forms of economic link such as the migration of labour, flows of capital or changes of ownership. Moreover, according to some theories, extra-regional sales are the main source of economic growth within a region.[1] The rather poor economic growth performance of many of the African and South American countries which pursued policies of economic protectionism during the 1950s–80s, along with the contrasting export-led 'Asian tiger' miracle economies of 1960–95, has sometimes been taken as evidence that 'open' or outward-orientated trading policies are the key to growth.[2]

The economic background: a small and sometimes poorly performing European region

It has to be stressed that Northern Ireland is an extremely small region (population 1.6 million) and that small region is placed within a much larger national economic and monetary union: the UK (population 58 million). The population size of Northern Ireland is, for example, about comparable to that of some of the larger English conurbations such as Birmingham, Liverpool or Manchester. This has profound implications for the subject at hand: Northern Ireland's extra-regional links.

In general small economies have higher ratios of export sales to total national income (GDP) than larger ones; contrast, say, the USA or Japan with Iceland or Luxembourg.[3] Thus one would expect Northern Ireland to have a relatively high ratio of external sales to regional GDP (see below). As a region within the UK, Northern Ireland has been highly integrated into the rest of the national economy in terms of most economic outcomes and policies.[4] Common rates of income and corporation taxes apply and similarly the same rates of social welfare benefits exist across the UK and the Minimum Wage is set at one national rate.[5] The banking and financial sector has been sufficiently developed and tied into the national sector to ensure that capital in Northern Ireland is available at much the same interest rate and on the same terms as in other UK regions.

In formal terms, policy-makers in Belfast, unlike their counterparts in Dublin, have hitherto lacked the autonomy to set either a separate fiscal (i.e. tax and spending) or monetary (money supply growth and level of interest rates) policy for Northern Ireland.[6] In fact, a case could be made for doubting the intellectual worth of considerations of the Northern Ireland economy as a *separate* region given the degree of openness to and integration with the rest of the UK. After all, far fewer books and articles have been written about the economy of Strathclyde or the West Midlands. Certainly, it would be a mistake to analyse the regional economy as if Northern Ireland were a quasi-independent state. There may be a political agenda present when the assumption is made, sometimes overt but sometimes implicit, that Northern Ireland should 'pay its own way' and if it cannot then it is ripe for either dissolution and/or collapse into the arms of its southern neighbour[7] or at least some hybrid constitutional status whereby policy making is harmonised between the two Irish economies.[8] Even during the Stormont years, 1921–72, the fiscal transfer from London to Belfast was a bone of contention.[9] In truth, the longstanding emphasis on the Northern Ireland economy as a region[10] probably is a product of the devolved form of administration which existed until 1972 and which may now be about to be restored, albeit in a very different form, from 1999 onwards.

Table 5.1 presents a summary of the recent economic performance of Northern Ireland compared to the rest of the UK and EU.

It is worth noting that Table 5.1 emphasises that compared to the UK and EU Northern Ireland is a relatively poor region with relatively high levels of unemployment (especially long term; see Chapter 3 for more detail on the possibly improved performance of the regional economy during the 1990s). By implication, one objective for policy makers might be to promote accelerated convergence between Northern Ireland the rest of the UK and EU economies. This, to a large extent, underlines the thinking contained within recent statements of

Table 5.1 Unemployment and GDP per capita in Northern Ireland and the Republic of Ireland compared to the rest of the EU, 1994–5

	Standardised unemployment (%) 1995*	Long term unemployment as % of total 1995*	GDP per hd, 1994 purchasing power parities (EU 15 = 100)[#]
EU 15 average	10.7	n.a.	100
Belgium average	9.4	61.8	114
Lowest region	6.9	46.7	91
Highest region	13.3	81.5	183
*Denmark average***	7.1	28.2	114
Finland average	18.1	29.9	91
Lowest region	6.2	n.a	91
Highest region	18.2	30.0	126
France average	11.2	42.6	108
Lowest region	8.7	40.5	87
Highest region	15.3	53.7	161
*Germany average****	8.2	47.8	110
Lowest region	4.9	39.6	196
Highest region	16.7	56.2	57
Greece average	9.1	50.9	65
Lowest region	4.5	50.7	57
Highest region	11.0	50.2	73
*Rep of Ireland average***	14.3	51.1	88

Table 5.1 (Continued)

	Standardised unemployment (%) 1995*	Long term unemployment as % of total 1995*	GDP per hd, 1994 purchasing power parities (EU 15 = 100)#
Italy average	12.0	61.5	102
Lowest region	6.0	43.8	131
Highest region	25.9	72.8	68
Luxembourg average**	2.7	24.0	169
Netherlands average	7.3	44.4	105
Lowest region	6.9	46.4	101
Highest region	8.9	47.4	102
Portugal average	7.1	48.7	67
Lowest region	4.6	67.2	48
Highest region	7.8	60.0	68
Spain average	22.7	54.4	76
Lowest region	7.8	60.0	58
Highest region	18.5	63.0	64
Sweden average**	9.1	n.a.	98
UK average	8.8	43.1	99
Lowest region	6.7	35.2	117
N. Ireland (also highest UK region)	13.0	51.6	80

Notes:
*Unemployment defined according to a standardised economic activity classification. Long term unemployed being those out of work for more than one year. (The regional long term unemployment and GDP per capita data correspond to whichever regions had the lowest or highest rates of *total* unemployment.)
GDP is a measure of the total value of goods and services produced during each year. Although GDP is often used in international comparisons, peculiarities of the Republic of Ireland economy imply that it is an inappropriate indicator of living standards (see below) which biases measured comparative productivity in an upwards direction. The purchasing power parity based calculations make allowance for variations in the cost of living.
**No sub-national regional breakdown was available.
***Including the former East Germany.
Source: Office for National Statistics (1997).

economic policy in Northern Ireland.[11] In fact, it is possible to look at the extent of economic links between Northern Ireland and other regions as both an indicator of relative competitiveness performance (export levels would be significant in this context) and also as a means to improve that performance (for example, through inward investment and the extent of external ownership).[12]

The level and geographical distribution of trade

Table 5.2 attempts to summarise the recent trading performance of the Northern Ireland economy by presenting estimates of the geographical composition of manufacturing sales during the first half of the 1990s.

The data shown in Table 5.2 are restricted to manufacturing but are highly indicative of the overall performance of the Northern Ireland economy. Whereas in the early 1990s external sales from manufacturing were greater than £4 billion, agriculture would then have contributed about another £500m and the other tradables (activities such as tourism and financial) something less than farming.[13]

Table 5.2 Northern Ireland manufacturing sector: Total sales, external sales and exports (£m, current prices). Percentage composition of sales in parenthesis

Year	1991–92 (%)	1992–93 (%)	1993–94 (%)	1994–95 (%)	1995–96 (%)
Total sales	6450 (100)	6827 (100)	7267 (100)	7848 (100)	8705 (100)
N. Ireland	2278 (35)	2425 (36)	2578 (35)	2631 (34)	2826 (32)
External sales	4172 (65)	4402 (64)	4689 (65)	5217 (66)	5879 (68)
Gt. Britain	2388 (37)	2422 (35)	2514 (35)	2614 (33)	2806 (32)
Export sales	1784 (28)	1980 (29)	2175 (30)	2603 (33)	3073 (35)
Rep. of Ireland	437 (7)	498 (7)	544 (7)	631 (8)	710 (8)
Rest of EU	786 (12)	879 (13)	916 (13)	1047 (13)	1242 (14)
Rest of World	561 (9)	603 (9)	715 (10)	925 (12)	1121 (13)

Note: These estimates were constructed using a variety of sources. The principal source was the Northern Ireland Economic Research Centre's survey of all manufacturing firms with 20 or more employees. This was augmented by the Annual Survey by the small firms agency (LEDU). To account for any underrepresentation of small firms, a number of small non-assisted firms with fewer than 20 employees were also surveyed. Overall coverage in the manufacturing sector is high, accounting for approximately 90 per cent of manufacturing employment in 1995/96 and about 45 per cent of manufacturing firms. Estimates for manufacturing firms are produced by grossing up by sector and size range.
Source: NIERC/DED/IDB (1997).

The total level of external sales increases from about 44 per cent of regional GDP in 1991/92 to 48 per cent in 1995/96. (It was assumed that non-manufacturing external sales increased from £700m to £800m during that period. The rates for exports properly defined, that is sales going beyond the UK, increased from about 20 to 26 per cent; assuming non-manufacturing exports increased from £400m to £500m.) This extent of openness to the rest of the world beyond the region is less than that of, say, Denmark, Netherlands and Belgium but greater than that of the UK as a whole (though, the UK on average would have a similar export ratio to that of Northern Ireland taken separately. In 1995 the UK export ratio was 28 per cent).

Throughout the first half of the 1990s the geographical composition of Northern Ireland manufacturing sales remained roughly stable such that about one-third were sold within the region, one-third to Great Britain and the remaining third were exports to the rest of the world (including the Republic of Ireland). However, as Table 5.3 confirms, during the first half of the 1990s sales to the Northern Ireland and Great Britain destinations increased more slowly than the average for all external sales and exports. During the period from 1991 to 1996 sales to the Republic of Ireland and the rest of the EU increased at three times the rate of growth of sales going to Great Britain. In part, Northern Ireland was participating in a general EU-wide and indeed global trend with rates of growth of international trade being higher than those for GDP, with the result that economies have become more open.

Table 5.3 Northern Ireland manufacturing sales growth (nominal terms), 1991–92, 1995–96

Geographical destination	Total % growth in nominal terms
Total sales	35
Northern Ireland	24
External sales	41
Great Britain	18
Export sales	72
Republic of Ireland	62
Rest of EU	58
Rest of the world	100

Source: As for Table 5.2.

Previous policy measures to promote co-operation between Northern Ireland and the Republic of Ireland

In recent years the nature and extent of economic links between Northern Ireland and the Republic of Ireland have probably been given more attention than any other type of link.[14] In one sense this degree of attention has been surprising since Northern Ireland remains a UK regional economy which is highly integrated within that national economy. However, the creation of institutions to promote increased economic co-operation has been viewed in some quarters as an essential component in an overall political settlement in Northern Ireland[15] and this has been official Anglo–Irish policy thinking from the Frameworks Documents[16] through to the 'three strand' multi-Party agreement which was eventually made in April 1998 and confirmed in the May 1998 referendum. One striking feature of the political economy of North–South co-operation in the mid to late 1990s is the number of parallels to developments about forty years previously when the then Republic of Ireland Minister for Industry and Commerce, Seán Lemass, declared, 'Ireland is too small a country not to be seriously handicapped in its economic development by its division into two areas separated by a customs barrier'.[17] During 1958–65, as in the 1990s, there was a tension between the anti-partitionist rhetoric of the Dublin Government and its fear that all-Ireland arrangements might harm Southern economic interests, while the Unionist leadership, for its part, often saw the co-operation agenda as a Trojan Horse for constitutional change but in practice was prepared to be pragmatic given pressure from the Northern Ireland business community.[18] In the contemporary debates it has been claimed that the current level of integration is less than would be reasonably expected and therefore there would be larger gains to both Irish economies through ever increasing integration.

Perhaps the main area of policy intervention in order to promote cross-border economic integration has been with respect to industry and trade.[19] The Confederation of British Industry and Confederation of Irish Industry have been working jointly at a sectoral level to identify opportunities for greater trade. Chambers of Commerce in Northern Ireland and the Republic of Ireland have sponsored schemes to promote cross-border trade. Development agencies have attempted to encourage local sourcing (for example by the multinational plants in Northern Ireland or the Republic of Ireland) on an all Ireland basis.

There has also been some pooling of research activities (for example by the Institute for Advanced Microelectronics which links universities in both economies).

In agriculture, fishing and forestry there have been some longstanding and successful initiatives.[20] For example, the common management of the Foyle Fisheries since 1952 and reciprocal fishing rights in coastal waters (this is of mutual benefit given the Northern Ireland specialism in shellfish and that of the Republic of Ireland in whitefish). Animal health programmes have also been run in parallel. Difficulties were however caused in the 1980s as divergent exchange rate movements and the consequent differences in prices to farmers provided incentives for disruptive and variable movements of animals across the border. (One consequence of the 1996–8 BSE crisis was that the Republic of Ireland sealed its border to prevent the movement of cattle from Northern Ireland to further processing in the Republic of Ireland.)

There are a number of institutional links between the financial systems in the two economies.[21] However, the breaking of the Irish pound–pound sterling parity in 1978 and the subsequent variation of the Republic of Ireland/UK exchange rate has made co-operation more difficult. This is even more true now as the Republic of Ireland is amongst the first group of members of the new European single currency but the UK has decided to exercise its opt-out for at least a couple of years.[22] Moreover, post-1979 the regulatory regime in Northern Ireland has probably moved further away from that in the Republic of Ireland. Both economies have a stock exchange but the Belfast exchange does not perform a capital raising function. Ironically, Republic of Ireland firms through their use of the one in Dublin are more integrated into the London exchange.

At the start of the 1990s eight per cent of the Republic of Ireland's out-of-state tourist revenue derived from visitors from Northern Ireland and the equivalent in Northern Ireland represented 17 per cent of total tourist revenues. Thus cross-Border tourist flows were especially important to the Northern Ireland economy.[23] There is already co-operation in terms of joint marketing and booking facilities and these were upgraded in late 1996.

In the early 1970s there was a 300 MW electricity interconnection which probably yielded a total benefit of IR £10 million annually in terms of pooling generation capacity and lowering marginal cost of supply.[24] Repeated terrorist attack brought an end to this form of co-operation which has recently been re-instated. Pollitt[25] notes that the main North–South interconnector was put back in place in March

1995 at a cost of £1.2m to NIE and £0.4m to the ESB. The savings to each system were £0.5m annually. Pollitt reckoned that in the long run annual capacity savings would be one per cent of total electricity generating costs on the island of Ireland. A number of standby links between electricity supply in the north–west of Northern Ireland and the Republic of Ireland have always been maintained and the feasibility of interconnection of gas supplies in the late 1990s is being considered.[26]

A number of formal and informal links exist in the area of transport[27] such as the joint operation of the Dublin–Belfast railway. Northern Ireland firms use the ports of Rosslare and Waterford and Republic of Ireland firms use Larne harbour.

There is therefore a mass of initiatives which seek to promote economic co-operation. These differ in the way in which government is involved. Some schemes are sponsored by local government, others by semi-state organisations, central government or supranational agencies (mainly the EU). In aggregate the measures are quite small relative to the total size of the economies. They tend to reflect piecemeal reaction to circumstances rather than some grand design. Measures to promote Northern Ireland–Republic of Ireland economic co-operation have thus been allowed to develop in a pragmatic and decentralised way.

The next section of this chapter considers the contention that the extent of cross-border trade is 'too small'. The multi-party Belfast agreement which was finally negotiated on 10 April 1998 will probably not herald a quantum leap in the extent of common policy making and administrative, economic and social integration between the two Irish economies. This outcome may have been surprising given that the Frameworks Documents[28] had ambitious plans for cross-border executive bodies with the role of harmonising policies and economic outcomes and also with an internal 'dynamic' with respect to their range of functions. Whilst the early draft agreement from talks chairman, Senator George Mitchell, seemed to envisage very extensive powers for all-Ireland political authorities,[29] the final agreement adopted a tentative tone as to which areas of possible co-operation might be placed within the scope of the North/South Ministerial Council.[30] Up to six entirely new implementation bodies are to be created during June 1998–June 1999 (subject to the overall constitutional package being adopted). It appears the Ulster Unionist negotiators succeeded in their objective of maintaining the principle that any agencies operating at an all-Ireland level should be strictly accountable to the Northern Ireland Assembly.

The current extent of cross-border trade: do international comparisons suggest the existing level of integration is too small?

Trade between the two Irish economies provides the most visible manifestation of their inter-relationship and this area has been stressed by those who claim large benefits from further linkage between the two economies.[31]

In fact, as Table 5.4 illustrates, the extent of trade appears small both in absolute terms and relative to the size of the two economies. (Table 5.4 also shows that a Republic of Ireland trade surplus relative to Northern Ireland has been a longstanding feature but in neither case is the scale of exports within Ireland large relative to total GDP.) This conclusion has been reinforced by a detailed study of the export destinations of Northern Ireland manufactured products.[32] Of total sales of £6.5 billion in 1991–2, seven per cent were directed to the Republic of Ireland and in 1995–6 of £8.7 billion of sales eight per cent went to the Republic (see Table 5.2). However, Scott and O'Reilly also cast some doubt on whether the extent of trade integration between Northern Ireland and the Republic of Ireland is actually lower than would be expected given that both are very small markets within a world or even EU perspective. For example, in proportional terms the trade flows between various Scandinavian economies were of a similar size.[33] Or, as MacEnroe and Poole[34] noted, in 1991 Northern Ireland sold about £120 of manufactured goods to each person in the Republic of Ireland compared to Northern Ireland sales of only about £40 per head to Great Britain. At least on this measure there was already

Table 5.4 Trade between NI and the ROI (cross–border merchandise exports)

Year	From Northern Ireland		From Rep. of Ireland	
	£m (current prices)	% of GDP	£m (current prices)	% of GDP
1960	7.4	2.4	20.3	3.7
1972	30.9	2.9	66.9	2.9
1991	496.2	4.7	789.5	3.3
1994	537.0	4.4	722.0	2.5
1995	632.0	4.8	789.0	2.6

Sources: 1960–91: Simpson (1993). 1994–95: based on a narrower definition of trade, manufacturing only; and for the financial years 1993–94 and 1994–95: Irish News (26 March 1997), 'A single island economy'.

stronger trade integration between the two Irish economies than there was between Northern Ireland and the rest of the national UK market. It is thus strange that Michie and Sheehan[35] (p. 247) should feel able to comment that 'The two economies remain poorly integrated'. They go on to qualify, and in fact weaken, this statement by adding, 'this reflects the limits of co-operation achievable under two different national jurisdictions, in other words, under current constitutional arrangements'. In other words, their objection to the *status quo* is much more a political than economic point.

Other economic links: interregional links at the level of the firm

Apart from the levels of trade across the border between Northern Ireland and the Republic of Ireland and, indeed, the trade flows with the rest of the UK and the rest of the world, there are some other economic links which should ideally be considered. These include the nature and extent of inward investment and the possible scope for mergers, acquisitions and partnerships between enterprises in Northern Ireland and Republic of Ireland to gain greater economies of scale.

(a) Extent of external ownership

Table 5.5 illustrates that historically Northern Ireland manufacturing has been more dependent on branch plants of foreign firms than has been the case for industry in Great Britain. The relative importance of the branch plant economy in the region has sometimes been used to explain the prevalence in Northern Ireland of 'production platforms', that is basic production facilities with few of the functions, such as research and development, marketing and higher management, which generate higher levels of value added.[36] It is certainly true that industry has been characterised by relatively low rates of spending on R and D (total R and D spending in Northern Ireland in the early 1990s was equivalent to only 0.5 per cent of regional GDP whereas in the UK as a whole, and in the major western economies, the rate of spending was about 2 per cent.[37] However, as Table 5.5 also shows, since the late 1980s the multinational sector in Northern Ireland first declined in relative size and then increased substantially so it is less likely that a 'branch plant syndrome' can be used to explain the relative weakness of manufacturing. Moreover, relative to at least Northern Ireland indigenous firms, inward investment in Northern Ireland has been relatively intensive in R and D spending (a 1991 survey of Northern

Table 5.5 Relative importance of foreign owned manufacturing plants in Northern Ireland and Great Britain (% of all manufacturing)

	Gross value added		Employment		Investment	
	NI	GB	NI	GB	NI	GB
1973	31.2	14.3	17.9	10.6	33.3	15.1
1979	30.0	20.3	22.7	13.9	`37.4	21.2
1981	30.1	18.1	21.5	14.7	42.7	25.1
1983	19.6	18.6	16.3	14.5	35.7	22.7
1984	27.7	19.6	18.1	14.1	26.3	20.2
1985	18.2	18.1	13.5	13.6	20.4	21.1
1986	21.2	16.9	13.5	12.7	26.7	19.5
1987	26.4	17.8	13.2	12.8	34.0	20.1
1988	22.8	17.7	12.6	12.9	17.3	20.9
1989	27.6	20.5	12.2	14.7	23.4	26.8
1990	33.2	21.4	19.9	15.9	40.9	26.6
1991	38.7	21.2	21.8	17.0	42.2	33.2
1992	38.1	23.0	22.1	17.8	43.9	31.2

Source: Author's calculation based on Census of Production.

Ireland R and D indicated that externally owned firms were more likely to be spending on R and D, 46 per cent, compared to indigenous (29 per cent).[38]

(b) Inter-firm linkages at an all-Ireland level

By global and European standards firms in either Irish economy are usually relatively small. Does this matter and could there be large gains through mergers, acquisitions and alliances on an all-Ireland basis? Standard economic theory notes the importance of economies of scale. As output rises the average cost of producing each unit of that output often drops. Could a lack of such economies of scale explain the weak competitiveness performance of Northern Ireland manufacturing? In 1985 the average (median by employment) plant size in Northern Ireland manufacturing was only about 70 per cent of that in Great Britain, and in the Republic of Ireland about 60 per cent. As two small economies it is not surprising that firms in Northern Ireland and the Republic of Ireland are also generally relatively small and that there is a small representation of medium and larger sized enterprises (those employing more than, say, 499 persons).

However, as Table 5.6 illustrates, the Republic of Ireland now has three manufacturing companies placed within the list of Europe's top 500 companies by market capitalisation whereas Northern Ireland has

Table 5.6 Development of large PLCs; Northern Ireland compared to small European economies, 1997 (number of companies within Europe's top 500 by market capitalisation, end of 1997)

	NI	RoI	Switz	Belg.	Den	Swed	Austr	Neth	Nor
Manufacturing	0	3	5	4	2	6	2	7	5
Non-manufacturing	0	0	8	7	3	3	3	4	4
Total	0	3	13	11	5	9	5	11	9
Total adj. for NI's pop.**	0	1.3	3.1	1.8	1.6	1.7	1.0	1.2	3.4

**Actual total adjusted downwards according to the ratio between the size of that country's population and that of Northern Ireland.
Source: *Financial Times* (22 January 1998).

none (the origin of a company being determined by the location of its headquarters). Once adjustment is made for relative national/regional population size it would appear that if Northern Ireland had been as successful as the Republic of Ireland or any of the small continental economies illustrated in Table 5.6, then it would have had at least one representative in Europe's top 500. If it had been as successful as either Norway or Switzerland there would have been three.

Table 5.7 confirms that even by the standards of the Republic of Ireland, Northern Ireland locally controlled manufacturing firms have relatively small turnovers (and one of the companies on this list, Shorts, has in recent years become part of an international group, whilst the second ranking company, Powerscreen, at the time of writing, is still in the midst of a financial crisis).

The Republic of Ireland has indeed been somewhat more successful than Northern Ireland in developing big, indigenously controlled PLCs. This might prompt the suggestion that perhaps the road for Northern Ireland companies to scale economies in the European market would be through merger with, or acquisition by, Republic of Ireland companies. There are, however, two things which qualify the seemingly impressive achievement of the Republic of Ireland in constructing giant companies. First, it is a recent development driven by overseas acquisitions on the part of two companies (CRH and Jefferson Smurfit) as well as merger and transformation into PLC status of dairy co-operatives (building up the Kerry Group). Second, the Republic of Ireland does not yet appear to have been successful in developing any very large non-manufacturing companies.

Table 5.7 Largest Northern Ireland-controlled manufacturing firms (by turnover) compared to the three largest Republic of Ireland companies (taken from Europe's top 500 by capitalisation), 1996–97

NI company	Turnover ($m)*	Sector	RoI company	Turnover ($m)*	Sector
Shorts	660	Aerospace	Jefferson Smurfit	3800	Packaging
Power-screen	490	Engineering	CRH	3600	Materials
United Dairy Farmers	420	Dairying	Kerry Group	1800	Dairying
Lamont	200	Textiles			
Desmond & Sons	190	Clothing			
Harland & Wolff	190	Shipbuilding			
Boxmore	140	Packaging			
O'Kane Poultry	130	Meat processing			
Brett Martin	90	Building products			
Galen	60	Pharmaceuticals			

*Using the September 1997 average market exchange rate.
Source: Belfast Telegraph (18 February 1998).

At the same time, it is worth stressing that an increasing amount of cross-border acquisition of companies has been taking place albeit almost all of this has involved Republic of Ireland companies buying up firms in Northern Ireland. Rafferty[39] makes three points in this regard:

(1) While a number of Republic of Ireland companies have now built up substantial interests in Northern Ireland, there has been little movement in the opposite direction.
(2) Apart from two major banks, AIB and Bank of Ireland, Republic of Ireland PLCs with substantial interests in Northern Ireland include CRH, Fitzwilton, Fyffes, Grafton, Heiton, Smurfit and United Drug. Large private companies with Northern Ireland interests include Glen Dimplex, Easons and Musgraves.
(3) The largest company with roughly equal amounts of profits deriving from both sides of the border is Ulster Bank. Castlemahon Foods, listed at 263 in the Republic of Ireland's *Business and*

Finance Top 1000 may be the largest company in the Republic of Ireland with a Northern Ireland parent.

Table 5.8 emphasises the much greater penetration of Republic of Ireland ownership into Northern Ireland than *vice versa*.

To summarise, the data in Tables 5.6 and 5.7 suggest the possibility of gains from increased scale through mergers with, or acquisitions by, Republic of Ireland companies. Table 5.8 indicates that this process has already started. Such developments might be politically unpalatable to some Unionists in Northern Ireland though this resistance might be reduced if the April 1998 political agreement does stick.[40] Some of the objections to increased Republic of Ireland ownership in the Northern Ireland market would be reduced if there were some takeovers in the opposite direction. In fact, the fears on the Northern Ireland side are not simply those of political participation. There is a concern that part of the Northern Ireland food processing sector is going to be reduced to the status of a mere supplier of raw materials to the much larger enterprises south of the border (e.g. some of the very big dairy co-ops and PLCs in the Republic of Ireland have bought over operations).

Alongside the increased presence of Republic of Ireland enterprises in Northern Ireland, the grocery and retailing sector has since the mid

Table 5.8 Ownership of the top 100 companies in Northern Ireland and Republic of Ireland

	Top 50	51–100	Top 100
Northern Ireland			
Indigenous	22	34	56
Republic of Ireland	9	7	16
UK	13	5	18
USA	2	2	4
Others	4	2	4
Total	50	50	100
Rep. of Ireland			
Indigenous	31	32	63
Northern Ireland	0	0	0
UK	5	3	8
USA	9	8	17
Others	5	7	12
Total	50	50	100

Sources: *Ulster Business Top 100* (August 1994) and *Business and Finance Top 1000* (January 1994) quoted in Rafferty (1996).

1990s witnessed the arrival of the big Great Britain multiples. This development is producing a complex pattern of social, economic and environmental costs and benefits: cheaper bread and petrol, job losses in Northern Ireland's traditional bakeries and food processors and the belated arrival of the English-style out-of-town shopping centre.

Conclusion

It is important to stress that this chapter has *not* considered a number of important extra-regional links. For example, the transport connections between Northern Ireland and the rest of the world and whether their cost, frequency and reliability impedes cost competitiveness (probably not as large a negative factor as has traditionally been argued).[41] Northern Ireland is a region with a history of exporting some of its surplus labour to the rest of the UK (without net outmigration unemployment rates would have been even higher). More recently, commentators have begun to worry that outmigration may erode the region's stock of human capital to the extent that those who leave are those with above average levels of qualifications.[42] Differential migration rates may also go some way to explain the persistent difference between Catholic and Protestant unemployment rates[43] and may also have long-term implications for voting patterns. There are some connections between the wage rates set in Great Britain and counterpart levels in Northern Ireland, whether through the operation of national wage bargaining or the national minimum wage from 1999 onwards.[44]

In addition to considerations of the overall extent of trading and co-operative links between the two Irish economies there has also been a recent debate as to whether there might be large gains to economic integration concentrated within the so-called Belfast–Dublin economic corridor.[45] Whilst strongly competitive clusters or corridors of economic activity probably do exist in various parts of the western world and some of these do cut across frontiers (for example, Vancouver–Seattle or the region around Basel) it is unlikely that Belfast–Dublin displays many of the preconditions which are probably necessary for such developments: world class research and development facilities, a large number of internationally competitive manufacturing firms and a high density of good transport links.

What this chapter has attempted to establish is the nature and extent of trading links between Northern Ireland and the rest of the world. Particular attention was given to the extent of trade with the

Republic of Ireland. Despite claims to the contrary, it is by no means clear that the amount of this is less than would be reasonably expected. For a considerable number of years Northern Ireland has had a trading deficit with the Republic of Ireland, in recent years this has been paralleled by a capital in-flow in the sense that local companies are being taken over by those from the Republic of Ireland.

Notes

1. H. Armstrong and J. Taylor (1993), *Regional Economics and Policy*, London: Harvester Wheatsheaf.
2. D. Lal (1997), *The Poverty of 'Development Economics'*, Hobart Paperback No. 16, London, Institute of Economic Affairs.
3. NIEC (1998), 'Regional economic and policy impacts of EMU: The case of Northern Ireland', *Research Monograph No. 6*, Belfast, Northern Ireland Economic Council.
4. J. Michie and M. Sheehan (1998) 'The political economy of a divided Ireland', *Cambridge Journal of Economies*, vol. 22, pp. 243–59, consider the extent of statistical co-integration between the growth rates of Northern Ireland, Great Britain and the Republic of Ireland. On this basis they claim to find that the Northern Ireland growth rate is poorly integrated with either economy and therefore, in their view, is in a somewhat anomalous position as a place apart. I wonder how far this result is sensitive to the peculiarities of Northern Ireland's performance in the 1990s. In particular, as other commentators have noted, in the early 1990s the recession in Great Britain was very deep whereas Northern Ireland passed through 1990–2 without a decline in output (NIEC, 1993 'Northen Ireland and the recent recession: Cyclical strength or structural weakness?' *Report No. 104*, Belfast, Northern Ireland Economic Council). This difference of outcome has been variously attributed to the absence of a 1980s house price-based boom in Northern Ireland and the relatively higher growth of public spending in the region in the early 1990s compared to Great Britain. Michie and Sheehan have thus not proven that Northern Ireland is not integrated with the rest of the UK in trading and policy terms.
5. NIEC (1998), 'The impact of a national minimum wage on the Northern Ireland economy: A response to the low pay commission', *Occasional Paper No. 9*, Belfast, Northern Ireland Economic Council.
6. The Republic of Ireland as another small open economy, but also as an independent state within the EU, may have more policy autonomy than Northern Ireland but that autonomy is not absolute. To the extent that there has been an exchange rate target, whether the parity link to the pound sterling during 1922–78 or the *de facto* Deutschemark standard for much of the period of European Monetary System membership since 1978, then the ability to operate an independent monetary and interest rate policy has largely been lost. However, the punt was substantially devalued in early 1993 and since then, as the celtic tiger economy has boomed, short term interest rates

have been maintained at levels about twice those in the recession bound German and French economies. As a member of the single currency club from January 1999 onwards the Republic of Ireland will surrender this ability to set interest rates which are appropriate to the stage of the domestic economic cycle. In this sense, the Republic of Ireland will be in the same relation to the rest of the continental EU economies as Northern Ireland now occupies with respect to the rest of the UK monetary union. There could be severe problems for the Republic of Ireland as it is forced to reduce its interest rates to the lower continental levels whilst being in the middle of an inflationary boom (*Economist*, 1998, April 11).

7. R. Rowthorn and N. Wayne (1988), *Northern Ireland: The Political Economy Conflict*, London, Puto Press; R. Munck (1993), *The Irish Economy*, London, Puto Press.
8. J. Bradley (1996), 'Exploring long-term economic and social consequences of peace and reconciliation in the island of Ireland', *Forum for Peace and Reconciliation Consultancy Studies*, No. 4, Dublin, Stationery Office; J. Michie and M. Sheehan (1998), 'The political economy of a divided Ireland', *Cambridge Journal of Economics*, Vol. 22, pp. 243–59.
9. T. Wilson (1955), *Ulster under Home Rule*, Oxford University Press.
10. Isles and Cuthbert (1957), *An Economic Survey of Northern Ireland*, Belfast, HMSO; T. Wilson (1989), *Ulster: Conflict and Consent*, Oxford, Blackwell.
11. DED (1990), *Northern Ireland Competing in the 1990s: The Key to Growth*, Belfast, Department of Economic Development. Also DED (1995), *Growing Competitively: A Review of Economic Development Policy in Northern Ireland*, Belfast, Department of Economic Development.
12. NIEC (1998), 'Competitiveness and industrial policy in Northern Ireland', *Research Monograph*, No. 5, Belfast, Northern Ireland Economic Council.
13. D. M. W. N. Hitchens and J. E. Birnie (1994), *The Competitiveness of Industry in Ireland*, Aldershot, Avebury.
14. R. Munck (1993), *The Irish Economy*, London, Puto Press; Hitchens and Birnie (1994), op. cit.; D. W. M. N. Hitchens and J. E. Birnie (1997), 'The potential for a Belfast–Dublin economic corridor', *Australasian Journal of Regional Studies*, Vol. 2, No. 2, pp. 167–87; M. D'Arcy and T. Dickson (1995), *Border Crossings: Developing Ireland's Island Economy*, Dublin, Gill and Macmillan; J. Bradley (1996), 'Exploring long-term economic and social consequences of peace and reconciliation in the island of Ireland', *Forum for Peace and Reconciliation Consultancy Studies*, No. 4, Dublin, Stationery Office; Michie and Sheehan (1998), op. cit.
15. P. Bew, H. Patterson and P. Teague (1997), *Between War and Peace*, London, Lawrence and Wishart.
16. *Framework Document* (1995), 'Frameworks for the Future', London and Dublin, Government of the UK and Government of Ireland.
17. Speech to the Oxford Union, 15 October 1959.
18. M. Kennedy (1997), 'Towards co-operation: Seán Lemass and North–South economic relations', *Irish Economic and Social History*, Vol. XXIV, pp. 42–61. By 1958 there was co-operative management or administration of schemes such as the Foyle Fisheries, Erne hydro electric, cross-border electricity links and Belfast–Dublin railway line.

19. A. W. Gray (1992), 'Industry and trade' in Government of Ireland, *Ireland in Europe: A Shared Challenge*, Dublin, Stationery office, pp. 35–63; Hitchens and Birnie (1994), op. cit.
20. A. Matthews (1992), 'Agriculture and natural resources', in Government of Ireland, *Ireland in Europe*, op. cit., pp. 65–93.
21. R. Kinsella (1992), 'Financial Services' in Government of Ireland, *Ireland in Europe*, op. cit., pp. 95–118.
22. NIEC (1998), op. cit.
23. J. Fitzpatrick and J. McEniff (1992), 'Tourism' in Government of Ireland, *Ireland in Europe*, op. cit., pp. 119–52.
24. M. McGumaghan and S. Scott (1981), 'Trade and Co-operation in electricity and gas', *Understanding and Co-operation in Ireland*, Paper IV, Belfast and Dublin, Co-operation North.
25. M. Pollitt (1997), 'The restructuring and privatisation of The electricity supply industry in Northern Ireland – will it be worth it?', *DAE working Papers Amalgamated Services*, No. 9701 (revised), Cambridge, DAE.
26. F. Convery (1992), 'Environment and energy', in Government of Ireland, *Ireland in Europe*, op. cit., pp. 175–97.
27. J. Crowley (1992), 'Transport', in Government of Ireland, *Ireland in Europe*, op. cit.
28. Op. cit.
29. The proposed all–Ireland political authorities were to be free standing in the sense that they were not in any way accountable to a Northern Ireland Assembly and would derive their legislative authority and, presumably funding arrangements, from Dublin and London. Paragraph seven of the Strand Two (i.e. Northern Ireland–Republic of Ireland relationships) proposals of the original Mitchell draft said: 'For the areas listed in annex C, where it is agreed that the new implementation bodies are to be established, the two governments are to make all necessary legislative and other preparations to ensure the establishment of these bodies at the inception of the agreement...such that these bodies function effectively as rapidly as possible' (D. Trimble, 'Ulster should say "yes"', *Daily Telegraph*, 13 April 1998). The Unionist fear was that once such bodies came into being a united Ireland government would inevitably grow from the embryo.

    'Annex C (of the Mitchell draft) listed eight bodies: Annexes A and B also listed respectively 25 and 16 other areas for immediate cross-border co-operation. Some of these were modest, but others included the harmonisation of further and higher education and general hospital services, as well as the creation of all-Ireland bodies to run trade and the arts' (Trimble, op. cit.).
30. The 10 April agreement listed the following dozen areas as ones were co-operation through the North/South Ministerial Council might be possible:

    (1) agriculture – animal and plant health.
    (2) Education – teacher qualifications and exchanges.
    (3) Transport – strategic transport planning.
    (4) Environment – environmental protection, pollution, water quality and waste management.
    (5) Waterways – inland waterways.

(6) Social security/social welfare – entitlements of cross-border workers and fraud control.
(7) Tourism – promotion, marketing, research and product development.
(8) Relevant EU Programmes such as SPPR, INTERREG, Leader II and their successors.
(9) Inland fisheries.
(10) Aquaculture and marine matters.
(11) Health – accident and emergency services and other related cross-border issues.
(12) Urban and rural development.

31. CII (1990), *Newsletter*, May, Dublin, Confederation of Irish Industry; *Banking Ireland* (23 September 1992), 'Belfast–Dublin New Economic Axis'.
32. R. Scott and M. O'Reilly (1992), 'Exports of Northern Ireland Manufacturing companies 1990', *NIERC Report*, Belfast, Northern Ireland Economic Research Centre.
33. A similar point can be made by drawing a comparison with trade flows within the Iberian peninsula. In 1986 Spanish exports to Portugal were 2.2 per cent of its total and in 1997 still only 5.4 per cent (*Economist*, February 14, 1998) and Portugal's population is about three times that of the Republic of Ireland and six times that of Northern Ireland.
34. G. MacEnroe and W. Poole (1995), 'Manufacturing: Two plus two makes more than four', in D'Arcy and Dickson, op. cit.
35. Michie and Sheehan, op. cit.
36. R. I. D. Harris (1991), *Regional Economic Development Policy in Northern Ireland 1945–88*, Aldershot, Aveburey.
37. NIEC (1993) 'R and D activity in Northern Ireland', *Report*, No. 101, Belfast, Northern Ireland Economic Council.
38. DFP (1993) *Northern Ireland Structural Funds Plan 1994–1999 Technical Supplement*, Belfast, Department of Finance and Personnel.
39. M. Rafferty (1996),'Northern Ireland and the Republic of Ireland: A Contrast at firm level', in P. Gillespie (ed), *Britain's European Question: The Issues for Ireland, Seminar Papers*, Dublin, Institute of European Affairs, pp. 83–5.
40. In the mid 1990s the Ulster Unionist Deputy Leader John Taylor MP opposed what he thought was a possibility for the Republic of Ireland's airport operators to buy out the Belfast City airport.
41. NIEC (1994), 'The implications of peripherality for Northern Ireland', *Report*, No. 111, Belfast, Northern Ireland Economic Council.
42. D. M. W. N. Hitchens, K. Wagner and J. E. Birnie (1990), *Closing the Productivity Gap: A Comparison of Northern Ireland, the Republic of Ireland, Britain and West Germany*, Aldershot, Gower–Aveburey.
43. G. Gudgin and R. Breen (1996), 'Evaluation of the ratio of unemployment rates as an indicator of fair employment; *Research Report*, No. 4, Belfast, Central Community Relations Unit; J. Bradley (1997), 'Evaluation of the ratio of unemployment rates as an indicator of fair employment: a critique', *Economic and Social Review*, Vol. 28, No. 2, pp. 85–104.
44. NIEC (1998), 'The impact of a national minimum wage on the Northern Ireland economy: A response to the low pay commission', *Occasional Paper*, No. 9, Belfast, Northern Ireland Economic Council.

45. Cooper and Lybrand/Indecon (1994), '*A Corridor of Opportunity; Study of the Feasibility of Developing a Belfast–Dublin Corridor,* Belfast and Dublin, Confederation of British Industry and Irish Business Employees Confederation; Hitchens and Birnie, (1994) op. cit.; Bradley (1996), op. cit., Hitchens and Birnie (1997), op. cit.

6
For Richer or Poorer: the Social Impact

Quintin Oliver

In the 1975 referendum, campaigners against the United Kingdom remaining in the European Economic Community coined the slogan 'leave Europe – join the world'. They argued that the then six member states were merely 'a rich man's club'. Rich man's club or not, the debate about the quality of life for citizens within the European Union, about equity and distribution of resources, about equality and human rights, continues unabated.

In this context, how has Northern Ireland fared, as a region within the United Kingdom within the European Union? Comparisons might be easier if a similar country or region had stayed outside the Union, but no such examples can easily be found. Norway, which twice voted in referendums against EU membership, is very different because of its oil reserves and its Nordic relationships. Switzerland is also different because of its financial services industry, tourism and propinquity to strategic markets.

Although it is easy to extract statistics for Northern Ireland as a region of the United Kingdom, its geo-political sensitivities, the Troubles and a range of other factors mark it out as something very different and probably unique. (It is separated by sea from the member state of which it is a part, but has a land border with another member state with which it shares the island. At the start of this period it shared a common currency with the rest of the island, but no longer.) Its special situation has been explicitly recognised in its Objective One status for aid from the Structural Funds, despite not meeting precisely the criteria laid down.

Economists and statisticians can measure the Structural Funds, plot graphs of economic growth and draw learned conclusions from public opinion polls and attitudinal testing. To measure quality of life, and socio-political impacts, however, is rather more difficult.

Even the terminology can be confusing. In the United Kingdom, the 'Social' Fund is a rather unpopular part of the benefits system, whereby needy applicants may apply for loans *in extremis*. 'The Social' is also popular slang for the Social Security Benefits Office and the benefits system in general. On the other hand, the European Union's Social Fund, which many here think refers to social projects, in the lay sense of the word, deals mainly with employment training. A European definition of 'social', drawn from *Access to Social Europe*, November 1997, includes 'social cohesion, free movement of workers, freedom of establishment and recognition of diplomas, employment policy, education, vocational training of youth, living and working conditions, and safety and health at work'. In assessing in this chapter the social impact of EU membership on Northern Ireland, we are using the accepted, broader, British/Irish terminology of 'social', as in social policy.

Jacques Delors, then European Commission President, said in 1987, as he tried to elevate the significance of his European project to one of the rather more recalcitrant member states, that within a decade, 80 per cent of all decisions affecting social and economic questions in EU member states would be made in Brussels. This was used by Eurosceptics in Britain and elsewhere, in their relentless hostility to European integration, as a threatened loss of sovereignty, and a take- over of national decisions by the European 'super-state'. Others, however, saw it at least as a spur to understanding and analysis of where decisions might best be made and how areas lagging behind in development might be accelerated towards or above the average.

Delors himself, on a visit to Northern Ireland in November 1992, expressed his pleasure (*Irish Times*, 6 November 1992) that the debate about the European Union in Northern Ireland was not just about Structural Funds but, as importantly, about structural policies. The fabled crock of gold at the end of the rainbow has often distorted debates about the European Union and its role and helped spin a web of misinformation about Brussels' real powers. As other chapters in this volume attest, the quantum of European funding is modest, certainly less than five per cent of other Northern Ireland public spending, whereas the dynamic of European policy and of European decision-making has less quantifiable but perhaps more significant impacts on life and society in Northern Ireland.

It is not just the language which has come to dominate our discourse. 'Social inclusion', 'subsidiarity', 'marginalisation' and 'partnership' have all entered our lexicons but, more importantly, the concepts behind them have led to significant improvements in the way in which people's lives here can now be led.

When Northern Ireland joined the EEC in 1973, as part of the United Kingdom, structural funding was in a nascent stage of development. The European Social Fund (ESF) provided modest assistance for training, the European Regional Development Fund (ERDF) had been agreed in principle, but was at an embryonic stage. It was only during the 1980s that the mechanism of approving operational programmes under the Community Support Frameworks developed. Even at an earlier stage, when the prosperity of the original six-member European Economic Community was indeed increasing, it was clear that some regions were lagging behind and required special extra resources, which would, it was hoped, improve economic performance and standard of living. But it was to be 'additional', rather than incorporated within member states' pre-existing budgets, and was to have a distinctly European dimension, often in the form of a transnational element to each programme. By the 1980s, programmes special to Northern Ireland were beginning to emerge. In 1979 Belfast and Naples were designated as the only two sites in the Community for experimental integrated operations programmes; in 1983 an Urban Renewal Regulation uniquely allocated 100 million ecus to Belfast over a three year period. More recently the 1995 Special Support Programme for Peace and Reconciliation (SSPPR) followed that pattern of special treatment for Northern Ireland, because of its political and social problems.

The manner in which European aid came to Northern Ireland and the structures through which it was arranged and dispensed also began to evolve during this period, from a starting point entirely dominated by government departments. The first significant involvement of players and actors external to government in the Structural Funds came with the development of the 1989–93 Community Support Framework (CSF) for Northern Ireland. At least some outside government were asked for their views, albeit at short notice and with little attention seemingly paid to those views. However, the development of the 1994–9 Single Programming Document (SPD) was distinctly more transparent and open, partly because of Delors' personal engagement with the Northern Ireland question and generally because of a more rigorous requirement by Brussels for local consultation. Drafts were issued, conferences held, roundtables organised and a process of winning understanding and commitment to the principles behind the SPD was started. Concepts such as 'bottom-up development', 'local development', 'partnership-building' and 'community infrastructure' permeated the Single Programme, although with less operational impact than some had hoped.

A radical and, with hindsight, almost prophetic Common Chapter appeared in both the Northern Ireland and Republic of Ireland plans submitted to Brussels. This recognised that there were economic and social challenges on both sides of the border which would benefit from joint and parallel actions. It identified transport, energy and community infrastructure as such issues; however, the absence of a concomitant budget or delivery mechanism left the chapter rather high and dry in terms of implementation on the ground.

Five examples of social progress

But the promise of the 1994–9 Single Programme, in terms of openness and broad community involvement, was only really delivered with the Special Support Programme for Peace and Reconciliation which followed upon the August 1994 IRA cease-fire. With Delors' personal involvement in the dying months of his ten year presidency, this came to fruition in 1995, moving to full-speed-ahead implementation in 1996 and the following years. It is in the Special Support Programme that the concepts of 'social inclusion', 'partnership' and 'bottom-up development' take real root.

As already indicated, there is no easy or simple way to measure social progress in a region resulting directly or indirectly from the fact of European Union membership. Some indications may be derived, however, from examination of social progress made in five defined areas – rights and equality, partnership, social inclusion, civil dialogue and transnational networking.

Rights, equality and non-discrimination

It is widely agreed, even amongst the more feminist women's groups, that the role of the European Union in promoting and extending women's rights has been significant, especially in more conservative and socially backward countries. The reference in the Treaty of Rome to equal pay for men and women has been the foundation stone for many actions, directives and legislation on gender equality, covering equal pay for equal value, discrimination at work, sexual harassment, part-time work, maternity and family leave. The Amsterdam Treaty takes these rights further in terms of the anti-discrimination clause, extending similar principles to those with disabilities, racial minorities including Travellers, and other disadvantaged groups. Whilst rights remain theoretical unless access to justice can enforce them and unless economic equality renders them realisable, the rights framework provided by the European Union is certainly well advanced.

Partnerships for progress

The model of partnership, enshrined in several European institutions, is born of the model of capital and labour meeting with government to reach consensus. It has already challenged traditional concepts of public or private corporations, or municipalities, acting on behalf of, rather than for or with, communities by trying to engage those local communities as the authors of their own change, rather than being merely the objects of actions by others, however well-meaning. The typology of partnerships is messy. Chuck Sabel, Chicago-based academic and expert in regeneration strategies, in his evaluation for the OECD of the southern Irish examples, describes them as enjoying 'fragile democratic legitimacy' and as having an 'anomalous administrative status'. But he, and others, recognise that these partnerships fulfil a gap between the citizen and the state, including the European Union, which politicians have for years been striving to fill. Sabel concluded they were also 'extraordinarily innovative'. As local and regional government atrophies and as citizens become more disenchanted with governments and politicians in general, models like these are popular and potentially significant as creating a new form of political structure, not undermining the electoral process, but rather reinforcing it.

In Northern Ireland, that has certainly been the case. While many politicians found it difficult to talk to each other within the all-party talks format, or even in local Council chambers, they were able to work together around partnership tables, with their structured three-way format, engaging multi-party political representatives, the voluntary/community sector and a third category of 'others', made up of local statutory bodies, employers, trade unions and independents. All commentators on the District Partnerships in Northern Ireland created under the European Special Programme for Peace and Reconciliation, have noted their political impact in terms of creating a neutral forum for representatives of the two main communities in conflict, within which they could meet and negotiate; there may, however, yet be questions about their service delivery impact or administrative efficiencies. Indeed, the model is now moving towards that promoted by Paul Q. Hirst's concept of 'associational democracy'. The development of partnerships did not come solely through the SSPPR, but predated it through the rural LEADER Programme, the area-based strategy in the Republic of Ireland, the economic development programme under the

Single Programming Document, administered by District Councils and by the Department of the Environment in Northern Ireland, through 'vision' partnerships in the cities of Armagh, Belfast and Derry.

Social inclusion, combating exclusion

The concept of social inclusion was developed in France in the early 1970s as a counterpart to the purely economic analysis of poverty. Its beginnings could be seen in the first European Poverty Programme of the late 1970s and early 1980s where, for example, it was explained that 'a shortage of material resources still keeps many citizens apart from the rest of society'.[1] The Second Programme of the European Communities to Combat Poverty followed after a pause from 1986 to 1989, moving towards area-based approaches to combat poverty, but still targeting groups of individuals, such as older people, lone parents, Travellers and those living in isolated rural areas. Allegedly because of British hostility to the term 'poverty', the third European Programme eschewed the P-word, but also overlooked the increasingly popular Greek and Roman titles (e.g. Leonardo, Socrates, Ergo or Leda), instead plumping for 'Medium-Term Community Action Programme to Foster the Economic and Social Integration of the Economically and Socially Less Privileged Groups' (1989–94). This, the Third Poverty Programme, introduced the concept of integrated local development, elevated the significance of the participation of affected groups and insisted on the practice of partnership. In Northern Ireland, the Brownlow Community Trust, the Programme's sole beneficiary, became a shining example across Europe of what can be done in a local community to combat disadvantage through energy, vitality and above all partnership of the key players, including the local community, which was the subject of attention in the first place. Just as the Brownlow Community Trust has survived, albeit under a different title, after European funding had been exhausted, so it is estimated that the District Partnerships, under the guidance of the Northern Ireland Partnership Board, born of the SSPPR, will survive that programme's demise. It is likely that they will continue as a bridge between the ordinary citizen, the 26 elected local councils and the new Northern Ireland Assembly and the North–South Ministerial Council, created under the Stormont Agreement of April 1998, endorsed in referendums on both parts of the island in May 1998.

Civil dialogue for civil society

The European institutions have for long had structured relationships with capital (employers) and labour (employees through trade unions), but as the intensity of the conflict between capital and labour has softened and as the vertical structures between the citizen voting every few years and the decision-makers in government and the EU have become less rigid, so the mechanisms for debate and dialogue have had to adjust and adapt. Again, prefiguring the Belfast Agreement with its innovative consultative Civic Forum, the European Union's move towards civil dialogue is creating a new form of discourse. In a speech to the first European Social Policy Forum in Brussels in April 1996, European Commissioner for Social Affairs, Pádraig Flynn, explained: 'We have *political* dialogue through the Council of Ministers at the European level, we have *social* dialogue through our three-way discussions with employers and trade unions, now we will move to *civil* dialogue with representatives of the burgeoning non-governmental organisations (NGO) sector.'

This model was also prefigured by the SSPPR with its Consultative Forum, comprising 80 representatives of the social partners, including one quarter from the voluntary/community sector, to advise, criticise and give feedback on the operation of the Special Programme in the twelve northern counties of the island. The Civic Forum of the Belfast Agreement enshrines such an advisory relationship in constitutional measures and binds the Assembly to develop a structured relationship with the Civic Forum, rather than as mere external lobbyists. In the hierarchy of advice, consultation and negotiation, the Civic Forum sits at the second level. A similar mechanism is anticipated under Strand Two of the Belfast Agreement to complement the North–South Ministerial Council. No other part of the United Kingdom or Ireland has such an arrangement and none, regrettably, has developed elsewhere from Flynn's 1996 pronouncements, enunciated again at the second European Social Policy Forum held in Brussels in June 1998.

Transnational exchanges and networks

One of the great ambitions of Monnet and Schuman was to increase the flow of interaction between the peoples of Europe. Subsequently many European programmes have required the inclusion in projects of transnational exchanges and transnational elements. At the same time there has been an explosive growth[2] in the number of European networks of NGOs and other associations working across national boundaries to lobby the institutions of the European Union and to seek changes in policy. Both these trends have been evident in Northern Ireland, and both have undoubtedly speeded up collaboration on the island of Ireland, since in the former case it is easier to find a partner project in the south of the island than in the south of the continent. (The fact that both parts of the island have enjoyed Objective One regional status has helped, since many funding programmes are weighted towards Objective One collaboration). Policy collaboration was also assisted during the Thatcher years by the insularity and isolation of British representations, thereby making Irish linkages more attractive. In addition this process was aided by the highly developed networking skills at European level of the Republic. Simple logistical reasons of distance and cost also encouraged relationships on an all-island basis.

At times the networking tail tended to wag the project dog, and it became a standing joke in voluntary sector circles that as each deadline for project submissions neared, the fax would become red hot with potential partners seeking to bind them into a consortium. Northern Ireland and the Republic were always popular choices, since both were Objective One regions in the north of Europe, and both are English-speaking. Although many turned out to be 'paper partnerships' only and to have been poorly brokered or worked through, some genuinely innovative and developmental relationships were struck with mutual benefits accruing to both or all partners.

The development of the NGO sector at European level certainly impacted on Northern Ireland, but, in reverse, Northern Ireland and actors from Northern Ireland also contributed significantly to that development. In 1991, for example, the eight European NGO networks dealing with poverty, women, HIV and AIDS, health promotion, mobility, disability, rural issues and rural women were not only influenced by Northern Irish participants, but were led by them, with Northern Ireland people holding office as president or vice-president. Northern Ireland's position as a corner of one member state on the border of another, convulsed by civil strife, perhaps impelled some to seek external engagements with alacrity. It certainly equipped many social activists with the sorts of skills which made European networking and lobbying less onerous.

The Common Chapter in the Structural Funds Plans (1994–9) for the two parts of the island could also be said to have been nudged into place by European requirements and in turn it can be said to prefigure Strand Two of the Belfast Agreement on cross-border collaboration. Lobbying for its inclusion was a high priority of the voluntary and community sector. Again, however, in the views of its proponents, its implementation left much to be desired. The SSPPR was the eventual vehicle for realisation of many of its aspirations, at least in the social field.

Would it have happened anyway?

The past twenty-five years have seen undeniable development, change and growth in the five areas listed above, most of it readily deemed to be progress. To what extent has this progress resulted from the impact of European factors? Or would it have happened anyway?

Codification of rights

Although there has been a general trend over the period for rights to be codified and enshrined in legislation, charters, directives and conventions, the pace of development in Europe has certainly had an impact on Northern Ireland. The celebrated Dudgeon case, which resulted in legal equality for homosexuals in Northern Ireland, came about as a result of legal action taken through the Human Rights mechanism of the Council of Europe, but action or threat of it based on European Community law has led to changes in equal opportunities, public appointments and equal pay practices. That said, however, the development of fair employment legislation in Northern Ireland since 1976, outlawing discrimination on grounds of perceived religion or political opinion, would undoubtedly have developed in any case, probably with US influence, and has only been partially enshrined into European law with the Amsterdam Treaty.

Partnerships

Some might say that Northern Ireland is now 'over-partnershipped', with LEADER II rural development partnerships, peace partnerships in District Council areas, vision partnerships in Armagh, Belfast and Derry cities, sub-city partnerships in north, south, east and west Belfast, and a host of other alliances and coalitions dubbed partnerships. Certainly it is unlikely that the concept and practice of partnerships would have come about with such a vengeance without the European dimension. Partnerships have developed in the United States, but they tend to be bi-lateral between the private and the state sectors with limited or no involvement of the non-profit or NGO sector. This again is an area where Northern Ireland's experience, developed to some extent from the early partnerships in the Republic of Ireland in the late 1980s, has now had an influence across Europe. It is anticipated that the Agenda 2000 project will use the Northern Ireland structured three-way partnership model for dispensing Structural Funds in other European member states. The consultative Civic Forum, enshrined in the Belfast Agreement, owes much to a European source – the SSPPR's Consultative Forum, and may be set up following a similar pattern.

Social inclusion

The development of a social inclusion agenda has certainly come from Europe, and has perhaps facilitated the debate on such questions in Northern Ireland, because of the very fact that it is a European issue. At times it has been deemed unfashionable to import into Northern Ireland experiments essentially designed for Great Britain; if they were seen to be 'European', they carried an additional *cachet*. Developments in the United States, with its very divided society and economy, and little effort to promote social inclusion, have been less significant in this field. The new Blair government in the United Kingdom, however, has vigorously embraced the concept of social inclusion, with the early establishment of a Social Exclusion Unit at Downing Street and social inclusion networks in Scotland and Wales. Northern Ireland, at the time of writing, has yet to follow suit, partly because many of the programmes and mechanisms for promoting social inclusion are already in place, including the Targeting Social Need (TSN) and new TSN (1998) policies designed to target government resources to areas of greatest need and thereby to reduce the socio-economic differentials between Northern Ireland's two main communities – Protestant/unionist, and Catholic/nationalist. Significantly in this context, 44 per cent of the resources of the Special Support Programme for Peace and Reconciliation have been allocated to social inclusion projects.

Civil dialogue

It is possible that the concept of civil dialogue would have developed in Northern Ireland without impetus from the European Union. Under direct rule from London there was an obvious democratic deficit in the governing of Northern Ireland, with almost no input from locally-elected representatives, and many argue that the NGO sector began filling some of this vacuum, and occupying some of the space between individual citizens and the state. Tom King MP, Secretary of State for Northern Ireland in the late 1980s, once remarked that 'the voluntary sector can reach parts of the province which others, including government, cannot'. It is difficult to say, however, whether those developments were in turn influenced by the European concepts of social partnership and of civil dialogue. In any event it may be that Northern Ireland has had as much influence on European developments as they have had on Northern Ireland, with key interlocutors from the European

Anti-Poverty Network, the third European Anti-Poverty Programme and other alliances taking leading roles in the European debates, leading up to and at the European Social Policy Forums in 1996 and 1998.

Transnational partnershipping and exchanges

Cheaper travel, improved communication and globalisation have all created imperatives towards movement of people and ideas, but the structured approach to transnational collaboration fostered by the European Union has undoubtedly had a significant impact in Northern Ireland. It has lifted the horizons of Northern Ireland participants and may well have stimulated new thinking both on our position in Europe and our conflict at home. Although building transnational partnerships was sometimes seen as a necessary chore to achieve funding, it also led to significant learning opportunities and exchange of information and expertise.

What didn't happen?

Has Northern Ireland's position within the European Union narrowed or limited some horizons as well as widening others? Again, it is extremely difficult to argue about the past, even with hindsight, but it is possible to suggest that some things might have happened, but did not, over the past twenty-five years because of the province's position within the EU.

First, in one way, Europe may have helped protect our cultural insularity, our 'Britishness/Irishness'. The radical government of Margaret Thatcher and the eighteen years of Conservative rule were certainly significant in this respect, but it could be argued that outside the European Union Northern Ireland might have had to make wider and different relationships, perhaps only on an East–West basis with Britain or also on a West–East basis with the US. Commonwealth links might have been enhanced, trading links with non-EU countries and exchanges of people and ideas with a wider range of cultures and systems might have resulted.

Second, economic and social cohesion might have been more quickly accelerated onto the agenda, especially if the stultifying process of Europe proceeding to economic and monetary union had not taken place, causing downward and deflationary pressures on the economies of Europe. If the World Bank could agree in the early 1990s that social and economic justice had to be at the core of economic interventions, perhaps these would have come to Northern Ireland before the late 1990s.

Third, the benefits and social protection systems of Northern Ireland might have developed differently had the UK not been hostile to including them within the European remit. 'Elsewhere in Europe' Hirch argues, 'the language (of debate) is not of a welfare state to help the poor, but of a generalised system of social protection that creates solidarity.'[3] He continues in his analysis by suggesting that social security is 'a tool for organising a stable social and economic system', as indeed it has been used, with European assistance, in the former fascist countries now in EU membership – Greece, Portugal and Spain. Hirsch concludes that

> the recent political rhetoric for more market deregulation, consumer freedom, labour mobility and flexibility and for the abolishment (sic) of minimum wage and income levels can hardly hide its plea for an American implantation in this European model. The US model rests indeed on less government intervention. It focuses on low labour costs but yields lower labour productivity and low unemployment rates, but provides also a low level of social protection. Together with the low wages, this limited degree of social protection generates a high poverty incidence and complex situations of social exclusion.

Conclusion

It is obviously impossible to turn the clock back and to test how Northern Ireland might have fared outside of European Union membership. Similarly, the impact of a radical and reforming Conservative government under Margaret Thatcher cannot be disaggregated from the calculation. Had Northern Ireland been outside the UK but inside Europe, or outside the UK *and* outside Europe, things would indeed have been very different. Likewise, Northern Ireland's relationship with the Republic of Ireland would also have had a colossally different impact.

That said, however, the range of funding programmes and policy frameworks provided by the European Union has undoubtedly had a beneficial impact, however modest, on the quality of life in Northern Ireland. Even if the quantum has not been affected, thanks to arcane additionality rules, the fact that European programmes brought different voices and decision-makers around the table itself made a difference.

Indeed, the argument of many in the social policy field during the last two decades has been 'but they do it in Europe and if it's good enough for Europe, surely we should be doing it here in Northern Ireland'. For many years social policy activists have argued for 'mainstreaming', drawing the lessons from experimental and innovative

European programme projects and incorporating them into domestic policy and programmes. Successful mainstreaming can be traced in the fields of community infrastructure, social inclusion and, perhaps shortly, in the use of partnerships to deliver services. In structural terms the SSPPR's Consultative Forum can be seen to have prefigured the Civic Forum.

Less tangible, but equally significant, has been the importation of ideas, attitudes and approaches from the European Union. The Anglo-Saxon model of development has thus been moderated by other European models and styles. Even the simple fact of taking participants from different sides of the Northern Ireland conflict to a European venue, as happened in the secret talks in Duisburg in 1988 involving members from four main parties, has had indirect, but perhaps weighty, side effects, in that particular case helping to open the way to formal inter-party negotiations. The genesis of the Northern Ireland Centre in Europe is another example, begun as a political reconciliation exercise in the early 1990s and ending, *inter alia*, in the creation of an outpost to give Northern Ireland interests a voice in Brussels.

As this chapter has argued, the flow of benefits has been two-way, with the frequent involvement of Northern Ireland social policy activists in European debates and arguments. It is perhaps significant that a number of the individuals now assuming positions of responsibility in new cross-community bodies in Northern Ireland came to prominence first in EU-funded social projects. The fact that many of them are women is also, perhaps, eloquent testimony to the beneficial effects of Europe.

Notes

1. *Europe Against Poverty*, Commission of the European Communities, June–July 1982.
2. B. Harvey (1995), *Networking in Europe: A Guide to European Voluntary Organizations*, 2nd edition, London, National Council for Voluntary Organizations.
3. D. Hirsch (1997), *Social Protection and Inclusion: European Challenges for the United Kingdom*, York, Joseph Rountree Foundation.

7
The Sectoral Impact: European Rules and a Changing Environment

J. S. Furphy

The word 'environment' can mean the immediate local area within which a person lives, moves and has cultural ties, or it may include all the natural external factors influencing our life – air, water, soils, landscape and wildlife. The European Union has approached environmental issues from this latter, wider, perspective but has of necessity had to deal with them in a piecemeal fashion. This chapter deals primarily with the impact of European Directives on the natural environment, though water and air matters are dealt with less comprehensively.

Following the introduction of a European Community Directive, member states must produce new or amending legislation to ensure compliance with the Directive. Northern Ireland is part of the United Kingdom, but has its own law-making facility, and therefore the UK cannot claim compliance until legislation in the province conforms – usually somewhat later than the production of equivalent legislation in Great Britain.

The impact of European Directives dealing with nature conservation has to be seen in the context of the history of Northern Ireland's own conservation legislation. By accession in 1973, several significant pieces of legislation specific to Northern Ireland had been put in place.

Early domestic legislation

The first conservation measure introduced by the Parliament of Northern Ireland was the Wild Birds Protection Act (Northern Ireland) 1931. This far-seeing Act was based on the principle that all wild birds should be fully protected from shooting, trapping or commercial exploitation, except for a few which were regarded as quarry species during an open season and some which were classified as pests.

In the following year, a measure dealing with the protection of grey seals was passed, but its provisions were never put into effect as the threat of local extermination of the seals receded as the population slowly rose.

Most of the Game Laws predate the Wild Birds legislation, but it is difficult to consider them as true conservation measures in that many of their provisions deal with the protection of property, i.e., game birds and animals, rather than the overall protection of fauna. However, they do deal with close seasons and the burning of vegetation in which game birds breed (particularly red grouse *Lagopus scoticus*), both of which have clear environmental benefits.

The Amenity Lands Act (Northern Ireland) 1965

In 1965 the first measure to deal with comprehensive conservation of the natural environment entered the statute book – the Amenity Lands Act (Northern Ireland). It provided for countryside conservation – through the establishment of amenity areas and Areas of Outstanding Natural Beauty – and for nature conservation through nature reserves and areas of scientific interest. It is significant to note that this Act was framed primarily as a planning measure, that activity being at the forefront of so much government thinking in the 1960s.

Need to develop new legislation

By the mid-1970s it was apparent that the rapid rate of environmental change was such that certain of the provisions of the Amenity Lands Act, the Wild Birds Protection Acts and the Game Laws were unable to prevent species, habitats, landforms and landscapes from damage. Government's advisory committees recommended that new, all-embracing environmental legislation was needed, in order to provide long-term protection to the most significant aspects of our flora, fauna and countryside.

It seemed that the timing was propitious in that the UK Government was beginning to implement the recommendations of the Ramsar, Bonn and Bern Conventions and the EC had announced its intention to produce a Directive on the Conservation of Wild Birds. However, when the United Kingdom Government decided to prepare new wildlife legislation for England, Wales and Scotland, preparatory work on the guidelines for new legislation for Northern Ireland stopped under the arrangements then in place under Direct Rule.

Until 1972, Northern Ireland had its own parliament based at Stormont, which produced domestic legislation. While in most cases this was basically similar to that current in Great Britain, there were many instances where Northern Ireland legislation was ahead of, or differed significantly from, that across the Irish Sea. When Direct Rule was established, Northern Ireland legislation was now introduced as Orders-in-Council at Westminster and, by and large, it followed on the introduction of similar measures in Great Britain, albeit with suitable alterations to take account of local situations.

The Birds Directive and conformity with existing legislation

When the European Commission began to prepare Directive 79/409 on the Conservation of Wild Birds, all existing relevant legislation in member states was examined. It is a tribute to those who originally prepared the Wild Birds Protection Act (Northern Ireland) 1931 that the general provisions of the Directive bear such a strong resemblance to that Act. In many cases the Directive demands stronger protection, but both provide for the total protection of all wild birds at all times other than for specified exceptions. They allow for the setting aside of specially protected areas where birds may rest, feed or breed unmolested. Each allows sport shooting of certain quarry species during an open season. Only last minute action removed from the Directive a schedule of species regarded as pests and which could be taken at any time, which would have been another similarity. One area of difference is that of sale – totally prohibited under the Wild Birds Protection Act but allowable regarding certain species in the Directive.

It was not until some months after the date by which compliance with the Directive was required that the Wildlife and Countryside Act 1981 (applicable only to Great Britain) was passed. In that piece of legislation, the opportunity was taken to deal with a wide range of issues in addition to the requirements of the Directive and Conventions, including provision for a new organisational structure.

The 1985 Orders

Work on Northern Ireland's equivalent Order-in-Council recommenced at that stage in the Department of the Environment in Belfast (DOE), but, for a variety of reasons, finalisation took rather a long time, putting compliance with the Birds Directive well behind schedule. Primarily, the new Northern Ireland legislation was designed to cover a wider range of matters than were dealt with in the Wildlife and Countryside Act. The procedure for preparing legislation meant that much work had to be completed before the proposed Draft Order began its progress through the timetable set out under Direct Rule operations. The draftsmen had to take on board the views of the statutory advisory committees, those of other bodies with interests in conserving nature and the countryside and those of the public – a record number of submissions were received in the DOE at the stage of public consultation.

The delays caused by these factors did however have the advantage of allowing the avoidance of shortcomings and failings which quickly became apparent in the operation of the Wildlife and Countryside Act. By the time the Draft Orders were ready, the Northern Ireland Assembly, a non-legislative consultative body which sat from 1982–6, had been established; the Orders were extensively debated in that chamber where a number of useful minor amendments were made before the final debates at Westminster.

As it transpired, two Orders-in-Council were required to cope with the needs of the various international measures and the additional local aspects. These, both passed in 1985, were the Nature Conservation and Amenity Lands (Northern Ireland) Order and the Wildlife (Northern Ireland) Order. By their entry to the Statute Book, it was generally considered that the United Kingdom now complied with the requirements of the Birds Directive.

Effects of the Birds Directive – species conservation

Earlier legislation already mentioned gave a considerable degree of protection to all bird species, and few changes in the basic aims of the legislation can be attributed directly to the needs of the Birds Directive. The schedule of pest species was reduced and the conditions regarding their taking were tightened – they can now be taken only with the express wish or permission of the landowner. Controls on taxidermy were strengthened, making the activities of legal operators more straightforward and enabling easier detection of offences. The old legislation did not permit the keeping of birds for activities such as falconry, and one of the new aspects introduced as a result of the Directive was the legalisation of that activity, which conversely then also allowed for its control. Previous to 1985, falconers could not use native species for the purpose of their sport, though it was practice for some of them to use birds which had been injured or imprinted to such an extent that they could not be released into the wild. Some falconers were skilled in being able to rehabilitate injured birds into the wild, something which, too, was previously illegal but had been tolerated in the interests of the welfare of the birds.

The previous legislation did not specify the ways by which birds could be taken, nor did it list any weapons the use of which was prohibited. This changed in the Wildlife Order, where, following the terms of the Directive, a number of weapons and means of killing or taking were declared illegal. Perhaps most publicity surrounded the banning of the repeating shotgun; however this was a weapon very little used by reputable wildfowlers.

The schedules of protected species caused much debate, with hunters and landowners feeling that some species scheduled for protection did not warrant it because of the damage they caused. In particular, Cormorant *Phalacrocorax carbo* was generally considered a pest to fisheries interests, but following the line set out in the Directive, it did not appear on the list of birds on the 'open' list. A few years later, this 'open' list itself came up for scrutiny, when the European Commission decided that a strict interpretation of the Directive meant that no such list could be legal, but that pest species required a form of derogation instead. Accordingly, birds previously on the 'open' list can now only be taken under licence, though a form of general licensing is being operated, obviating the need for individual landowners to request a licence each time they wish to control a particular species on their land.

Effects of the Birds Directive – habitat conservation

It was in habitat conservation that the Birds Directive made the greatest impact on domestic legislation. Prior to 1985, three methods existed for the statutory protection of habitats – bird sanctuary, nature reserve and area of scientific interest. The former involved the declaration that an area was subject to a non-shooting regime, with all birds being protected; in some cases certain pest species could still be taken. This method of protection depended for its success entirely on the goodwill of the landowners and, in reality, few important sites became Bird Sanctuaries. As the Wild Birds Protection Act provided for no form of control on development, recreation, or other activities on sanctuaries, it was clear that they fell far short of what was required in the Directive. The Wildlife Order provided for a category with much stronger protection – the Wildlife Refuge – but it too does not conform to the needs of the Directive, being designed to protect sites which are not necessarily of the highest conservation quality.

A major cornerstone of environmental legislation the world over has been the setting aside of areas to be managed primarily for the purposes of nature conservation. In Northern Ireland, as in many other countries, the term for such land which has been acquired, leased or subject to a management agreement is nature reserve. The guarantees provided by state ownership or management control should be sufficient to cover the requirements of the Directive, but practical difficulties mean that this is not necessarily the case. Nature reserve designation is applied to a limited number of sites – those which are either the very best examples of habitats, or which hold significant populations of important species, or which provide particularly good opportunities for education, study or research. Government would find it difficult to justify acquiring other than this limited range of sites both because legislation suggests that nature reserves are very special places and also because of the administrative burden which would result – larger sites of conservation significance have so many owners that acquisition by other than compulsory means could take several years to complete.

The Area of Scientific Interest (ASI) category was introduced in the Amenity Lands Act; it was in effect a form of planning control. Consultation was required between planners and governmental conservationists on all planning applications submitted within ASIs. However, it became clear that many of the threats to ASIs were coming from activities not covered by planning legislation, and when the Directive appeared, this class of protection was deemed to be inadequate to meet its requirements. As a consequence, the Nature Conservation and Amenity Lands Order introduced the very much stronger Area of Special Scientific Interest (ASSI) category. Similar in principle to the British Site of Special Scientific Interest (SSSI), it differed from that category in a number of ways, the most significant of which was that a declaration took effect immediately on notification, whereas in Britain there was a three month period for consultation with landowners or other interested parties.

The Directive introduced the category of Special Protection Area (SPA), calling for virtually total protection to be afforded to the principal sites used by a range of species considered to be at special risk and which are listed in Annex I to the Directive. In addition, member states must take similar steps to protect regularly occurring migratory species by ensuring that their normal stopping-off locations are protected; wetlands are to be particularly targeted. While the Directive gives no detailed instructions as to how member states are to achieve this level of protection, the control of development and prevention of pollution and disturbance are considered to be the most significant steps towards implementation.

Impact of the Birds Directive on planning matters

Since 1972, planning in Northern Ireland has been centralised in the Department of the Environment, within which one particular agency, the Environment and Heritage Service (EHS), deals with conservation. This allows co-ordination of action regarding SPAs through administrative arrangements. Planning matters relative to SPAs fall into two categories – strategic planning and development control. The former has been met through the preparation of Area Plans, covering sub-regions of the Province with the boundaries being those of District Councils. At the public consultation stage, the Department produces its outline proposals, which are then debated at several fora, with invariably, a public inquiry. The proposals define constraints and opportunities provided by conservation designations such as SPAs, and at inquiries voluntary organisations have consistently urged the Department to follow closely the Directive's requirements. There have been two public inquiries where the attitude of the voluntary movement has been particularly effective.

In the text of the draft Antrim Area Plan, the Department made clear the need to conserve the natural resources of Lough Neagh, which at that stage was a Ramsar Site but not an SPA. Following representations from the Royal Society for the Protection of Birds, a form of words was produced which greatly strengthened the sense of the Department's approach to the matter of development within the entire area, and which has since become the basis for the standard Departmental statement in subsequent Area Plans.

When the Plan for the Belfast Area was being considered, it was discovered that the Belfast Harbour Commissioners held a deemed planning consent allowing them to develop an area for port-related purposes, even though two lagoons within this area lay inside the Inner Belfast Lough ASSI, a probable candidate SPA. This revelation evoked such strong opposition from several voluntary organisations that the Department decided to produce a Local Plan for the Harbour Area. In its preparation there were many discussions between the Harbour Commissioners, the voluntary bodies and the Department. During this period, the importance of the site to the total SPA network was constantly stressed; the probable outcome of the Department's failure to protect the site, given the adverse interpretations placed by the European Court on development proposals from other Member States affecting SPAs, was regularly quoted.

There were two major consequences. First, the Department introduced an amendment to the Nature Conservation and Amenity Lands Order closing the loophole so that the holding of a deemed planning consent was no longer a valid reason to undertake development in an ASSI. The second had a bearing on subsequent developments on the ground. At the opening of the public inquiry into the Local Plan, it was announced that all parties had agreed a way forward by which one of the lagoons would become a nature reserve, with a further area being developed as a nature park with the emphasis on education. These two projects have since been completed, with considerable grant-aid from the EU; the entire scheme has earned great commendation and has been used as a example to other ports with high nature conservation interests.

Implementation of the SPA programme

Work towards implementing the SPA programme has been very slow in Northern Ireland. Several reasons can be put forward to account for this. One is that of resources; EHS has always been small and historically priorities have been given to conserving sites and species under threat rather than to the implementation of an overall plan. However, with the passing of the 1985 legislation, a new impetus was given to the work through the new facility to undertake province-wide surveys leading to the identification of sites worthy of a conservation designation. Prior to this, sites were notified as ASIs or designated as nature reserves on the basis of best information available. The undertaking of this new survey work called for the appointment of additional scientific staff and for the adoption of a new approach. This culminated in the publication of a plan 'Target 2001' which set out the basis for site selection and gave an indication of how the service would implement its obligations as spelt out in international and domestic legislation.

As part of the overall survey work a study was commissioned to identify those sites which would qualify for classification as SPAs; because of the international dimension and the desire to consider such sites as part of a wider network, the study involved the whole of the island of Ireland. This approach flowed from the European Commission's encouraging of work of a cross-frontier nature where this has obvious environmental or economic benefits. The survey identified ten sites which met the agreed criteria including some which straddle the political frontier.

The policy of the UK Government towards classification/designation of sites under international measures has been that they must first be designated appropriately under domestic legislation before they receive their international designation. In Northern Ireland the minimum classification to satisfy the Directive is ASSI, introduced only in 1985. Therefore all sites identified in the all-Ireland survey had to be declared ASSIs before they could be classified as SPAs. The exceptions were sites which were already ASSIs and known to qualify as SPAs because of their breeding populations of species listed under Annex I of the Directive, and two were classified for this reason – Sheep Island and Swan Island.

Given the land ownership situation in Ireland generally, where properties are small and grazing rights may be shared by a large number of individuals, the declaration of large lacustrine or coastal ASSIs is a herculean task. The first large site to be declared as an ASSI, Strangford Lough, had over four hundred owners and occupiers, all of whom had to be visited and supplied with the required documentation; confusion and a desire for debate led to a series of public meetings where fears about the proposed designation were voiced. These led to further debate on the overall control of such a diverse area, and today the Department is advised by a Strangford Lough Management Committee which includes, among others, representatives of bodies which originally objected to the ASSI designation. This Committee has worked with the Department on further designations which have followed, including Marine Nature Reserve, Ramsar Site and SPA, which combined with the Area of Outstanding Natural Beauty landscape designation means that Strangford Lough is one of the most comprehensively designated sites in the British Isles.

The sites which have been designated as SPAs by 30 June 1998 are:

- Carlingford Lough
- Lough Neagh (including Lough Beg)
- Upper Lough Erne
- Larne Lough (including Swan Island, originally classified separately as SPA)
- Pettigoe Plateau
- Rathlin Island Cliffs
- Sheep Island
- Strangford Lough

Those where consultations are still in progress are Belfast Lough and Lough Foyle. Carlingford Lough, Lough Foyle and Pettigoe Plateau each have a cross-border dimension.

Conformity with the Birds Directive

After the introduction of the 1985 Orders, it was believed that Northern Ireland's domestic legislation now conformed to the wishes of the EC regarding habitat conservation. On site protection as required for SPAs, the Nature Conservation and Amenity Lands Order provided that the Department could compulsorily acquire an ASSI, or part of an ASSI, where it was clear that a legal agreement with the landowner over the site's management was not possible, or where the landowner had contravened the conditions of an agreement and was not able to, or not prepared to rectify the damage. This method of securing the conservation interest of a site provided the means of ensuring the viability of an SPA – though as with all legislation, it was to be the practical outworking of the legislation that would be the real test of its effectiveness. To date the Department has not found it necessary to acquire any land in this way.

The Habitats Directive

The Directive on the Conservation of Natural Habitats and of Wild Fauna and Flora (the Habitats Directive, 1992) had a much greater immediate impact on conservation in the United Kingdom than did the Birds Directive; this is probably true of all Member States. The principal aim of the Directive is to maintain biodiversity throughout Europe.

The Birds Directive left it open to Member States as to how its various clauses were to be interpreted; this led to wide variations in practice, particularly as the Directive did not lay down criteria for site selection nor did it prescribe the form domestic legislation should take to ensure compliance. These defects were largely addressed in the Habitats Directive which is a much more comprehensive document.

Implementation of the Special Areas of Conservation selection requirements

The Directive lists a series of habitats to which its provisions apply and where designation as candidate Special Areas of Conservation (SAC) is the probable outcome. Certain habitats considered to be at such immediate threat are listed as priority habitats, the conservation of which is virtually mandatory, although a member state may be able to argue that should it hold a high proportion of the sites in such a habitat it can select only a proportion of them by way of compliance with the Directive.

The Directive introduced the concept of Natura 2000 sites to bring SPAs and SACs under one general heading. Perhaps surprisingly, the two declarations do not have identical effects; nor do SACs subsume

138 *A changing environment*

SPAs, a unifying move which would have made the system less confusing. In domestic legislation, SPAs and SACs are grouped together under the title 'European Sites'. Each Member State had to submit its list of candidate SACs by June 1995, giving a period of three years for the completion of all preparatory work. In the case of Northern Ireland this meant undertaking surveys of the habitats listed, quantifying the results, discussing the priorities within the United Kingdom context, declaring qualifying sites to be ASSIs where this was not already the case, modifying boundaries of existing ASSIs, re-declaring former ASIs as ASSIs, re-negotiating management agreements to take account of the more stringent requirements of the Directive, preparing new and amending existing legislation.

Clearly such a range of tasks was beyond the capabilities of the Environment and Heritage Service without a massive injection of resources. As this was not forthcoming, a major re-adjustment to Target 2001 was necessary, setting aside a number of declarations, restructuring survey work and offering an increased number of tasks to outside contractors. It was recognised that concentration on this new work could lead to a significant loss of existing or potential ASSIs through damage caused to them in the interim; no data exist to prove that this fear was realised, though there is anecdotal evidence to show that this was, sadly, the case.

The extensive work undertaken in EHS, which called for a high degree of dedication and expertise, resulted in a list of candidate SACs being provided as part of the United Kingdom's first tranche of submissions in June 1995. Subsequent additions have been made following declaration of sites as ASSIs and amendments to the lists of habitats provided by the Commission. The full list of sites presented to the Commission is:

- Ballynahone Bog*
- Black Bog*
- Cuilcagh Mountain*
- Fairy Water Bogs*
- Garron Plateau*
- Garry Bog*
- Pettigoe Plateau*
- Slieve Beagh*
- Teal Lough* (all peatlands)
- Magilligan*
- Murlough (both dunes)

- Derryleckagh (fen)
- Eastern Mournes (grassland/heath)
- Magheraveely Marl Lakes (calcium-rich oligotrophic waters)
- Largalinny (old oakwood)
- Monawilkin (limestone grassland)
- Strangford Lough (shallow sea lough)
- Upper Lough Erne (eutrophic lake)
- Rathlin Island (sea caves)
- Lough Melvin (mesotrophic lake).

*Sites with an asterisk are those which include a priority habitat or species within the terms of the Habitats Directive. All these sites are now ASSIs and the registration called for in the Directive has been completed – no mean task given the huge number of landowners and other parties who had to be notified.

The Commission's response to this list of candidate sites, now overdue, is keenly awaited.

Problems posed by the Habitats Directive

The habitats quoted in brackets above do not follow the listing given in the Directive. That was drawn up under the Corine habitat classification, which did not lie comfortably with the classification used in Northern Ireland. This led to a number of anomalies. On first examination of the EC's list of habitats where sites must be considered for candidate SAC status, two of Northern Ireland's prime sites did not qualify – Strangford Lough and Rathlin Island. Such omissions tended to diminish the respect and enthusiasm with which conservationists viewed the Directive generally, as it indicated that preparatory work was undertaken in the absence of a detailed knowledge of the conservation issues throughout the EC area. Detailed discussions at United Kingdom level and with the Commission have resulted in some of the anomalies being rectified, and both the sites mentioned were eventually added to the list of candidate SACs.

The requirement that a high proportion of sites within particular habitats be proposed for classification caused other problems. Northern Ireland holds a goodly proportion of the United Kingdom's high quality lowland raised bogs. Proposal for SAC classification of all our ASSIs would have meant that the geographical spread of such bogs throughout the United Kingdom would have been uneven, and so a selection of the Northern Ireland sites was made, the sites being chosen to represent the range of variation found within the province.

140   *A changing environment*

The best United Kingdom examples of marl lakes lie close to, and some actually straddle, the border between Northern Ireland and the Republic of Ireland. In the terms of the Directive, they clearly warrant SAC status, but there are many better examples (in biological terms) elsewhere in the Republic. Those in Northern Ireland have been protected by ASSI status for a number of years, but there has as yet been no statutory protection for those in the Republic. The effective conservation of these lakes therefore rests with their appearance on the list of candidate SACs put forward by Dublin, which action should result from the many fruitful meetings between officials of EHS and the National Parks and Wildlife Service.

Similarly, confusion was caused by the appearance of 'turlough (Ireland)' in the list of habitats to be specially targeted. Did this mean that the three small examples in Fermanagh should be put forward for protection at the European level? This has proved to be the case, though it can be argued that they fall short of the quality of the poorest examples likely to be put forward from Dublin.

These examples highlight a weakness of the Commission's policy in placing so much reliance on the selection of sites on a state by state basis; selection made on the basis of biogeographical areas and site quality within those areas should have given a coverage more justifiable in overall conservation terms; even using the British Isles as a biological unit would have given a more balanced final listing.

Conservation in the marine area is called for in the Directive, but there is little uniformity in the approach of member states to the control of maritime activities. There are several aspects where domestic legislation is unable to deliver the requirements of the Directive, and where only co-operation at Community level, or between individual countries, would provide the opportunity for full conformity. It is to be hoped that the declaration of Marine Nature Reserves under the Nature Conservation and Amenity Lands (Northern Ireland) Order 1985 plus internationally-agreed marine controls will provide adequate safeguards to this most threatened and poorly appreciated habitat.

A particularly tricky situation relates to excessively rare species where publication of their localities could attract undesirable attention from collectors who could easily and rapidly exterminate them. There is therefore a marked reluctance on the part of both professional and amateur workers to arrange for the conservation through legislation of these habitats – in direct contravention of the wishes of the Directive.

Cross-frontier dimension

The European Commission promotes cross-frontier co-operation in all matters relating to Directives, and the above cases have been fully discussed between the statutory bodies in Belfast and Dublin, who have shared technical and scientific expertise at all levels as well as discussing the overall policy implications of the Directives. This co-operation has proved mutually advantageous in many ways, and contacts have been widened to cover other aspects of nature conservation. As a result of the work undertaken in the selection of candidate SACs and other aspects of implementation, there has been a greatly increased level of co-operation and understanding at all levels within the United Kingdom's official conservation agencies.

The Habitats Directive and planning issues

One further aspect of the Habitats Directive required legislative provision. The requirement to maintain European Sites at a favourable conservation status called both for detailed monitoring of habitats and species, and for a very strict implementation of planning controls. These were effected through the Conservation (Natural Habitats, etc.) Regulations (Northern Ireland) 1995, which dealt with the operation of controls on all European Sites.

The planning controls were further spelt out in a significant document 'Planning and Nature Conservation'. Produced in 1997 by the Planning Service in co-operation with EHS, it sets out how local and international nature conservation interests are treated in both development planning and development control situations. Two tables in the Annexes set out how the Planning Service considers development proposals affecting international sites and how it deals with permitted development rights in European Sites. In each case the clear message is that planning permission will only be granted where there are reasons of overriding public interest, and, where a site hosts a priority habitat or species, permission will be granted only after consultation with the Commission.

Environmental Assessments

EC Directive 85/337 on the Assessment of the Effects of Certain Public and Private Projects on the Environment calls for assessments to be made before a decision is taken as to whether planning permission should be granted relating to certain types of project which are likely to have significant environmental effects. In this case the domestic legislation means that the Planning Service requires an environmental impact statement to be submitted for many of the classes of project listed in the Directive.

Environmentally sensitive areas

Natural, or more accurately, semi-natural habitats have benefited from another group of designations flowing from an EU measure. These are the Environmentally Sensitive Areas (ESA) which are administered by the Department of Agriculture for Northern Ireland (DANI). One of the aims of the Regulation, part of the Common Agricultural Policy, is to encourage farming practices which are consonant with conservation. In an ESA, a landowner is given grants to carry out certain environmentally-friendly operations, or to alter his farming practice in the interests of conservation. ESAs are selected by virtue of their landscape, ecological or historical importance. Five exist in Northern Ireland – the Mournes and Slieve Croob; Antrim Glens, North Coast and Rathlin; West Fermanagh and Erne Lakeland; Slieve Gullion; and the Sperrins. For some years conservationists had expressed concern that grazing levels in upland grasslands and heathlands in particular were too high and resulted in habitat loss; one of the tangible benefits of the ESA scheme is that grazing pressures have been reduced in several areas, with farmers being compensated for the loss of productivity.

Other environmental directives

The Community has produced a plethora of Directives in the areas of water and air pollution. These represent a direct response to what is considered by most experts to be one of the greatest threats to the environment – degradation through pollution. Northern Ireland has not experienced some of the spectacular levels of pollution seen in parts of mainland Europe, largely because it is virtually devoid of mineral resources and does not have a history of major industrial developments. Its water and air do, however, suffer from a range of pollutants, some of which have their origin in agriculture, with others resulting from domestic and vehicular smoke emissions. Water pollution is a major cause of concern; with so many streams and lakes, detection of offences and carrying out of remedial action is often difficult. Much of the focus of domestic environmental legislation has been on the control of discharges into watercourses in order to lessen the potential for pollution incidents. Implementation of domestic legislation is largely the responsibility of EHS and the District Councils.

The European Union has been particularly active on water quality issues, producing over 25 Directives. These include, in particular, the control of discharges of dangerous substances into watercourses and the maintenance of high water quality standards, those standards being related to the use to which the particular water source is to be put.

Many of the general provisions of two related Directives – 75/440 concerning the quality required for surface water intended for the abstraction of drinking water, and 79/869 regarding sampling and analysis of such water – were already in force in Northern Ireland when the Directives were formally implemented. The general effect of the Directives has been to hasten improvements in water abstraction methods and to highlight minor inadequacies in existing domestic legislation. The Directive 80/778 on drinking water quality standards has been partly implemented in Northern Ireland.

One Directive which has received much public acclaim is that dealing with the quality of bathing waters – for both public health and amenity reasons. In common with many other areas, sewage disposal into the sea was practised in Northern Ireland, but over recent years this has ceased to be commonplace. The Directive has given greater impetus to this process; sixteen bathing waters have been identified where regular monitoring of a series of parameters takes place.

A most important Directive is that dealing with urban waste water treatment (91/271). It seeks to reduce the pollution of waters generally by sewage, industrial waste water and rainwater run-off. It sets standards for the collection, treatment and discharge of such water. It also deals with controls over the dumping of sewage sludge, including provision for the cessation of dumping at sea. It has been implemented in Northern Ireland through a Statutory Rule made in 1995.

Air quality directives

The EU tackled the issues of air quality rather later than was the case with other environmental matters. This was partly the result of upheavals caused by oil-related crises, but also because of the very complicated interactions of matters affecting air quality.

In Northern Ireland, it was realised that a significant factor adversely affecting air quality was smoke from domestic sources, and this had been addressed in the Pollution Control and Local Government

(Northern Ireland) Order 1978. In 1982, the UK Government wrote to the Commission stating that, in its view, this measure fulfilled the formal requirements of the EC Directive on Air quality – smoke and sulphur dioxide. However, the Commission gave a reasoned opinion that this was not so, as limit values were not included; this is still the case.

Compliance with other air quality Directives is variable, partly dependant on their applicability to Northern Ireland.

Problems in meeting deadlines for conforming to directives

Northern Ireland has been very tardy in having legislation in place by the dates set out in European Directives. The House of Commons Select Committee on the Environment, reporting in 1990 on Environmental Issues in Northern Ireland, commented adversely on the delays in putting EU Directives into effect. The Committee stressed the fact that the European Court of Justice had ruled on this aspect, and had not accepted the explanation for the delays afforded to the Court by the UK Government. This explanation gave the rather complicated system for introducing legislation in Northern Ireland as the major cause of delays. Under Direct Rule, production of Northern Ireland legislation normally does not begin until similar legislation has been introduced in Great Britain. There then follows a 64 weeks (minimum) period of inter-Departmental and public consultation before the legislation is finally processed through Parliament.

Some of these difficulties have been met to some extent. Recently it has been found possible contemporaneously to bring forward certain items of legislation for Great Britain and Northern Ireland; this method of working, however desirable, requires considerable co-ordination and is probably only achievable with smaller measures where the subject matter does not require separate treatment on either side of the Irish Sea.

In its response to the Select Committee Report, the Department also quoted the shortage of resources as a reason for delay. EHS is small and suffers from chronic high work pressures; because its work covers such a wide range of subjects, many of its staff are experts in relatively narrow fields, and cannot be easily moved around to enable the Service to cope with changing demands. There seems little likelihood of the resource situation improving in the short term, with the inevitable consequence that delays in implementing Directives are likely to continue.

Conclusion

The 'man in the street' will have little appreciation of the changes brought about to the environment as the result of European Directives. He may notice in his everyday life that air is purer, water more potable, and minor changes seem to have been made to the installation of central heating and plumbing fixtures. He is unlikely to pay much attention to the impacts of the Habitats Directive on the protection of birds, but may just have learnt that planning applications inside SACs and SPAs are rather more rigorously assessed than had been the case in the past. Publicity from the voluntary movement may make him realise that Directives have some significance as they are regularly used in support of calls for improved habitat protection.

It is probably among the agricultural community that there is greatest awareness of the environmental changes brought about through EU influences. ESAs have been welcomed by farmers, many of whom privately express concern at the speed of change, especially of the adverse effects on wildlife, the landscape and also the cultural aspects of the rural scene produced by the current rates of fertiliser application, increased mechanisation, and field enlargement. In the areas of our earlier ESAs, one can today see that the farmers' initial response has produced rapid changes, particularly to the landscape, with the planting of small woodlands, the improvement of hedges and the renewal of traditional stone-wall field boundaries; there is a general feeling that there is more wildlife around than there was ten years ago. Research work sponsored by the Department of Agriculture would support these general impressions, though it is still too early to be certain that these improvements will be sustained. What is of real benefit is that farmers now realise that nature and countryside conservation are legitimate uses of their living environment and can, and must, be integrated into all land-use activities. What they also find palatable is that they are now receiving conservation advice from agriculturally-trained staff – even though that advice may not differ from, or indeed may be less detailed than that provided by staff from EHS or voluntary organisations.

The Conservationist will have welcomed most, if not all of the changes brought about by EU Directives. In particular, he will have been encouraged by the strength of the Habitats Directive and by the speed of Government's response to its requirements. He will feel, perhaps, that the range of habitats selected for SAC status is not the most relevant in the local scene, and may feel that not enough sites have been proposed for this status by EHS. However, he will be encouraged by the strictures placed on the decision-taking process on planning applications within European Sites – though he will reserve judgement until he sees these strictures operating. He will also be encouraged by the development of environmentally-friendly agricultural schemes. He may be a little concerned that there is no sign of the EU showing a deep interest either in the conservation of geological features or of landscapes – even though he knows that the latter subject is fraught with difficulties.

The impact of European legislation on Northern Ireland legislation has been considerable and in overall terms, beneficial with the preparation of new legislation and the improvement of existing measures. For the Government Services, they have meant much additional work, some of it with little direct benefit to the environment. For example, implementation of the Habitats Directive involved considerable administrative work in site designation, including the informing of many hundreds of owners, occupiers and others. In particular, the re-designation of sites in order to allow full conformity with the Directive added little to their actual protection but occupied much administrative time. A great deal of detailed scientific survey was accomplished over a couple of years, although it largely provided evidence to support existing qualitative assessments of individual sites rather than identified new ones. In order to accommodate all of this, work already programmed had to be set aside, perhaps resulting in the loss of quality of some sites prior to their declaration under domestic legislation. Staff were placed under even greater pressures to meet the deadlines set by Brussels for what was a gargantuan task, given the resources available to them.

A major positive benefit has been that stronger protection is now afforded to a wide range of habitats and species. This is the case even where the site has not yet received the benefit of a European designation, as it is the policy of the United Kingdom Government to follow the wishes of the European Union and consider all matters relating to a proposed European Site as if it were already designated as such. All government Departments must now bear this in mind, whereas in the past DOE would have had to persuade other Departments of the merits of the conservation case regarding any particular proposal.

Various other benefits have flowed, including providing the impetus for assembling a vastly increased amount of data on important sites – a factor essential to the proper consideration of biodiversity issues. EHS has been encouraged and enabled to promote conservation at the international level – European Nature Conservation Year 1995 achieved much good publicity and many young people were enthused as a result. The appreciation in Great Britain and Europe of the valuable work already being achieved in Northern Ireland and of the significance of some of its internationally important sites has also increased. Links with the statutory conservation agencies throughout the British Isles have been greatly strengthened.

Regrettably, the European Commission has never yet met face to face with EHS – a service whose staff deserve great credit for the quantity and above all the quality of work which has been produced in meeting European requirements. Had such an encounter taken place, the Commission may have been made aware of difficulties in translating some of the principles applicable in Europe to a small country on its fringes, where cultures are such that Directives may be seen as invasive, of difficulties in operating in a situation where domestic conservation priorities are often, with justification, seen as being more urgent than is the production of legislation to conform with European Directives, and where, as in Northern Ireland, the opportunities for co-operation between Departments and the voluntary sector are such that a great deal of conservation benefit can proceed from goodwill rather than through compulsion.

8
Europe and the Northern Ireland Problem
Dennis Kennedy

On the 22nd of January 1972, in the Palais d'Egmont in Brussels, Ireland and the United Kingdom signed the Treaty of Accession to the European Communities. Jack Lynch for Ireland and Edward Heath for the United Kingdom made speeches in praise of a new Europe based on the unity of its peoples, on understanding and friendship.

Ten days later a mob of Mr Lynch's citizens attacked and burned the United Kingdom's Dublin embassy. In the year between the signing of the Treaty of Accession and the entry of both countries into the European Community in January 1973, more than 450 people died in terrorist related violence in the island of Ireland.

Violence had begun in Northern Ireland in 1969, the year in which the Hague Summit had cleared the way for the commencement of negotiations between the European Community and the United Kingdom and Ireland on their applications for membership. In 1970 and 1971, as intensive negotiations continued in Brussels and Luxembourg, the violence in Northern Ireland increased to its crescendo in 1972, and bi-lateral relations between the United Kingdom and Ireland deteriorated to their nadir in the burning of the embassy.

After 25 years of shared EU membership, the United Kingdom and Ireland were still involved in the same unsolved problem of Northern Ireland. The year 1998 saw significant progress, giving some grounds for optimism, but the fact that this latest and longest violent phase of the problem began coincidentally with the approach of Ireland and the UK to EC membership is as remarkable as is the fact that a quarter of a century of shared membership, it would appear, did little to solve the problem.

Remarkably, the speeches in January 1972 contained no mention of Northern Ireland and its troubles. In the prolonged accession negotiations in 1970 and 1971 no one – the Irish, the British, nor anyone in the Community – made any reference whatsoever to the events in Northern Ireland. In its White Paper of April 1970, on the implications for Ireland of membership of the EC, the Dublin Government saw no need to refer to Northern Ireland, not even in chapters specifically on the Constitutional and Legal Implications, and on the Political Implications.[1] Similarly, two years later the White Paper of January 1972, on the outcome of the negotiations, avoided any reference to Northern Ireland, or to relations with the United Kingdom, even in a brief discussion of the meaning of political union in Europe.[2]

Yet in this period the Northern Ireland problem was irresistibly becoming an issue, not for just one state, the United Kingdom, but for two. Ireland had, with the highest profile possible, sought in 1969 to internationalise the issue by having it inscribed as an item on the agendas of the United Nations Security Council and General Assembly. Mr Lynch as Prime Minister repeated his Government's contention that partition and continued United Kingdom retention of Northern Ireland were at the root of the problem.

While more complex than a territorial dispute between the two states, the Northern Troubles were essentially based on the claim of Irish nationalism to the whole territory of the island, including that portion universally recognised as part of the United Kingdom – a claim enshrined in the Irish Constitution.[3]

While never raised explicitly in negotiations or speeches, the territorial dispute had its subtle reverberations. The United Kingdom in its official documents of the time constantly refers to 'the Irish Republic' as its fellow-applicant.[4] The Irish Government documents speak of the 'United Kingdom', but never the *United Kingdom of Great Britain and Northern Ireland*. Some of these points were made less subtly in the key drafting committee of the negotiations. If the chairman called for a comment from the representative of the 'Irish Republic', or even of the 'Republic of Ireland', as happened on occasions, the unbending Irish diplomat on the committee was given to remaining silent, looking around, even peering under the table, and, if pressed, pointing out that no such state was represented, but if the chairman wished him, as representative of *Ireland* to comment, he would do so.

Away from formal contacts and Brussels negotiations, others were making explicit connections between imminent membership of the EC and Northern Ireland's crisis. One of the most strident voices in opposition to Irish membership in the run-up to the 1972 referendum was that of militant Republicanism; accession would mean final acceptance of partition, and formal recognition of Northern Ireland. In Northern Ireland, Unionism in general, and Paisleyite Protestantism in particular, saw the Treaty of Rome and all its works as the passport to perdition and a united Ireland.

Even someone who could claim much greater insight into the nature of European integration, and who was subsequently to be Irish Foreign Minister and Taoiseach, Garret FitzGerald, saw EC membership in 1972 as possibly the most important single factor influencing events in Ireland in a positive direction in the years ahead, by which he meant both peace and Irish unity.[5] EC membership would not be a panacea, he wrote, but 'such influence as membership of the Community will have is likely to be uniformly directed towards easing that path to a united Ireland'. Much of his argument was based on his view that EC membership would lessen the obvious economic benefits of remaining within the UK, while Northern Ireland's interests in the Community would much more closely correspond to those of the Republic than to the general UK interest.

He also suggested that modifications of national sovereignty within the Community would mean any future transfer of Westminster powers over Northern Ireland to an Irish Federal Government in Dublin would lose some of its 'emotional impact', if much power had already passed from Westminster to Brussels anyway.

There was an obvious anomaly between the total absence of any official reference, by anyone, to Northern Ireland in the context of EC membership, and the general assumption in Ireland that the two main preoccupations were, in a variety of ways, closely interlinked. Various factors can help explain this.

Initially British Governments maintained that Northern Ireland was an internal United Kingdom problem, and therefore no concern of Dublin, let alone of the United Nations or the European Community. Dublin also had strong reasons, of a domestic political nature, for keeping all mention of Northern Ireland out of its European dealings. While the referendum on EC membership was, in the event, passed easily in May 1972, there had been fears that, against the background of intense violence in the North, an extreme nationalist backlash could put the vote in jeopardy. To try to raise the North in Brussels, and be told again that it was an internal United Kingdom affair, was seen as unwise.

There was also the view, shared by both London and Dublin, that the European Economic Community, as it then was, had no mandate to act in relation to a situation such as that in Northern Ireland. It had not been raised by the European Commission in its formal examination of the applications of both countries for membership, and it was not raised by any of the existing member states. No one wanted Brussels intervening in internal affairs of member states, even if such a course had been envisaged in the Treaty of Rome, which it was not.

The United Kingdom did not long maintain its position that Northern Ireland was a purely internal affair. By September 1971 Heath was entertaining Lynch at Chequers, and less than a month later he had convened a tri-partite meeting of himself, Lynch and Northern Ireland's Prime Minister Brian Faulkner, conceding thereby an Irish dimension to the problem. By late 1973 this policy line had been taken much further, and the Dublin Government's role as the 'second guarantor' in Northern Ireland was effectively embodied in the Sunningdale Agreement.

However, even if Ulster had become a bi-lateral concern between London and Dublin, neither side showed any desire to go further and make it a European matter. The only mention in the Sunningdale Agreement (December 1973) of the European Community is a suggestion that the proposed Council of Ireland, as part of its harmonising and consultative role, might undertake 'important work relating, for instance to the impact of EEC membership'.[6] It is noteworthy that, in a flurry of constitution drafting, and with both countries in the first flush of enthusiasm for EC membership, there was no looking to the Community for assistance, or for a way of using the new relationship to help build a solution. Both sides, it seemed, saw the problem, and its solution, as bi-lateral.

If the European Community seemed to have little or no relevance in 1973 and 1974, when the violence in Northern Ireland was at its worst, and when ideas for a solution were apparently fluid, it is hardly surprising that the EC receded further into the background as the stalemate of direct rule and the long IRA terrorist campaign continued through the 1970s.

Roy Jenkins' *European Diary*, for instance, which covers the years of his presidency of the European Commission from 1977 to 1981, makes no reference in its 600 hundred pages to the Northern Ireland problem.[7] Jenkins had good reason to be well aware of Northern Ireland. As Home Secretary in the 1960s he had had Cabinet responsibility for the province's affairs. In January 1979, while President of the Commission, he was at the centre of a security alert when police discovered an IRA plot to assassinate a senior British representative in Brussels. Also in 1979 he came in person to Belfast to open the new Commission office there. (Ivor Richard, now Lord Richard, who succeeded Roy Jenkins as a UK nominee on the Commission from 1981 to 1984, cannot recall any discussion at Commission level of the poltical problem of Northern Ireland, or of any role for the EC in it, other than in the context of regional aid. Nor can Lord Tugendhat, who was a UK nominee on the Commission from 1977 to 1984.)[8]

Even when Margaret Thatcher and Charles Haughey moved Anglo–Irish relations towards a new institutional plane by their agreement in London in December 1980 to 'give special consideration to the totality of relationships within these islands' and decided to commission joint studies to that end, the European dimension was missing. The studies were to look at citizenship rights, security matters, economic co-operation and measures to encourage mutual understanding, but not, specifically, European Community affairs.[9] A year later Mrs Thatcher and Mr Haughey's successor, Dr FitzGerald, formally established the Anglo–Irish Intergovernmental Council (AIIC) to give 'institutional expression' to the unique relationship between their two countries. Their joint statement to this effect contained no reference to the EC.[10]

In 1983 the Steering Committee of the Anglo–Irish Intergovernmental Conference published a report on the range of cooperation and contacts between the two countries since 1981. One paragraph in a lengthy report is entitled Anglo–Irish Cooperation in the European Community and Political Co-operation. It makes no reference to Northern Ireland.[11]

Perhaps more significant is the Report of the New Ireland Forum, which sat in Dublin in 1983 and 1984 to consult 'on the manner in which lasting peace and stability could be achieved in a new Ireland, through the democratic process' and to report on possible new structures and processes to achieve this. The four main nationalist parties on the island participated – Fianna Fail, Fine Gael and Labour from the Republic, and the SDLP from Northern Ireland. The Forum received numerous written and oral submissions from a wide range of individuals and organisations, and produced its report in May 1984.[12] It contained no substantive reference to the European Community.

The report did, in its introduction, note that the continuation of the conflict in Northern Ireland, more than 30 years after the beginnings of European efforts to set aside ancient quarrels and work together in the EC, represented a dangerous source of instability in western Europe, and a challenge to European democratic values. But in the ensuing consideration of the nature of the problem, of the identities and attitudes of the people involved and of a new Ireland which might take account of 'present realities and future requirements', there is no discussion, and scarcely a mention, of the European dimension.

By mid-1984 the Northern crisis had been raging for 15 years, and both the United Kingdom and Ireland had been partners within the European Community for more than a decade. Judging from the Forum Report, the EC was still largely irrelevant to the problem.

A year later came the Anglo–Irish Agreement, the most significant landmark in Anglo–Irish relations for half a century. It contains only one passing reference to the EC and that in a preliminary paragraph expressing the wish to develop close co-operation between the UK and Ireland 'as friendly neighbours and as partners in the European Community'. There is no mention of the European dimension in the mandate given in the Agreement to the Intergovernmental Conference on cross-border co-operation on economic matters.

In a detailed account of the Agreement and the background to it, published two years later, its chief architect, Garret FitzGerald, again omits entirely any reference to the European Community – as a factor in Anglo–Irish relations, as an inspiration for the Agreement, or as model for its institutional structure.[13] Similarly in his later autobiography where he deals at length with the negotiating and working of the Agreement, the European Community is absent.[14]

When the Agreement was formally reviewed in 1989 the drive to complete the Single European Market was in full swing, and the Official Review document did record that the two Governments agreed that the Intergovernmental Conference could provide a 'valuable forum for both sides to consider and assess the cross-border implications of the Single Market'. There was no suggestion of any broader coordinating role.[15]

Since then the mechanisms of the Agreement – the Conference and the Secretariat – seem to have played little or no part in coordinating approaches to the EC. Nor for many years was there much evidence of effort to coordinate approaches outside the Agreement.

It would seem therefore that, right up to the end of the 1980s, and even into the 1990s, there was no expectation, in Brussels, London or Dublin, that the European Community had a special role to play in helping solve the Northern Ireland conflict, or that the context of membership of the European Community had anything other than a very general influence on the situation.

This was to change in the early 1990s. In the Brooke–Mayhew inter-party talks on the future of Northern Ireland, in 1991 and 1992, the European dimension was considerably enlarged. Europe also featured prominently in several submissions to the independent Opsahl Commission in 1992. It was repeatedly asserted, by the SDLP and others, that the Anglo–Irish Agreement was inspired by the example of European integration, and that its institutional framework was modelled on that of the European Community. In 1995, the Frameworks Documents put forward by the United Kingdom and Irish Governments as the basis for a solution in Northern Ireland, placed considerable emphasis on the European dimension.

What brought about this apparently sudden discovery of Europe in relation to the Northern Ireland problem? And what was the basis for this new assumption that the European dimension was somehow central to the whole issue?

There had long been, of course, another and different European dimension to the situation in Northern Ireland. Edward Heath, we are told, had been deeply embarrassed in the course of 1972 by the images of apparent British military repression in Northern Ireland being flashed on TV screens around the world, and particularly in the European Community of which both the UK and Ireland were shortly to become members.[16] This growing awareness in London, and in Dublin, of steadily increasing international interest in events in Northern Ireland, and of the importance of taking account of opinion in Washington, Brussels and elsewhere was to become a significant factor in the handling of the issue by London. It has been well documented and analysed by Adrian Guelke, in his *Northern Ireland: The International Perspective*.[17]

While Washington, and possibly individual European capitals, were more important in this regard than the European Community *per se*, the directly-elected European Parliament after 1979 became a frequently used forum for public scrutiny at European level of the Northern Ireland problem, and for discussion of what responsibility the European Community had as regards it, and what actions it might or could take.

At a practical level this probably helped ensure a modest increase in regional aid going to Northern Ireland, most notably in the form of the special Urban Renewal Regulation of 1983. But it could be argued that it also made more obvious the very limited role the European Community could play as regards Northern Ireland. The Parliament's decision in 1983 to ask its Political Affairs Committee to draw up a report on the situation in Northern Ireland, including its political aspects, was groundbreaking. It was perhaps the first time an institution of the European Community had taken formal notice of the political situation in Northern Ireland, and it was a move opposed not just by Ulster Unionists, but by the United Kingdom Government, which declared it interference in the internal affairs of a member state.

The resulting Haagerup Report, adopted by the Parliament in 1984, indeed constituted an EC intervention in the problem, in that it advocated, albeit discreetly, lines of political action not acceptable to Unionists in Northern Ireland, or at that time, to the United Kingdom Government.[18] As Guelke notes, the Parliament's action in 1984 added to the pressure on London to accept the policy line that led, in 1985, to the signing of the Anglo–Irish Agreement.

But that was political pressure on the parties involved. The Parliament was much less successful in its attempt to persuade the EC to involve itself more directly. The Haagerup Report acknowledged that the EC had no competence to propose changes in the constitution of Northern Ireland, and that any intervention could only be economic and social, but even there the Parliament's call for the EC to assume greater responsibility for the province, and to produce an integrated development plan for it, based on a major Brussels cash contribution, produced no direct response.

The signing of the Anglo–Irish Agreement in 1985 brought fulsome endorsement from the Parliament, and from the President of the European Commission, Jacques Delors. After a rather embarrassing lapse of time, it also brought a modest European contribution to the International Fund for Ireland designed to assist reconstruction and reconciliation. At the end of the 1980s, when the Community came to reform its Structural Funds, the special difficulties of Northern Ireland were reflected in more generous treatment – though not spectacularly so – than strict economic criteria might have justified.

There was still, however, no indication that the European Community saw itself as playing any significant political role in resolving the Northern Ireland problem, or that either of the two Governments had any expectations in that direction. In non-governmental circles, however, there was growing interest. Some commentators were beginning to extol the virtues of a Europe of the Regions which they claimed to see on the horizon. In 1988, Richard Kearney, a Dublin academic, proclaimed that this Europe of the Regions offered the best, and perhaps the last or only hope for Northern Ireland. Is it not probable, he asked, that a lasting solution to the Ulster conflict is most likely to be found in a new Europe where the borders separating the nation states of Britain and Ireland would be transcended in favour of a federation of equal and democratic regions?[19]

John Hume, the SDLP leader and MEP since 1979, regularly pointed to post-war Europe as an example to follow in terms of reconciliation among former enemies. Can we not learn the same lesson, he asked his party's annual conference in 1988; can we not sit down with former foes, with those whom we distrust, and hammer out our institutions which will settle our relationships and preserve our differences?

It was in the Northern Ireland inter-party talks of 1991 and 1992 that the European dimension to the Northern Ireland problem, and its solution, were pushed centre stage, both by the nationalist SDLP and by the Irish Government.

Hume, in his opening statement on behalf of the SDLP on 17 June 1991, said that the changing shape of Europe was a dynamic context which had profound implications of the most far-reaching kind. Later that day the SDLP delegation told the talks that the European Community had changed the nature of sovereignty and signalled an advance on the nation–state concept. Northern Ireland could take its place in the vanguard of this advance if the talks proved successful.[20]

The inter-party talks of 1991 were short-lived, but when they resumed in 1992, now under Sir Patrick Mayhew, the SDLP immediately returned to the theme of Europe, a paper of 5 May declaring that the European Community offered both an example and context in which diversity of identity could fully respected. A week later it added, in its submission on New Political Structures (11 May 1992), 'The SDLP...believe that the European Community institutions offer an accessible and persuasive model of how new arrangements for Northern Ireland might be shaped, allowing, of course, for necessary adaptations to local circumstances.' The party then tabled a formal proposal including an Executive Commission to run Northern Ireland, a Parliamentary Assembly with functions similar to those of the European Parliament, and a Council of Ministers which would comprise Ministers from the South and Commissioners from the North, and would have overall responsibility for matters affecting the whole island. The most radical aspect of the proposal was that the six-man Executive Commission would be made up of three elected members, and three nominated – one each by the British Government, the Irish Government and the European Community.

The SDLP paper was leaked to the press, and became the subject of public controversy. Within the talks it drew criticism from all the other parties. The Ulster Unionists said the proposal envisaged something very different from the European model. In the EC context, they pointed out, each country surrendered a part of its authority on the same basis but the SDLP paper proposed that only Northern Ireland should give something up. The UK Government also felt the SDLP proposal did not entirely fit the EC model.

Clearly there was no chance of the SDLP proposal being accepted, but relations between Northern Ireland and the EC were now high on the agenda, and merited their own Annex to the Sub Committee Report of 10 June 1992. This was mainly concerned with how any new institutions in Northern Ireland would deal with Brussels, but the sub-committee also recognised that it would be open for new institutions in Northern Ireland to promote the case for further innovation in the representation of regions in Community institutions and the recognition of regional interests in Community policies. The SDLP believed that the possibility of a more direct relationship between new Northern Ireland institutions and the institutions of the EC was a matter which should be explored.

When the Irish Government entered the talks at Strand 2, in June–July 1992, it largely restricted itself to the usual generalities about a common European identity and the removal of barriers, but it did hint at more radical lessons that might be learned from Europe:

> We are living through times of unprecedented change in human society and political structures alike. The development of the European Union promises to transform our political and economic environment. Issues of sovereignty and borders no longer mean what they meant in the days of Lloyd George. The European Community offers new points of reference, new possibilities free of the connotations of the past. These could be invaluable assets, if we chose to use them, in the process of agreeing our relationships in this island we are destined to share.

Another Irish Government paper, of 28 August 1992, stressed the need to build on common bonds 'across the divide in Northern Ireland and between both parts of Ireland'. Progress towards European union, it said, created unprecedented challenges and opportunities for both parts of Ireland, and its impact would, in many areas, dictate a joint response.

In the same exchange the SDLP returned with enthusiasm to its European theme, praising the role of the EC in fostering cross-community and cross-border co-operation in Ireland. The Party was convinced that new structures in Ireland should have 'a capacity to represent common Irish interests to the European Community and to other international organisations and agencies as appropriate'.

In a submission of September 1992, the SDLP sought an intellectual link between its own nationalist aspirations and the process of

European integration:

> The context in which the aim for Irish unity is now expressed is in many respects radically different to what it was seventy years ago. Today, both parts of Ireland share membership of the European Community which is uniting people in an unprecedented experiment in continental democracy. To achieve its aims the European Community is overcoming barriers of history, geography, language, nationality and religion. The people of Ireland, North and South, are making a significant contribution to this process in ways which cannot fail to impact positively on relationships within the island itself. The SDLP believes, therefore, that as we plan new structures for future relationships between the people of Ireland, we should be conscious of the principles and experiences of the European Community.

The paper gives some indication of ways in which Irish unity might find expression 'radically different' from the original demand for full political independence and total separation for the island as a whole. One was the shared sovereignty and respect for difference at the heart of the principles on which the EC was founded. In the new Ireland this had to ensure, in the words of the document, quoting from the New Ireland Forum Report, the right of nationalists to effective political, symbolic and administrative expression of their identity, and the same, of course, for Unionists.

Still in the context of finding radically new ways of giving expression to Irish unity, the document proposed the establishment of a North–South Council/Council of Ministers 'as an expression of relationships between the people of the whole island'. As one of its special functions, the Council would have responsibility with respect to European Community issues with implications for the whole island. Thus, in regard to some aspects of European Community membership, Irish unity would be achieved.

Public attention at the time of the Brooke–Mayhew talks was focused on the SDLP's rather startling proposal to have a European nominee on the six-man Commission it suggested as an executive for Northern Ireland. But that was always a long shot.[21] (President Delors, on his first visit to Belfast in 1992, made it clear that the Commission had no mandate for such a political role.[22]) More significant was the underlying message, contained in the then confidential proceedings of the talks, that the European dimension was somehow now a central element in any future Northern Ireland settlement, particularly for nationalists, and that they saw in it a new way of pursuing Irish unity, albeit a new type of Irish unity.

Throughout the inter-party talks the United Kingdom Government remained cautious about the European dimension, intervening to remind the participants of the UK's overall responsibility for Northern Ireland within the EC, and pointing out that it was not possible to give the province a seat at the EC's Council of Ministers, as some of the more enthusiastic delegates seemed to be suggesting. This lower key approach was reflected in the Downing Street Declaration of December 1993, which had only two brief references to the European dimension. It stated the British and Irish prime ministers considered that 'the development of Europe' would, of itself, require new approaches to serve interests common to both parts of the island of Ireland, without attempting to indicate what particular development they had in mind, or what the new approaches might be. The Declaration went on to say that the two governments would seek to create new 'institutions and structures to enable the people of Ireland to work together in all areas of common interest'.[23]

Expectations regarding the European dimension increased during the negotiations leading to the Framework Documents in 1995. It was reported that the Irish Government was pressing for a very radical European dimension indeed, including the possibility of the Dublin Government actually representing Northern Ireland in certain circumstances in the Council of Ministers. In the event that did not happen, but the European dimension to the Frameworks was large, though somewhat confused, showing indications of conflicting priorities between London and Dublin. However, much of the SDLP thinking and rhetoric from the Brooke–Mayhew talks found its way into the Frameworks, often with a striking similarity of phrasing.

At the outset, in the first, internal, framework document, the British Government puts down a familiar marker on the legal limits imposed as regards new NI institutions, and new North-South links, in their dealings with Brussels. Any such arrangements must respect the British Government's responsibility for the whole of the UK in the European Union and before the European Court of Justice.[24]

It is in the main document, A New Framework for Agreement, that Europe looms large. In the context of the proposed new North–South institutions to cater for 'present and future political, social and economic interconnection on the island', the document states, 'specific arrangements would need to be developed to apply to EU matters'. Any EU matter relevant to administrations North or South could be raised for consideration in the new North–South body.

Paragraph 26 continues:

> Across all designated matters and in accordance with the delegated functions, both Governments agree that the [North/South] body will have an important role, with their support and co-operation and in consultation with them, in developing on a continuing basis an agreed approach for the whole island in respect of the challenges and opportunities of the European Union. In respect of matters designated at the executive level, which would include all EC programmes and initiatives to be implemented on a cross-border or island-wide basis in Ireland, the body itself would be responsible, subject to the Treaty obligations of each Government, for the implementation and management of EC policies and programmes on a joint basis. This would include the preparation, in consultation with the two Governments, of joint submissions under EC programmes and initiatives and their joint monitoring and implementation, although individual projects could be implemented either jointly or separately.

These proposals were radical in terms of how Northern Ireland as a region would relate to the European Union and of how EU programmes would be drafted and implemented in Northern Ireland. The concept set out, of 'an agreed approach for the whole island' on European Union matters, went far beyond anything previously envisaged, though legal obligations were invoked as a reminder of practical limitations in the actual implementation of such ideas.

No such inhibitions were mentioned, however, in the section dealing with Northern Ireland's 'wider relationships'. Paragraph 19 reads:

> They [the Governments] agree that future arrangements relating to Northern Ireland, and Northern Ireland's wider relationships, should respect the full and equal legitimacy and worth of the identity, sense of allegiance, aspiration and ethos of both unionist and nationalist communities there. Consequently, both Governments commit themselves to the principle that institutions and arrangements in Northern Ireland, and North/South institutions, should afford both communities secure and satisfactory political, administrative and symbolic expression and protection.

This paragraph repeats almost verbatim the claim put forward in Brooke–Mayhew by the SDLP, that nationalists had a legitimate right to 'effective political, symbolic and administrative expression of their identity', wording taken from the New Ireland Forum Report of 1984.[25]

It seemed to be stating that Northern Ireland's dealings with the EU must respect the 'full and equal legitimacy' of the nationalist identity and sense of allegiance, and that the two Governments were committed to institutions or arrangements for relations with the EU which afforded 'satisfactory political, administrative and symbolic expression and protection' to the nationalist identity and sense of allegiance.

On the one hand it was possible to see such arrangements affording a new expression of Irish unity, as advocated by the SDLP in the Brooke–Mayhew talks, but it was difficult to see them operating under anything less than joint authority, which the two governments had repeatedly ruled out. The New Ireland Forum Report, the definitive document of nationalist thinking, makes it clear that this 'parity of esteem', as regards identity and sense of allegiance, and their satisfactory expression, could be ensured only by, at the very minimum, joint Irish–British authority over Northern Ireland.

The dream of instituting an 'expression of Irish unity' through giving the Irish state and its Government in Dublin a role in handling the external relations of the whole island, however unrealistic, has long appealed to nationalists. One of the powers as regards Northern Ireland that Garret FitzGerald felt, in 1972, might possibly be transferable within the EC from London to Dublin was foreign affairs.[26]

This approach is based in part on the assertion that Northern Ireland's interests within the EU are more closely aligned to those of the Republic than they are to those of the UK generally, and that therefore the Government of the Republic might more appropriately and efficiently represent Northern Ireland in Brussels. A variation on this theme came more recently from the (Dublin) Institute of European Affairs, in *Issues, Opinions, Implications,* a report focused on the 1996 EU Intergovernmental Conference. The Institute considered the policy options for Dublin regarding Northern Ireland and the EU in a situation where the United Kingdom continued to resist further European integration, and extended its (then) practice of opting out of major policy areas, and made the following suggestion:

> Northern Ireland could be designated as a special region of the Union entitled to choose whatever Community policies suited its

regional interests from among the policy packages applying separately to the Republic and to the UK. This idea has been already advanced on the grounds that economic growth could be enhanced by allowing the Northern Ireland economy to dine à la carte off the EU policy menu.[27]

Another publication in 1996 from the same influential Institute, based on a project headed by Dr FitzGerald, argued that Northern Unionist politicians might find it opportune to support this idea of 'sovereignty sharing by the Irish state in a key area of external policy'.[28] *Britain's European Question; The Issues for Ireland*, credited Sir David Fell, then Head of the Northern Ireland Civil Service, with the 'imaginative proposal' that Northern Ireland be treated as a special case for the purposes of EU policy, suggesting that Northern Ireland's best interests might be served by aligning in different policy areas with the Irish or British positions, choosing, issue by issue, which suited it better, and also of raising the question of both Dublin and Belfast delegating the management of their relations with the institutions of the EU to some new North–South body.

Sir David, speaking at seminars in Belfast and Dublin,[29] had referred publicly and somewhat non-committally to these proposals, but in private had offered the opinion that given sufficient imagination and political will, the idea of Northern Ireland dining à la carte in Brussels was possible. This was clearly taken as an indication of UK Government willingness to contemplate such an arrangement.

The ability of nationalists to put forward very radical proposals as regards Northern Ireland's external relations while ignoring entirely the extremely serious constitutional implications for unionists was well illustrated in a 1997 speech by Michael O'Kennedy, one of the Republic's most experienced politicians who has served as Foreign Minister, and as European Commissioner. In July 1997 he said the European Union 'can and must' play a major part in shaping the future Ireland:[30] He claimed that the people of Northern Ireland had been effectively deprived of any meaningful or influential role in the European Union, through their representatives having no place at the Council of Ministers or at the European Council.

He repeated the argument that within the EU there were many areas where the interests of Northern Ireland were much more closely aligned with those of the Republic than with the rest of the United Kingdom. He then proposed that the elected representatives of Northern Ireland be accorded formal access to Ireland's delegations at the Council of Ministers. This could, he said, eventually develop into a shared role with the Republic in all negotiations affecting the direct interest of the people of Northern Ireland.

Despite such flights of fancy, the Belfast Agreement of April 1998, negotiated among all the parties in Northern Ireland and the two Governments, had little radical to say on European matters, compared to the Framework proposals of 1995. In 1995 the North/South body was to have 'an important role...in developing on a continuing basis an agreed approach for the whole island in respect of the challenges and opportunities of the European Union.' In 1998, the North/South body is deemed merely 'an appropriate forum to consider institutional or cross-sectoral matters' in relation to the EU.

Conclusion

Two main themes emerge from this survey of the Northern Ireland crisis and its twenty-five years within the European Union:

- The persistent belief, or assertion, that both the example of the European Union, and the fact of membership of it, can indeed facilitate a settlement in Ireland;
- The limited ability, or inability, of the European Union to act in any significant way to help resolve the problem.

Irish nationalist attitudes towards European union have always included a vague idea that the inclusion of both parts of the island of Ireland within a European Community destined for 'ever closer union' must, inevitably, provide a favourable context for their own aspiration towards a united Ireland.

At a more rational level, it was argued that the removal of barriers to trade, to free movement of goods, people and services and the levelling up of economic and social conditions, would all facilitate moves towards reunification by removing practical obstacles to it. Greater commercial and social intercourse in the island, plus a growing shared sense of European identity, would also help. Beyond this was the view, frequently asserted by John Hume, that the whole European project was about solving the problems of division in Europe by creating innovative structural arrangements which would allow former enemies to live and work together in a framework leading to union.

As was seen in the Brooke–Mayhew talks, the assertion that the problem in Ireland is akin to that in post-war western Europe, and that the legal and institutional structure of the EU is an appropriate model to follow, is far from convincing. The essential issue in Northern Ireland is not relations between a group of states, or even between two states, but the administration of one small region of one state, against the background of an essentially territorial dispute. The institutional model of the EU may have been in the minds of some of those who negotiated the Anglo–Irish Agreement, but the parallels are untrue, and were even more so in the SDLP 'European' model put to Brooke–Mayhew.[31]

There has been a persistent tendency among politicians from the Republic to overestimate grossly the importance to Northern Ireland of financial and other benefits from the EU. In terms of funding coming to Northern Ireland from outside its own boundaries and resources, the flow from membership of the EU has always been a modest fraction of that resulting from membership of the United Kingdom.

This is not to argue that the European dimension is irrelevant, or that the Anglo–Irish Agreement could ever have been signed if the United Kingdom and Ireland had not been partners within the EU. But it is to question seriously whether the European experience, or the EU institutional model, has any direct relevance to Northern Ireland.

Even so, should the EU have a role in the solution of the problem, if possible? We started by noting the coincidence in time between the outbreak of trouble in Northern Ireland, and the opening of the way for British and Irish membership of the then EEC. It is a stark truth that the problem, and the violence, have continued ever since; the most serious and sustained terrorist assault on the democratic process in western Europe over the past quarter of a century has been within the boundaries of the European Union.

At the outset there was a studied ignoring of the problem in any European context by all the parties – the United Kingdom, Ireland and the European Community. Initially the British regarded it as an internal affair; then it became an Anglo–Irish affair – in the first instance it could not be a European matter, in the second, as the two member states moved rapidly to a common position on it, it did not have to become one. As the high level of violence continued throughout the 1970s and into the 1980s it certainly aroused great concern in the other member states of the EU, in the European Parliament, and among some members of the European Commission. But this concern did not lead to any significant response. The European Commission did decide, in the 1980s, to set up a Northern Ireland committee consisting of the President, the British and Irish Commissioners, and the Commissioners for Regional Policy and Agriculture. In fact this group never met at Commissioner level.

Against the obvious anomaly of such a situation persisting within a Community 'founded to ensure the peace and prosperity of its member countries',[32] but with no EU action to intervene or help, must be set the reality of the legal framework of the EU, and the restricted mandate given to the European Commission, the initiator of action. It is extremely difficult to see what could have been attempted within the scope of treaties which were simply not written to cope with such situations.[33]

Even today, when the two member governments directly involved have elevated the European dimension to new prominence in discussion of the problem, and when the EU has, it would seem, moved towards much greater direct involvement through its Special Support Programme for Peace and Reconciliation in Northern Ireland, it is difficult to discern any distinctive, significant European contribution. In terms of its major policies, the EU has been modestly generous towards Northern Ireland, but nothing more.[34]

Where there has been intervention – endorsement of the Anglo–Irish Agreement by the Parliament and by the President of the Commission, contribution to the International Fund for Ireland, the Special Support Programme – it has usually been in support of action already taken elsewhere, mainly by the two governments. The much publicised Special Support Programme, essentially a gesture of support in the wake of the first terrorist cease-fires, is largely geared to tackling social deprivation, in the hope that this will assist the process of reconciliation and recovery and the search for a negotiated settlement by improving the environment within which that settlement is being sought. In its creation of local area partnerships it could be argued that European intervention has introduced a new mechanism to promote wider participation in the affairs of the community than has been possible through existing structures. The Special Programme is innovative and gives new substance to the European dimension to the Northern Ireland programme, but it hardly constitutes a significant initiative in the search for a solution.

The feeling that the European Union has, for whatever combination of circumstances and factors, never regarded the Northern Ireland problem as a main concern, or itself as having any significant role to play in its solution, is heightened by more recent interest at EU level both in combating terrorism, and in conflict within states rather than between them as the major threat to peace and stability. Invariably these topics are discussed without reference to Northern Ireland.

Middle East terrorism, events in former Yugoslavia and the prospect of enlargement have brought onto the broad EU agenda a range of matters long relevant to the Northern Ireland problem. These include not just the issue of how democracies should respond to sustained political terrorism, but the role of international arbitration on border disputes and the precise nature of the right of self-determination, and who can claim it.[35]

This new concern with old issues is neatly illustrated in Agenda 2000, where the European Commission proposes that applicant countries for EU membership must resolve any outstanding border disputes, by decision of the International Court of Justice if necessary, before they can be admitted.[36] Such a stance in 1970–3 would have presented the Irish Government with an interesting dilemma.

One of the many ironies of the Anglo–Irish approach at government level to the Northern Ireland problem has been the persistent tendency to accept the contention that Ireland is different, that the internationally-accepted approach outlined above is inadequate to the situation, and that the claimant state must be given some institutionalised representative rights in the territory claimed.

There is also an obvious anomaly between this view that the Irish situation is *sui generis,* requiring its own special responses, and the more general nationalist contention that the process of European integration, and in particular the institutions and mechanisms of the EU, provide both inspiration and model for a solution in Ireland. This gap is bridged, in nationalist thinking at least, by the assertion that the European Union has 'changed the nature of sovereignty and signalled an advance on the nation-state concept'.

In some ways it has, but many observers of European integration point to the survival of the nation–state, albeit in somewhat modified form, as one of the most remarkable features of that process. Integration has not made the nation–state redundant; indeed it has been argued that it has enabled the concept to be preserved in a radically altered world, and has helped the nation–states to find a way to live together in peace and combined economic growth.[37]

Europe has been invoked by nationalists as a way of dressing up an out-dated and discredited ideology in modern, progressive clothing. The ultimate solution to the problem of Northern Ireland, according to successive Dublin Governments, according also to the Irish Constitution, to the New Ireland Forum and to Northern nationalists, remains the simplistic one of unification of the island under an independent Irish state. This is plainly unobtainable, and in practical terms the demands of nationalism have centred on diluting British sovereignty over Northern Ireland, and instituting, in as formal a way as possible, a role for the independent Irish state in its government. The suspicion remains that even when presented as a local application of European integration principles, this is essentially pursuit of a nationalist goal, albeit an intermediate one, by other means.

Whatever the European Union should, or could, have done as regards Northern Ireland in the past, it remains the overall framework within which the problem continues. Membership of it has helped transform Anglo–Irish relations. Its rules and policies have facilitated commercial and other co-operation between North and South by removing barriers. (They have also created some new ones – currency for example.) In time, the exaggerated concepts of national identity which inflame the problem may be softened by a common European sense of identity, and offer a helpful background for the development of the fragile agreement of 1998.

Notes

1. *Membership of the European Communities: Implications for Ireland*, April 1970. Dublin: Stationery Office.
2. *The Accession of Ireland to the European Communities*, January 1972. Dublin: Stationery Office.
3. The explicit claim remains in Articles 2 and 3 of the Constitution, though the Belfast Agreement of 1998 envisages modification of it.
4. See e.g. White Paper (1971), *The United Kingdom and the European Communities*, London: HMSO.
5. G. FitzGerald, (1972), *Towards a New Ireland*, London: Knight.
6. O'Day, A. and Stevenson, J., (1992), *Irish Historical Documents since 1800*, Dublin: Gill & Macmillan, p. 229.
7. R. Jenkins, (1989) *European Diary 1977–81*, London: Collins.
8. Conversations with Lords Richard and Tugendhat, July 1998.
9. Communiqué of 8 December 1980, quoted in O'Day and Stevenson, op. cit. p. 235.
10. Communiqué from Department of Taoiseach 6 November 1981, Dublin: Government Information Services.
11. Joint Report of the Steering Committee of the AIIC to the Anglo–Irish Summit on Anglo–Irish Contacts and Co-operation, 3 November 1983.
12. New Ireland Forum (1984) *Report*, Dublin: Stationery Office.
13. G. FitzGerald, (1987), 'The Anglo–Irish Agreement', in Lynch, P. and J. Meenan, (eds), *Essays in Memory of Alexis FitzGerald*, Dublin: Incorporated Law Society of Ireland.
14. G. FitzGerald, (1991), *All in a Life*, Dublin: Gill & Macmillan.
15. The Review was published on 24 may 1989. Its text is reprinted in T. Hadden and K. Boyle, (1989), *The Anglo–Irish Agreement; Commentary, Text and Official Review*, London: Sweet & Maxwell.
16. J. Campbell, (1993), *Edward Heath: A Biography*, London: Jonathan Cape.
17. A. Guelke, (1998), *Northern Ireland: the International Perspective*, Dublin: Gill & Macmillan.

18. *Report of Political Affairs Committee on the situation in Northern Ireland*, (N. J. Haagerup) European Parliament Working Documents 1983–4, Doc 1–526/83 (19 March 1984).
19. R. Kearney, (1988), *Across the Frontiers: Ireland in the 1990s*, Dublin: Wolfhound Press.
20. All references to and quotations from the Brooke–Mayhew Inter-Party talks are taken from the record of talks published unofficially on the Internet in 1997 by the Cadogan Group at www.cadogan.org.
21. When Hugh Logue, the former SDLP Assembly-man then a European Commission official in Brussels, made his submission to the Opsahl Commission in early 1993, he proposed a set of institutions in Northern Ireland modelled on the those of the European Community, almost identical to the SDLP proposal to Brooke Mayhew. But he omitted the proposal to include an EC nominee as one of the six members of the executive Commission. Mr Logue was generally thought to have been one of the authors of the original SDLP paper, *A Citizens' Inquiry: The Opsahl Report on Northern Ireland*, Dublin: Lilliput Press, 1993, p. 214.
22. *Irish Times*, 4 November 1992.
23. Downing Street Declaration of 15 December 1993, Articles 3 and 9.
24. A Framework for Accountable Government in Northern Ireland, par 28.
25. New Ireland Forum *Report*, op. cit.
26. G. FitzGerald, (1972) op. cit. p. 108.
27. *1996 Intergovernmental Conference. Issues, Options, Implications*, Institute of European Affairs, Dublin, 1996. Chapter 26.
28. P. Gillespie, (1996) *Britain's European Question; The Issues for Ireland*, Dublin: Institute of European Affairs.
29. Held at Institute of European Affairs, Dublin, December 1993, and at Institute of European Studies, Queen's University, Belfast, September 1994.
30. M. O'Kennedy, (1997), Address to the Magill Summer School, 15 August.
31. For a discussion of these points see Kennedy, D., (1994), 'The European Union and the Northern Ireland Question' in B. Barton, and P. J. Roche *The Northern Ireland Question: Perspectives and Policies*, Aldershot: Avebury.
32. United Kingdom White Paper of July 1971, op. cit.
33. For a discussion of the hopes and disappointments of NI's EU experience see E. Moxon-Browne, (1992), 'The Impact of the European Community' in B. Hadfield, (ed.) *Northern Ireland: Politics, and The Constitution*, Buckingham: Open University Press.
34. See D. Kennedy, (1996), 'Europe's Concern' in M. Browne, and D. Kennedy, (eds) *Northern Ireland and the European Union*, The Institute of European Studies, Queen's University Belfast.
35. A. D. Rotfeld, (1997), 'Conflict is within States, not between them', in *How Can Europe Prevent Conflicts?* Philip Morris Institute for Public Policy Research, Brussels, November 1997. See also A. Alcock, (1994), *Understanding Ulster*, Lurgan: Ulster Society Publications, pp. 148–50.
36. Agenda 2000, the European Commission. 1997.
37. A. Millward, (1994), *The European Rescue of the Nation State*, London: Routledge.

9
The European Connection and Public Opinion
M. L. Smith

Since the end of the Second World War the United Kingdom has enjoyed neither a comfortable nor a clear relationship with the process of European integration. For more than fifty years the 'problem' of Europe, in the sense of the dilemma of choice which continental integration has presented to British policy, has consistently been one of the most central and divisive themes within British political debate. Given the importance of this debate about Europe, it is worth prefacing the analysis of public opinion in Northern Ireland that is the subject of this chapter with two, perhaps obvious, points: firstly, that it has been Westminster and Whitehall who have set the framework within which relations with Europe have developed; secondly, that this framework has seldom, if ever, been conceived in anything but broad terms of national interest. Whether it has wished this or not, Northern Ireland's response to Europe since accession to the EEC has been circumscribed by the context of the UK's frequently ill-tempered dialogue with the evolving European Community; a dialogue in which particular preoccupations about Britain's role in the wider world as well as Europe have played a large part. In many areas – for example, those of coping with economic decline and restructuring or of social issues – Northern Ireland has inevitably shadowed patterns across the UK as a whole. If this is so, it follows that perceptions of the benefits (or otherwise) that Europe may bring to dealing with these areas of concern have also, in their general outline, followed those in the UK. The attempt to identify specific and distinct perceptions must, therefore, first look at this shared, wider, context.

The features of those issues concerning European relations that the UK has believed to be central, and around which there has been a large measure of political consensus throughout the period since accession in 1973, have in fact varied little since the War. The UK's initial decision in the 1950s to stay outside the new economic grouping of the main west European states reflected a belief, argued tenaciously from 1945 on, that Britain stood at the intersection of three circles of involvement: the Atlantic, the Empire and Commonwealth and Europe, in all of which it was in her national interest to participate. Global trading relations, backed by a continuing British military capability, did not allow for exclusive or restrictive European entanglements. The failure, however, to sustain such a global policy in the face of American opposition and, most crucially, relative economic (in which must be included military) decline, made the option of an approach to Europe an inevitable one. The stages of the process toward joining, and subsequently confirming, membership in the European Communities are well known. They included the attempt to dissolve the new Economic Community of the 'Six' in a larger and looser European Free Trade Area (EFTA), the series of negotiations through the 1960s which were conducted by Conservative and Labour governments in turn and, after the accession of the UK in 1973, the re-negotiation of the terms of entry which culminated in the Referendum Campaign of 1975 and its two-thirds majority in favour of remaining in.

If public attitudes to the UK's gradual European engagement are to be understood, it is important to identify the connecting thread that runs through both the preparatory and post-accession phases. It would be wrong, if at times tempting, to read the UK's position toward Europe as simply reflecting and endorsing a strong current of chauvinism or anti-Europeanism. What appears as a persistent need to oppose the extension of European co-operation describes, rather, a fundamental and long-standing policy problem in relation to European membership. In essence it is that the nature of the interests which necessitated the original shift of the UK toward Europe was such as to require that they were defined almost exclusively in terms of economic benefits. What was in reality the end of a lengthy failure to maintain Britain's world status and relative prosperity was portrayed as the achievement of these goals by other means. Thus, while other European states sustained their embrace of European integration by recourse to 'myths' that fully justified the sacrifice of some areas of national initiative – Franco-German reconciliation that would make future wars impossible, the strengthening of fragile new democratic structures or protection from larger and dominant neighbours for example – for the UK the loss of key elements of national sovereignty which membership carried was an unwelcome, and reluctantly embraced, price for the advantages of access to an enlarged market.

From 1973 onwards, therefore, it would be a reasonable generalisation to say that it has been the twin issues of economic benefit and the protection of sovereignty that have set the terms of the UK's relations with the European Union. During the decade following the Referendum the initial premise of membership – that the development of a liberal trade and competition regime did not require any move toward the economic or political integration of Europe – appeared to have been secured. These were the years in which Mrs Thatcher's governments showed a robust determination not only to argue the corner of the UK's national interests against the European club but to block any progress toward supranationalism or the extension of powers to 'Brussels' above those of the individual sovereign member state. The key element in her presentation of these arguments was consistently that the focus of Britain's involvement in Europe must be to ensure a fair and open market from which the UK, above all, and as a direct result of her governments' successful neo-liberal policies, would benefit. It was this belief which encouraged her to endorse what was to prove a turning point in European development: the Single European Act (SEA), agreed at the end of 1985 and ratified in July 1987, which set the structure for the free movement of goods, persons, capital and services within the European Community.

The SEA ushered in a period of dynamism and turbulence in the discussion of European development both within the UK and widely throughout the Community. Above all it opened up – alarmingly so for some – those real steps towards economic and political integration which Britain had always resisted. The deliberations of the Delors Committee, created in 1988 to prepare a report on economic and monetary union (EMU), proved the first stage of a process that led to the Madrid agreement in 1989 to proceed further on this path and the subsequent embedding of EMU as the central plank in the Treaty of European Union of 1993. From the late 1980s onward, therefore, the growing continental emphasis on achieving monetary union as well as the endorsement of a raft of reforms that could be seen as passing more powers to 'Brussels' at the expense of the individual member states put Europe at the heart of political debate in the UK for the first time since the period around accession. In short, Europe became a serious focus of governmental and public concern.

Public opinion in the UK as a whole

The surveys of public opinion conducted throughout the Community by *Eurobarometer* show clearly (Table 9.1) that for most of the period

1978–94 only a minority of UK respondents believed membership of the EU to be a good thing and remained throughout largely unconvinced of the benefits that membership brought.

Table 9.1a/b provides broad evidence in support of a view that the terms of membership of the EU have been perceived both differently and less positively in the UK than they have throughout the Union as a whole. Indeed, the full individual country data in the *Eurobarometer* surveys show the UK to be invariably (with the partial exception of Denmark in the 1980s) the least positive respondent of all the member states.[1] What they also broadly confirm is that for UK opinion, European questions produced a greater volatility of response in the period from about 1987 onwards – the period we have identified above as that of turbulence caused by the first moves to greater European integration – than in the EU in general. From 1987 through to 1991, for instance, there is a sustained increase in the percentage of respondents believing the UK to be benefiting from membership, followed by a sharp (13 per cent) fall in 1992 at the time of the greatest uncertainties about the ratification of the Maastricht Treaty. This pattern is closely reproduced in the figures from 1989–91 charting approval for UK membership of the EU in which, for the first time since the UK's accession, a majority of respondents believe membership to be a good thing.

However, if these responses show the UK to have been the Community partner least convinced of the benefits of membership, it would not be correct to interpret them as a desire for the UK to leave the EU. The comprehensive British Social Attitudes (BSA) survey carried out in non-election years since 1985 shows, rather, a steady growth in support for continued membership.[2]

Taken together, both the *Eurobarometer* and BSA figures suggest that overall support for the fact of membership as well as for the perceived benefits it has brought showed a general upward trend until the early 1990s. If we aggregate in Table 9.1a those respondents who expressed a positive or a neutral view of UK membership, there is not only a clear rise in approval over time but also an acceptance rating of 75–78 per cent in the years 1988 to 1991.

Notwithstanding this general upward trend over two decades the surveys confirm that the issue of sovereignty has remained of higher concern in the UK than elsewhere in the EU. The sharp downturn in approval expressed after 1991 – and very clearly shown in the responses in Table 9.1b – is most cogently explained by the fact that it was precisely from this date that the direction in which Europe appeared to be moving was one that threatened the greatest erosion of

Table 9.1a How do you think of your country's membership of the EC (%)*

	1978	1979	1980	1981	1982	1983	1984	1985	1986	1987	1988	1989	1990	1991	1992	1993	1994
UK																	
good thing	39	29	24	27	39	36	38	38	42	46	48	52	53	57	44	43	43
neither good nor bad	25	25	24	27	26	30	25	28	26	25	27	25	24	21	26	30	28
bad	31	41	49	41	40	28	33	30	27	24	21	17	16	16	23	22	22
EC average																	
good	60	58	53	53	51	55	58	60	61	65	65	65	68	68	59	57	60
neither good nor bad	22	23	23	26	27	24	26	23	23	20	21	20	19	18	22	25	23
bad	10	12	16	14	15	13	11	12	10	9	9	8	8	8	13	13	12

Source: *Eurobarometer*. Trends 1974–94, pp. 71–88.
*Figures are in the last survey conducted in each year.

Table 9.1b Would you say your country has benefited or not from being a member of the EC? (%)*

	1978	1979	1980	1981	1982	1983	1984	1985	1986	1987	1988	1989	1990	1991	1992	1993	1994
UK																	
Yes	n/a	n/a	n/a	n/a	n/a	32	32	34	36	49	47	47	46	45	32	33	38
No	n/a	n/a	n/a	n/a	n/a	57	57	53	48	42	40	38	36	38	53	49	45
EC average																	
Yes	n/a	n/a	n/a	n/a	n/a	52	48	53	55	59	60	59	59	55	48	45	50
No	n/a	n/a	n/a	n/a	n/a	25	34	30	28	25	25	23	23	26	34	35	30

Source: Eurobarometer, Trends 1974–94, pp. 89–99
*Figures are the last survey conducted in each year.

Table 9.2 Respondents who think the UK should continue to be a member of the EC (%)

1985	1986	1987	1988	1989	1990	1991
56	61	63	–	68	76	76

Source: British Social Attitudes Survey, 1985–91.

Table 9.3 GB respondents saying as a member state, the UK's relationship with the EC should be (%)

	1991	1993	1994	1995
Closer	39	30	37	29
Less close	11	24	23	26
About right	41	36	34	39
Don't know	9	10	7	6

Source: British Social Attitudes Survey, 1991–95.

national sovereignties. This interpretation is strengthened by the responses given to questions posed by the BSA surveys from 1991 onwards which sought to address more directly the sovereignty issue (figures are given for Great Britain (GB) only):

The picture given in Table 9.3 is of a clear and sustained decline in support for closer relations with the EU, with between 23 per cent and 26 per cent of respondents after 1991 wishing for these to be less close. This movement is paralleled in the responses, shown in Table 9.4, to a question designed specifically to elicit a view of the economic benefits of greater integration:

In both tables the key period in which a dramatic erosion occurs in positive attitudes to EU integration and to its anticipated benefits for the UK is between 1991 and 1993. In neither case does the resurgence of support for integration in 1994 redress the hardening of negative or pessimistic attitudes.

That this shift describes a disturbance of the consensus in which EC membership was perceived as delivering economic benefits without fundamentally attacking the basis of UK sovereignty, is borne out by the exogenous contextual evidence. Firstly, the mid and late 1980s in Great Britain were, despite persistent high unemployment, years of economic growth and increasing levels of disposable personal income.

Table 9.4 GB respondents saying closer links with the EC would make the UK(%)

	1991	1993	1994	1995
Stronger economically	43	33	40	32
Weaker economically	13	22	20	20
Make no difference	31	32	29	39
Don't know	13	13	10	9

Source: *British Social Attitude Survey*, 1991–95.

Secondly, the bloodless change of regimes in eastern Europe in 1989, the apparently uncomplicated move to German reunification and the peace dividend expected from the ending of the Cold War, all helped to sustain a belief that developing European co-operation was both feasible and the stimulus to even greater prosperity. A context in which the integration of Europe was portrayed as continent-wide tended to divert attention from how radical and narrowly focused were the proposals coming from the Madrid summit and the Delors Commission. In consequence the implications of those proposals were put to one side and, encouraged by the government's advocacy of the 'widening' of the EU, did nothing to stop the wave of optimism that is reflected in the responses shown in Tables 9.1–9.4 up to 1991.

By contrast the period from spring 1992 onward placed both sovereignty and economic problems at the centre of public debate. The ratification process of the Treaty of European Union engendered a 'no' vote in Denmark and an embarrassingly small majority in favour in France. In the UK both campaigns were widely reported to be about the over-rapid ceding of sovereignty to an unelected and insufficiently democratic European bureaucracy. But overshadowing these doubts about the direction which Europe was taking was a real crisis of the UK economy which led to the débâcle of the UK's withdrawal in September 1992 from the European Exchange Rate Mechanism (ERM). The origins of this crisis lay partly in the high interest rates which reunification had imposed on Germany. These in turn impacted on a UK economy which, by June 1992, had been formally in recession for two years. In the face of a large, and growing, deficit on balance of payments together with predicted sharp increases in public sector borrowing requirements for 1993 and 1994, an overvalued sterling came under extreme speculative pressure in the currency markets. After a short and disastrously expensive attempt to defend the value imposed by ERM membership the UK withdrew from the mechanism in which it had participated since 1990. Wherever the real responsibility lay, one lesson was immediately drawn: that if the defence of the most potent instrument of a nation's ability to manage its own affairs could not be safeguarded within the existing arrangements of European membership, then how much more dangerous would be the union of currencies proposed in the process of EMU. Precisely because the ERM crisis conflated the two issues which had dominated UK attitudes toward European membership it proved to be both a litmus test of the persistence and depth of these attitudes and the point at which the steady rise in acceptance of the UK's relations with Europe was pinned back into something more cautious through the 1990s.

Public opinion in Northern Ireland: general trends alongside Great Britain

Having sketched the broad development of attitudes to Europe in the UK as a whole and, for specific questions, in Great Britain, it is time to turn to Northern Ireland. The aim of what follows will be to determine how closely Northern Ireland, as part of the UK, has shadowed the trends that have been outlined earlier. In particular this section will concentrate on trends in the 1990s. The choice of these years has partly been dictated by the availability and the quality of separate public opinion data for Northern Ireland. What follows will be based on the Northern Ireland Social Attitudes (NISA) surveys which, since 1991 – and in common with the BSA surveys – have included 'modules' dealing with Europe. The surveys are based on questionnaires given to a representative sample of 1400 (a number equivalent to the sample used for the whole UK by the *Eurobarometer* surveys), thus allowing a good geographical spread and derived analysis variables such as age and political identification of a size to allow meaningful analysis.[3]

The second reason for focusing on the 1990s is the hypothesis that these years, inasmuch as they cover the period of a real move to greater European integration, provide the best touchstone of embedded attitudes to Europe in those areas of concern which the Northern Ireland population might be expected to hold in common with their GB fellow citizens. This assumption can be tested by adding to the GB data already set out in Table 9.3, responses from the NISA surveys to the same question dealing broadly with the issue of retaining sovereignty. The responses are given in Table 9.5.

Table 9.5 Respondents saying as a member state, the UK's relationship with the EC should be (%)

	1991		1993		1994		1995	
	NI	GB	NI	GB	NI	GB	NI	GB
Closer	41	39	40	30	45	37	39	29
Less close	7	11	14	24	10	23	13	26
About right	41	41	34	36	37	34	38	39
Don't know	11	9	12	10	7	7	11	6

Sources: British Social Attitudes Survey, 1991–95; Northern Ireland Social Attitudes Survey, 1991–95.

What is immediately striking is how little the Northern Ireland (NI) response over the four surveys matches that in GB to the same questions. Both sets of respondents exhibit similar levels of approval for closer relations with the EU in the survey of 1991 which we have identified as the high point of general UK enthusiasm: there is only a 2 per cent variation between the two groups who wish the relation to be closer, and no difference in the proportions who believe the prevailing relation to be about right. But the subsequent responses show a significant divergence. In the first place the drop of 9 per cent which is registered in 1993 in the proportion of GB respondents who favour closer relations with Europe is not shared at all in NI. Secondly, this difference is sustained over time so that in the 1995 survey, while 2 per cent fewer in NI approve of closer EU links, 10 per cent fewer do so in GB. Both the overall pattern and the divergence between NI and GB responses is maintained if we add in the respondents who believe the relation with the EU to be about right.

The responses to the further question about the economic effects of greater integration produce similar patterns to those in Table 9.5. They are set out in Table 9.6.

A higher proportion of respondents in both survey groups hold a positive view about economic benefits than is the case in answer to the more general question about closer relations with Europe in Table 9.5. The most salient variation is the drop in confidence shown by the 1993 survey in which a similarly reduced proportion in both NI and GB (8 per cent and 10 per cent respectively) express the belief that EU links will help the economy. Given the focus of the question, this drop may well reflect the fact that the aftermath of the ERM shock was felt

Table 9.6 Would closer links with the EC make the UK (%)

	1991		1993		1994		1995	
	NI	GB	NI	GB	NI	GB	NI	GB
Stronger economically	50	43	42	33	48	40	47	32
weaker economically	10	13	16	22	12	20	11	20
Make no difference	27	41	31	32	32	29	32	39
Don't know	13	13	11	13	7	10	10	9

Sources: British Social Attitudes Survey, 1991–95; Northern Ireland Social Attitudes Survey, 1991–95.

equally across the UK as a whole. Support for this hypothesis is provided by the sharp rise (to 16 per cent) in 1993 in the proportion of NI respondents who believe EU membership to have a detrimental effect on the economy; a proportion which, in the other survey years, remains at about 10 per cent of respondents. In other respects, however, the pattern already described in Table 9.5 is closely reproduced. Thus the decline in confidence among GB respondents in the positive economic effects of EU links (11 per cent over the survey period) is not shared in NI (3 per cent drop). So too, the gap between the two jurisdictions widens from a 7 per cent greater positive assessment in NI in 1991 to a striking 15 per cent difference in 1995.

Two initial conclusions may be drawn from the comparative data laid out in Tables 9.5 and 9.6. Firstly, from a general European perspective, attitudes in Northern Ireland to relations with the EU are closer in their pattern to the UK as a whole (as set out in Table 9.1) than they are to those in the continental member states. Secondly, and by contrast, the decline in approval of the benefits for closer EU links which is so marked in the GB responses after 1991 is not shared by their Northern Irish counterparts. The ERM and Maastricht shocks which brought levels of support for Europe in GB back to those that were characteristic of the period before the mid-1980s appear to have had no such long-term effect on Northern Ireland opinion. On the contrary, NI opinion through the 1990s has remained both remarkably even and noticeably more enthusiastic about the relation with the EU than it has among fellow citizens across the water.

Issues in Ireland, Great Britain and Northern Ireland

The first and most obvious circumstance that distinguishes Northern Ireland from the rest of the UK is its proximity to the Republic of Ireland (ROI). Sharing a land border and, of course, common elements of history and culture, the two parts of the island have, while pursuing divergent paths, inevitably impacted upon each other. So too, both in turn have had constantly to define their position toward, or within, the UK. It may be supposed that this is no less true in terms of their relation to Europe than in other areas of opinion. Thus, before analysing specific features of opinion in Northern Ireland it is important to fix, at least in broad outline, what has been the evolution of European attitudes in the Republic. This we may do by setting out the ROI responses to the same *Eurobarometer* surveys that we have analysed for the UK in Table 9.1. These are given in Table 9.7.

The first point to note about these figures from each of the Tables is how much closer opinion in the Republic has been to the EU average than it has in the UK. Moreover, this opinion, as shown by the figures in Table 9.7a, has been consistently positive toward EU membership: in only five of the survey years has a majority of ROI respondents failed to indicate approval for membership; contrast this with the UK where a favourable majority has been registered in only three years in total. This difference is even more starkly pointed by the responses in Table 9.7b to the question about perceived benefits of membership.

The second noteworthy area is of a distinctive shift in ROI opinion compared with that in the UK. Although always more positive toward the EU than has been the case in the UK, opinion in the Republic in the first decade of the years surveyed tended in general to shadow or parallel movement in the UK. This is particularly so of the dramatic rise in approval from about 1987 onwards which we have already noted and have linked to the launch of what became the process toward greater integration. But what is more interesting is the divergence of opinion in the two states from this point. Whereas the argument about Maastricht and the ERM fiasco cut sharply into support for Europe in the UK, where a 13 per cent fall in approval both for EU membership and its benefits is registered between 1991 and 1992 and then sustained, this pattern is not reproduced at all in the Republic. Support for Europe there not only holds firm, producing a clear picture of approval which joins the late 1980s to the 1990s but, by the last survey year, reaches record levels.

Table 9.7a How do you think of your country's membership of the EC? (%)

	1978	1979	1980	1981	1982	1983	1984	1985	1986	1987	1988	1989	1990	1991	1992	1993	1994
Ireland good thing	63	58	47	49	47	42	47	55	58	64	72	69	76	76	73	73	82
EC average good thing	60	58	53	53	51	55	58	60	61	65	65	65	68	68	59	57	60
UK good thing	39	29	24	27	29	36	38	38	42	46	48	52	53	57	44	43	43

Table 9.7b Has your country benefited from membership of the EC? (%)

	1983	1984	1985	1986	1987	1988	1989	1990	1991	1992	1993	1994
Ireland Yes	36	61	67	71	79	79	75	85	80	80	80	90
EC average Yes	52	48	53	55	59	60	59	59	55	48	45	50
UK Yes	32	32	34	36	49	47	47	46	45	32	33	38

Source: Eurobarometer, Trends 1974–94.

A detailed commentary on the reasons for such a divergence lies outside the scope of this chapter. In general, as the figures in Table 9.7b would suggest, opinion in the Republic has consistently given a high value to the benefits of EU membership. The basis of such approval – which has been far higher than in the EU as a whole – may be attributed to two elements in the relationship. Firstly, it appears to reflect the financial benefits of European funding under the Structural Funds and other programmes which have contributed in a visible way to the Republic's modernisation and economic development. Secondly, it reveals a clear appreciation of the opportunities in influence and patronage which the process of European integration has offered since the mid-1980s to a small member state prepared to play the European game. In short, opinion in the Republic has been particularly favourable to European developments precisely because they have added to, rather than detracted from, the possibilities and achievements opened to the sovereign nation state.

What relevance do these broad trends in the Republic have to our understanding of Northern Ireland? If the figures for opinion in the Republic are placed alongside those for GB/NI given in Tables 9.5 and 9.6, it is clear that in one key respect Northern Ireland resembles the Republic more than it does the attitudes expressed in GB: namely that the level of enthusiasm for the benefits of European relations is sustained after, and in spite of, the ERM and Maastricht shocks. What this suggests is that there are factors in relation to their approach to Europe that the two parts of the island have in common which transcend other differences between them and give Northern Ireland a distinctive profile within the UK. At first sight there is one obvious such factor. Both the Republic and Northern Ireland were among the first recipients of funding as Objective One regions, a status which until 1994 made Northern Ireland unique in the UK. The perceived benefit of this privileged and substantial subsidy, especially after the widespread consultation exercise in 1993 to construct the Single Programming Document, is unlikely not to have had some positive influence on opinion in Northern Ireland similar to that (according to a reasonable interpretation of the figures in Tables 9.7a and 9.7b) experienced in the Republic. Nonetheless, although it can be argued that the fact of European funding may have contributed to minimising the importance of the ERM crisis in Northern Ireland, and thereby helped to explain the persistence of a relatively high level of approval for the EU, this alone does not go far enough in identifying the fundamental point of divergence between Northern Ireland and the rest of the UK. This is because the focus on funding as an explanatory factor of that divergence does not address what we have already hypothesised as the key long-term issue in shaping UK attitudes to Europe: that of sovereignty. As we have seen, it was not the question of economic benefits as such which sparked the downturn in British opinion after 1991 but an assessment of those benefits in relation to a process in which sovereignty was being challenged. In sum, if we are to understand what lies at the heart of Northern Ireland's divergence from the UK, it is to a fundamental difference in approaches to the defence of sovereignty that we should first look rather than to the direct effects of European funding.

Evidence that the variation between responses toward Europe in Northern Ireland and the rest of the UK may hinge on the importance that each respectively gives to the defence of national sovereignties within the EU is provided by the BSA and NISA surveys conducted from 1993 onwards. Both surveys included for the first time three questions which were prompted by the movement to greater European integration and allow a unique opportunity to identify distinctive attitudes in Northern Ireland. In the first question respondents were asked whether the UK should pursue a course of European unity or do its utmost to protect its independence. The responses are set out in Figure 9.1.

The columns show an unmistakable hardening of opinion in GB away from the desirability of European unity and a corresponding option for independence from the EU which, by 1995, is the expressed preference of 60 per cent of respondents. In strong contrast not only is there no majority in Northern Ireland in any of the three surveys in support of the idea of independence from the EU, but the preferred option remains the path of UK unity with Europe – a choice that shows some resilience within the overall pattern of declining Europeanism.

A similar divergence is shown in the answers to the second question in the surveys. Here respondents were asked to choose among six options relating to the future of the EU and which set that development between the opposite poles of a full re-establishment of UK sovereignty through its withdrawal from the EU or the submerging of that sovereignty in a single European government. Designed to allow a greater gradation in attitude to reveal itself than was the case in the answers reproduced in Figure 9.1 the questions, nonetheless, fall into two broad categories. Three questions offered the chance to express approval of European development: satisfaction with the status quo between the UK and the EU, an increase in EU powers, and the creation of a single European government. Two questions enabled disapproval

184 Europe and public opinion

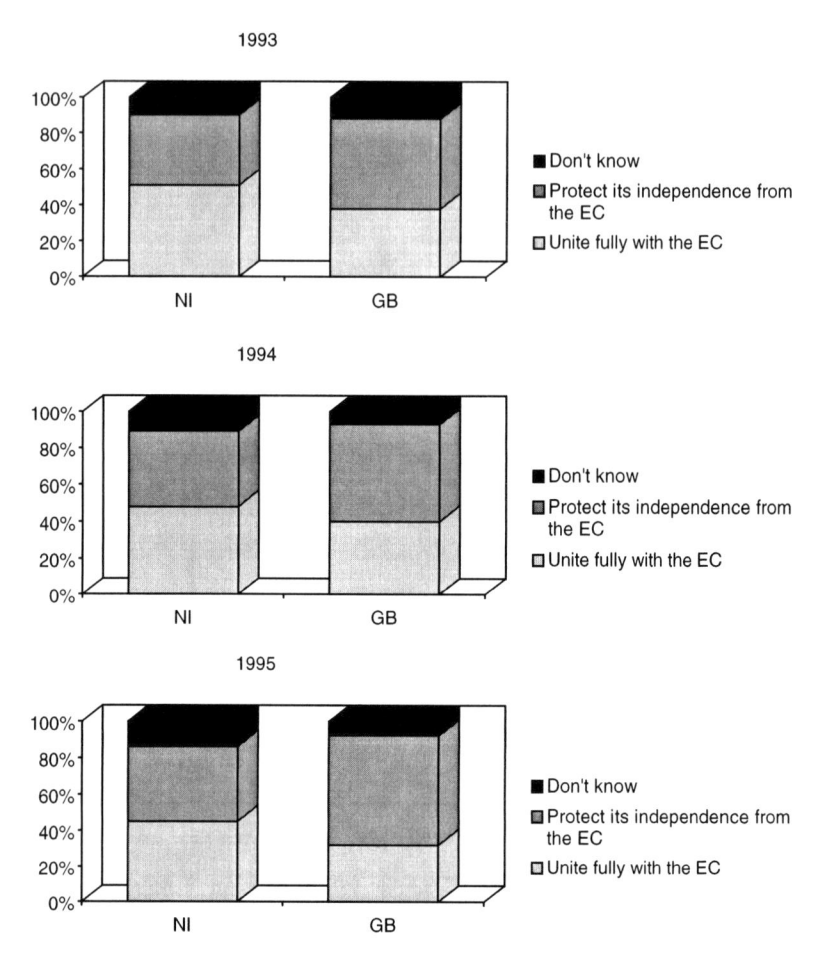

Figure 9.1 Respondents' views on whether the UK should do all it can to unite fully with the EC or whether the UK should do all it can to protect its independence from the EC
Sources: *British Social Attitudes Survey*, 1993–95; *Northern Ireland Social Attitudes Survey*, 1993–95.

to be registered: the reduction of EU powers, and UK withdrawal altogether from the EU; while indifference could be shown by opting to express no opinion. The results, tabulated by these categories of approval and disapproval, are given in Figure 9.2.

Given the greater range of options offered, it is perhaps not surprising that the proportion of respondents favourable to at least the current level of EU authority should be greater in both NI and GB than

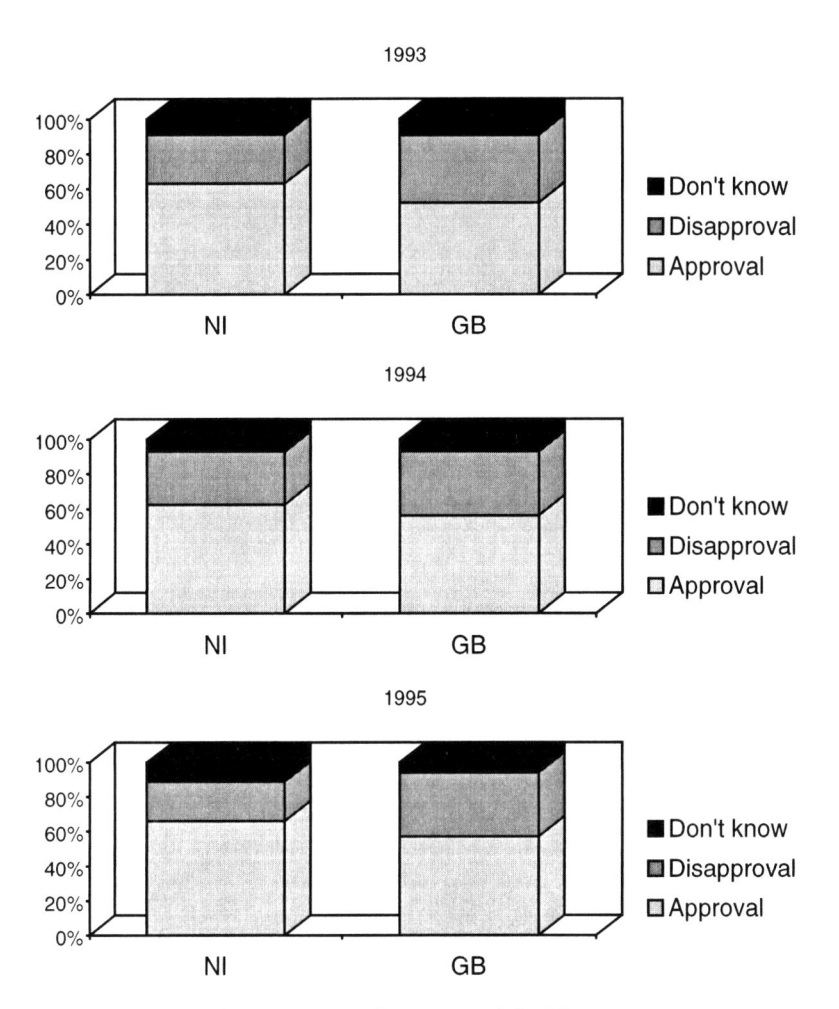

Figure 9.2 Respondents' views on the powers of the EC
Sources: *British Social Attitudes Survey*, 1993–95; *Northern Ireland Social Attitudes Survey*, 1993–95.

that which (as shown in Figure 9.1) had opted for full unity within the EU. What is interesting, however, is that even when respondents have the opportunity to avoid a direct confrontation with the issue of the importance of UK sovereignty in the future, there remains a clear divergence between NI and GB attitudes on exactly this point. Thus, faced with the possibility of choosing a future UK–EU relationship that continues the present one, 37–8 per cent of GB respondents across the

Table 9.8 Respondents' views on the future of the pound in the EC (%)

	1993		1994		1995	
	NI	GB	NI	GB	NI	GB
Single currency	23	14	25	17	22	18
Pound and European currency	15	17	15	18	17	18
Pound only currency	58	66	55	62	54	62
Don't know	4	3	4	4	7	3

Sources: *British Social Attitudes Survey*, 1993–95; *Northern Ireland Social Attitudes Survey*, 1993–95.

three surveys nonetheless chose those options which would defend UK sovereignty and reclaim powers from the EU. Among NI respondents this concern is expressed by 28–30 per cent – a proportion that falls to a low of 23 per cent in the 1995 survey.

The third question addressed the issue of sovereignty in terms of future control of the currency, asking respondents to choose between the desirability of moving to a single European currency, of retaining the pound as an independent currency, or of a hybrid system in which the two currencies would co-exist. Responses are set out in Table 9.8.

In general terms the distribution of answers to this question follows the lines of those in Figures 9.1 and 9.2 in which there is more concern for the preservation of sovereignty among GB respondents than there is in NI. Thus, the preferences in GB for a pound only currency (62–6 per cent) are closely in line with the proportion there who opt for UK independence from the EU; as might be anticipated, the proportion who choose this option in NI is 7–8 per cent lower. However, demonstrating how potent the emotions raised by questions of currency are, the level of concern among NI respondents about maintaining the pound is considerably greater than, for instance, the desire to protect the UK's independence from the EU, as given in Figure 9.1 (39–41 per cent per cent). Moreover, while this greater concern about the currency is most strongly expressed immediately following the UK's withdrawal from the ERM, it does not fall away in the two subsequent surveys.

Specific factors in Northern Ireland opinion

What is quite clear from the BSA and NISA questions taken as a whole is that there exists a large variation between Northern Ireland and the rest of the UK in attitudes to Europe when these are tested in terms of perceptions about maintaining or surrendering sovereignty within the context of EU membership. To explain this variation is not, however, completely straightforward. If we say that Northern Ireland opinion might best be seen as mirroring that in the Republic in its levels of approval for European membership, we are faced with the fact that it remains consistently closer to the somewhat cautious levels in the UK than it does to those expressed by its Southern counterparts. In this respect it would appear that NI citizens share the preoccupation with sovereignty that characterises UK attitudes as a whole and that this issue does, therefore, play a larger role in the formation of NI opinion than it does in the Republic. Against this, however, not only are NI responses to Europe more positive in absolute terms than they are in GB but, in distinction to the GB pattern, they have been maintained through the difficult years 1991–5 in which the relation between EU development and sovereignty has been most prominent.

To draw attention to the fact that Northern Ireland opinion shows affinities both with the Republic and the UK is, of course, to point to a very obvious truth about the political and social context in which it operates. In Northern Ireland sovereignty is itself contested – in the sense that competing national allegiances co-exist – and has long been the source of political conflict and the determinant of much of the primary political identification in the province. The division of the political landscape into two broad currents of 'unionism' and 'nationalism' expresses how definitive the issue is, since what separates them is not necessarily, or at all, matters of social or economic policy but a dispute as to the jurisdiction in which these policies should be conducted.

Given that the issue of whose sovereignty should rule in Northern Ireland remains such a central feature of political life, it might be supposed that part of the variation between NI and GB responses on Europe can be attributed to this particular factor. We should expect that the unionist current, even allowing for policy variations among its constituent groups, would be most attracted by the defence of what might be termed a traditional perspective of sovereignty: a disinclination to cede powers from Whitehall to Brussels. Equally, nationalist opinion, despite its broad wish to achieve a united, sovereign Irish state, might be expected to be attracted by the process of European integration precisely because of its erosion of the exclusive claims of the Union. These hypotheses would seem to be supported if crosstabulated according to party affiliation with the responses to the three questions designed to test attitudes toward greater EU integration

Table 9.9 Should the UK do all it can to unite with the EC or, should UK do all it can to protect its independence from the EC (%)

	Unite with EC	Independence	Don't know
1993			
DUP/OUP	37	54	9
SDLP/Sinn Fein	74	14	12
1994			
DUP/OUP	29	61	10
SDLP/Sinn Fein	75	15	9
1995			
DUP/OUP	24	62	14
SDLP/Sinn Fein	69	19	13

Source: Northern Ireland Social Attitudes Survey.

which were discussed earlier. The results are given in Tables 9.9 and 9.10 and Figure 9.3 in all of which respondents have been grouped within the two broad affiliations of unionism and nationalism composed of four mainstream political parties.

A clear, and increasing, majority of respondents who identify themselves with one or other of the two main unionist parties favour protecting the independence of the UK and oppose the move toward full European unity. As hypothesised, nationalist identifiers show an opposite, and even stronger, choice in favour of greater European unity. It is worth noting that the level of preference for UK independence among unionist identifiers closely mirrors the overall response in GB (as shown in Figure 9.1) where support for this option moves from 50 per cent to 60 per cent between 1993 and 1995. However, the opposition to EU unity is noticeably stronger among unionist identifiers than it is in GB, suggesting that for this group the threat posed to Northern Ireland by further integration is felt as immediate and unwelcome in its consequences and, therefore, a more urgent question than the somewhat abstract one of the protection of UK independence in general.

A similar division along party political lines is evident also in responses to the question about the evolution of greater or lesser powers in the EU. Figure 9.3 again shows the close shadowing of GB opinion by unionist identifiers and the high levels of support among nationalist identifiers for European integration expressed in their approval for maintaining at least the current level of EU powers.

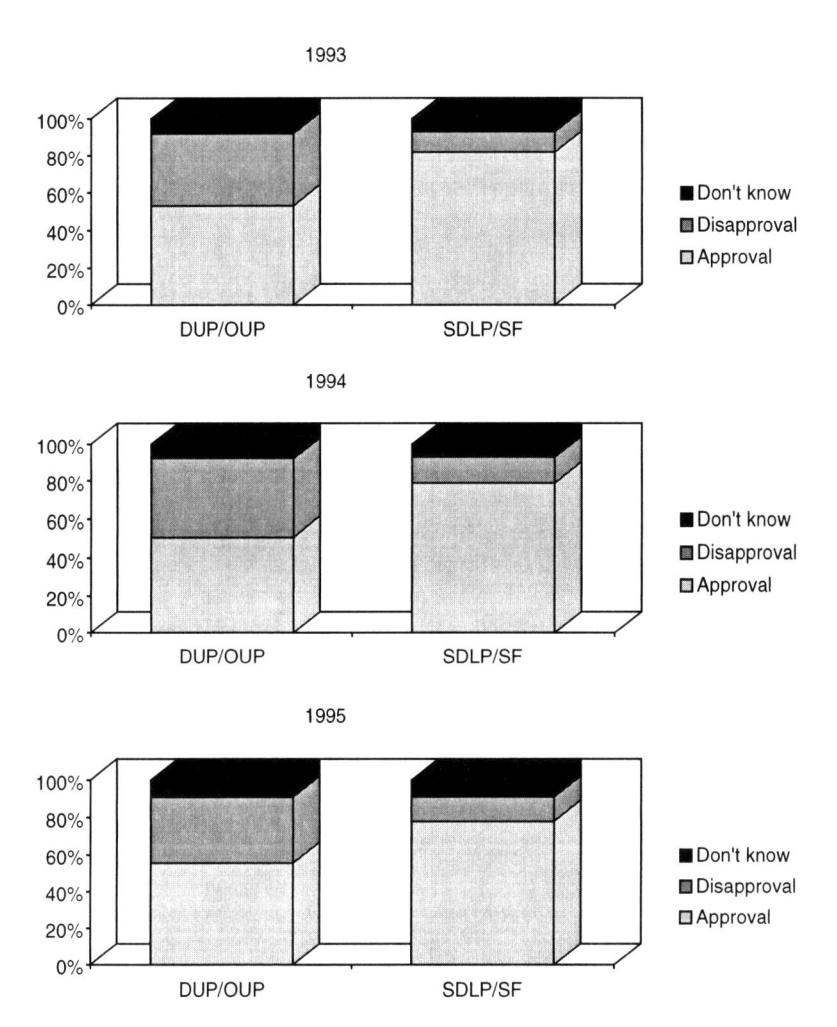

Figure 9.3 Respondents' views on the powers of the EC, by political party
Source: *Northern Ireland Social Attitudes Survey,* 1993–95.

Finally, the predominant role of party identification in determining attitudes to Europe is shown in the responses to the question about a future currency.

Here, as we analysed earlier in relation to Table 9.8, the fears that a change of currency raise in connection with personal economic cirumstances introduces a further variable into responses. This may explain

190 Europe and public opinion

Table 9.10 Respondents' views on the future of the pound in the EC (%)

	Single currency	Pound and Euopean currency	Pound only currency	Don't know
1993				
DUP/OUP	15	10	71	4
SDLP/Sinn Fein	39	23	34	4
1994				
DUP/OUP	14	12	70	4
SDLP/Sinn Fein	41	17	38	4
1995				
DUP/OUP	13	13	70	5
SDLP/Sinn Fein	33	19	42	6

Source: Northern Ireland Social Attitudes Survey.

the proportion of nationalist identifiers who express a preference for retaining the pound as the only currency; a proportion greater than might have been predicted from the responses to the two previous questions if this had been an issue seen only in terms of sovereignty. For unionist identifiers personal economic concerns may be disguised by being added to a general antipathy to abandoning the main symbol of a UK identity. Certainly, both the expressed desire to retain the pound and the opposition to a single European currency show a harder edge among unionist identifiers than among GB respondents as a whole.

From the evidence of these cross-tabulations it would appear that attitudes to Europe in Northern Ireland do correlate strongly to political identities which, in the particular circumstances of the province, are constructed around competing views of sovereignty. The three NISA surveys overwhelmingly support the case that the nationalist/ unionist division is determinant in the formation of a core position toward the question of UK–EU relations.

The surveys also indicate that the division, even if it remains of primary importance, is not static. While it would not be correct to say that there is a trend toward convergence of attitudes, there is a distinct shift over the three years toward less pro-European positions (positions which, we should remember, remain, nonetheless, consistently more favourable to Europe than they do in GB). This movement characterises the responses of both groups and is such as to leave the gap between them broadly constant. What is at first sight puzzling is that insofar as a hardening of attitude against European integration among unionist identifiers is consistent with what is the fundamental political concern of unionism, it is less to be expected among nationalist identifiers since it would seem to cut against those political aspirations of loosening UK sovereignty which underpin the nationalist position. In this case there is clearly a need to consider what other factors that partially transcend the unionist/nationalist divide may act on the expression of European opinion. To this end, and in view of the lack of space, we have selected one factor, tabulated from the NISA data, which can clearly be separated from political affiliation: namely age profile. It is with a brief summary of this indicative example that we will conclude this chapter.

First, however, there is one obvious additional factor operating on the formation of public opinion which is unique to Northern Ireland at this period. That is the effect of the specific political developments which occurred between 1993 and 1994. The most important outcomes of the intense political activity at this time were the Downing Street Declaration signed by the UK and Irish governments and the IRA ceasefire in autumn 1994. Both developments held the potential to create some movement toward what might be termed UK-centred preferences, especially among nationalists: the first by providing the reassurance of greater cross-border co-operation and a consequent diminishing of the urgency of changing Northern Ireland's status within the UK; the second by opening the prospect of a peaceful and secure future for Northern Ireland as part of the UK. It is, therefore, entirely plausible – if ironic – that the long desired 'peace process' may have had the paradoxical effect of diminishing the importance of Europe as a benchmark of divisiveness and bringing NI attitudes at least somewhat closer to those in GB. The extent to which this is either true or marks a long-term shift requires further specific research work.

What of the generation factor? We have tabulated all NI respondents' views on the alternatives of retaining UK independence or of pursuing European unity, by age band. The results are given in Table 9.11.

It would seem that if age is a significant factor in the expression of European attitudes it is evidently so only among both the youngest and oldest sections of society surveyed. Nonetheless, Table 9.11 does suggest that there is a striking variation in responses to the extent that the 18–24 age group registers a level of approval for European unity which is never less than 11 per cent higher than that of any other age group. Moreover, it is also consistently and by a wide margin the least concerned with retaining the UK's independence; indeed by the time

192 Europe and public opinion

Table 9.11 Respondents' views on whether the UK should do all it can to unite fully with EC or do all it can to protect its independence from the EC, by age group (%)

	Unite with EC	Independence	Don't know
1993 data			
18–24	72	22	6
25–34	52	37	10
35–44	51	44	5
45–54	52	41	7
55–59	61	24	15
55–64	31	52	17
65+	38	44	18
1994 data			
18–24	62	27	9
25–34	52	37	10
35–44	50	43	7
45–54	50	39	11
55–59	40	48	12
55–64	50	31	19
65+	29	58	13
1995 data			
18–24	71	20	9
25–34	41	46	14
35–44	46	45	10
45–54	44	41	15
55–56	42	40	18
55–64	35	50	15
65+	31	46	23

of the 1995 survey this group is the only one to express a pro-European choice in a proportion significantly above the NI average. At the other end of the age spectrum, as well as within the middle groups, the picture is less clear-cut although both of the oldest age groups, and particularly the over-65s, generally show the least favourable responses to European integration.

To explore further the strength of this dichotomy we have calculated the average of the responses by all age groups to the full range of questions asked on positive relations with Europe and have tabulated these together with the responses for three selected age categories: the youngest, the oldest and a middle group (45–54) chosen on the basis that its responses, as set out in Table 9.11, were closest to the mean over all three survey years. These figures are reproduced in Table 9.12.

Table 9.12 Attitudes to Europe among the 18–24, 45–54 and 65+ age group (%)

	18–24	45–44	65+	All
1993 data				
Closer links to the EC	59	41	26	40
Unite fully with the EC	72	52	38	51
Increased powers / single EC government	59	44	24	39
Single EC currency	30	22	15	23
1994 data				
Closer links to the EC	62	47	29	45
Unite fully with the EC	62	50	29	48
Increased powers / single EC government	57	37	25	39
Single EC currency	39	33	15	25
1995 data				
Closer links to the EC	54	35	25	39
Unite fully with the EC	71	44	31	45
Increased powers / single EC government	50	38	26	41
Single EC currency	22	27	14	22

This time an unmistakable picture emerges of a generational divide on the question of Europe. In all facets of European development except that of a single currency the 18–24 age group registers well above average support and the responses of its polar opposite, the 65+ group, although less strongly varying from the average of all the age groups, still fall well below. Of particular interest is the variation between the polar groups. With a low of 24 per cent in the 1995 survey in response to the question of the EU developing greater powers, including a single European government, and a high of 40 per cent in the same year in response to the prospect of full European unification, the pattern of variation is otherwise consistently close to the overall mean of 33 per cent. In short, on no European issue do the responses of the polar age groups begin to show any sign of convergence

The question remains whether these variations represent the effect of the community affiliations of the population surveyed or whether they have specific generational causes. In other words do similar generational responses occur when cross-tabulated with the three selected age groups are broad unionist and nationalist identifiers? An answer may be found in Table 9.13 which sets out the proportion of positive

Table 9.13 Political party identifiers' views that the UK should do all it can to unite fully with the EC, by age group (%)

	18–24	45–54	65+	All
1993 data [Political party]				
DUP/OUP	62	45	25	39
SDLP/Sinn Fein	89	91	67	74
1994 data [Political party]				
DUP/OUP	85	28	20	31
SDLP/Sinn Fein	74	85	68	75
1995 data [Political party]				
DUP/OUP	57	28	11	23
SDLP/Sinn Fein	79	71	64	69

responses to the question of whether the UK should unite fully with the EU.

Table 9.13 confirms that the core cleavage around attitudes to Europe remains nationalist/unionist identification. In each of the selected age groups nationalists give a higher level of pro-European responses than do unionists over the survey period. Yet real generational variations do emerge. As was suggested by the previous Tables, the over-65 age group in each political community is both the least favourably disposed to European integration and consistently registers a level of response beneath the average for its political group. In general, too, respondents in both the 18–24 age groups are most positive. However, it is when we look separately at the responses of each community that we can see some differences of pattern. If we start by comparing the three age groups of nationalist identifiers two points stand out. Firstly, although 79–89 per cent of respondents in the 18–24 age group support full unity with the EU, in two of the survey years the most positive responses are given not by this group but by the 45–54 year olds. Secondly, if we chart the gap between polar responses the variation moves from a high of 24 per cent in 1993, through 17 per cent in the second survey to only 8 per cent by 1995. In short, the evidence is that the pro-European responses of nationalist identifiers have increasingly converged. Community identification is more significant than generational difference.

By contrast the responses of unionist identifiers are increasingly divergent. The polar variation in this political community is 37 per cent in 1993, rising to 43 per cent in the third survey. So, too, the decline in levels of pro-European response describes an even curve through the age groups. But what is most striking is the clear generational gap between the 18–24 respondents and the other groups. Not only are young unionist identifiers the most pro-European by a wide margin, but the level of their responses places them closer in attitude both to their nationalist peer group and to nationalist respondents as a whole than to their own community. Indeed, in 1994 they register the highest pro-European responses of any age group in either community.

It would be imprudent to draw too wide conclusions from the highly circumscribed evidence above. Without a great deal more research we cannot say how far, if at all, the greater openness toward Europe among young unionists might be sustained in the face of the pull from traditional communal solidarity. Nor do we know whether their responses signify a long-term rethinking of the kind of relation that they wish to see between Northern Ireland and Europe. If the survey of opinion in this chapter has shown anything it is that, so far, membership of the European Community has not provided the context for change that it has done in the Republic and that its advocates would have hoped. Attitudes toward Europe have remained clearly divided along the lines of the two main political communities. Yet it is the distinctiveness of this divide that may in fact point the direction of a possible change. The context of Direct Rule from London and the corresponding absence of a normal political culture in Northern Ireland has meant that responses to Europe have been subsumed in a fundamental dispute about sovereignty. Both nationalists and unionists have thought of the process of European integration as primarily offering a mechanism that might help achieve, or hinder, their aspirations. All the survey evidence we have brought to this chapter confirms that it is not the economic or social effects of European integration that have formed opinion, but the extent to which integration is thought to loosen or strengthen the place of Northern Ireland in the UK. The creation of a new political culture, following the Referendum and elections to the Northern Ireland Assembly in 1998, offers at least the opportunity for a reassessment of the European relation. The economic effects of integration and the enlargement of the EU will inevitably play a large part in reshaping attitudes. But the context in which this will happen may be one in which calculations of benefit are made unmediated by the sovereignty question. This is not to suggest that the question will cease to exist in political life. Rather, that in an increasing number of areas of political decision and devolved responsibility which involve Europe, the issue may be transcended.

Notes

1. European Commission, *Eurobarometer Trends 1974–1994*, Office for Official Publications of the European Communities, Luxembourg, pp. 71–88.
2. I am indebted to Paula Devine of the Centre for Social Research, The Queen's University of Belfast, who was responsible for producing all the Tables and Figures from the BSA and Northern Ireland Social Attitude (NISA) surveys.
3. For a description of the methodology used in the NISA surveys see K. Sweeney and A. McClelland (1995) 'Technical Details of the Survey', in R. Breen, P. Devine and G. Robinson (eds), *Social Attitudes in Northern Ireland. The Fourth Report,* Appletree, Belfast, pp. 142–57.

Index

Accompanying Measures: Agri-Environment Regulation (2078/92) 80
acquisitions 104, 105, 106, 107, 108
additionality 7, 49, 52, 53, 54, 55, 57, 58, 59, 126
administrative reforms 43
Africa 94
age profiles 191–5
Agenda 2000 49, 64, 91, 123, 166
agri-environmental measures 91–2
agri-food 72–5, 81, 84, 86, 90–1
agri-money 80–2
agricultural development 56, 57
Agricultural Development Operational Programme (ADOP) 58–9, 62
Agricultural Fund 7
agricultural land market 82–4
agriculture 3, 5, 8, 41, 69, 71, 98, 101
air quality directives 143–4
Alpine area 33
Alsace 19
Amenity Lands Act (Northern Ireland) 1965 129, 133
Amin, A. 36
Amsterdam Treaty 118, 123
Andalucia 25
Anglo-Irish Agreement 55, 153, 154, 155, 164, 165
Anglo-Irish Intergovernmental Council (AIIC) 152
animal health programmes 101
Anti-Poverty Programme 125
Area Based Strategic Action Groups (ABSAGs) 88
Area of Outstanding Natural Beauty 136
Area Plans 134

Area of Scientific Interest (ASI) 133, 138
Area of Special Scientific Interest (ASSI) 133, 134, 135, 136, 137, 138, 139, 140
Argentina 71
Armstrong, H. 110
Assembly of European Regions 34
Assessment of the Effects of Certain Public and Private Projects on the Environment Directive 85/337 141
asymmetrical federalism 25, 27
Austria 15, 40, 106

Baden-Württemberg 34
Balkans 35
banking and financial sector 94–5
Basque country 20, 21, 25, 26
Basque ETA 18
Basque nationalists 22
Bavarian CSU 18
Beatty, C. B. 69
beef sector 76–8
Beef Special Premium 64
Belfast Agreement (1998) 102, 120–1, 123, 163
Belfast Area 134
Belfast/Dublin Economic Corridor 109
Belfast Harbour Commissioners 134
Belfast Lough 134, 136
Belgium 15, 25, 26, 28, 99, 106
Benelux area 33
Bern Convention 129
Bew, P. 111
Bird Sanctuaries 132
Birds Directive (79/409) 129, 130, 131–5, 136–7

Index

birth rates 3, 45
Blair, T. 27, 124
Bonn Convention 129
Borras Alomar, S. 37
bottom-up development 118
Bradley, J. 111
branch plant economy 104
Breen, R. 113
British Social Attitudes (BSA) survey 172, 175, 176, 177, 178, 179, 186, 287
Brittany 19, 20
Brooke–Mayhew talks 153, 158, 159, 161, 163, 164
Brownlow Community Trust 120
Brussels Capital region 26
Bryden, J. 90, 93
BSE crisis 8, 65, 77–8, 79, 84, 85, 101
Buckwell, A. 91, 93

Campbell, J. 167
capital stock 60
'carousel' 82
Caskie, P. 77, 92
Catalonia 20, 22, 25, 26, 34
Catholicism 109
central Europe 35
central government 2, 7, 8, 11, 12, 13, 22–3, 24, 27, 102
centralisation 28
Centre for Public Policy Research 56
Centre of Rural Studies 56
Chambers of Commerce 100
Chilton, S. M. 80, 92
Civic Forum 121, 123, 127
civil dialogue 120–1, 124–5
codification of rights 123
Cohen, A. 87, 93
Cohesion Funds 8, 54
commercial integration 9
Commins, P. 93
Committee of the Regions 12, 13, 31, 34
Common Agricultural Policy 8–9, 39, 46, 48, 55, 63–7, 71–9 passim, 91, 92
  and agri-money 81

assessment 66–7
beef sector 76–8
dairy sector 75–6
environment 142
farm households 86
land market 83, 84
pigmeat and eggs 79
poultrymeat 79
sheepmeat sector 78
subsidies, dependence and instability 85
Common Agricultural and Rural Policy for Europe (CARPE) 91
Common Chapter 122
community infrastructure 118, 127
Community Initiatives 47, 48, 54, 56, 88
Community Support Framework (CSF) programme 31, 55, 56, 59–63, 117
competition 29, 34, 35
Confederation of British Industry 100
Confederation of Irish Industry 100
Conservation (Natural Habitats, etc.) Regulations (Northern Ireland) 1995 141
Conservation of Natural Habitats and of Wild Fauna and Flora Directive (Habitats Directive) 137–41, 145, 146
  cross-frontier dimension 141
  planning issues 141
  problems 139–40
  Special Areas of Conservation 137–9
Conservation of Wild Birds Directive 129
Conservative government 27, 53, 125, 126, 170
consultative assemblies 27
consumer protection 5
consumer spending 60
Continental Shelf 40
Convery, F. 112
Cooke, P. 36
Cooper & Lybrand 114

Index 199

Corine habitat 139
corporation taxes 94
Corsica 19
Council of Europe 123
Council of Ministers 13, 77, 121, 156, 158, 159, 162
Council Regulation 724/75 52
Crowley, J. 112
cultural insularity 125
currency 186, 189–90
  see also Single European Currency
Curtin, C. 93

dairy sector 75–6
decentralisation 24, 28, 30
deconcentration 27
defence 26
Delors, J./ Committee/ Commission 116, 117, 118, 155, 158, 171, 176
Denmark 1, 46, 96, 99, 106, 172, 176
Department of Agriculture for Northern Ireland (DANI) 65, 87, 88, 142, 145
Department of Economic Development 57
Department of the Environment 56, 120, 131, 134, 146
Department of Finance and Personnel 7, 89
devaluation 85
development agencies 100
devolution 2, 10, 12, 14, 26, 27, 28, 30
Direct Rule 129, 130, 131, 144, 151, 195
Directive 75/440 143
Directive 79/869 143
Directive 80/778 143
Directive 91/271 143
Directive 268 78
directives 14, 29, 128, 136, 145, 147
District Councils 120, 123, 134, 143
  Partnership Boards 88

District Partnerships 119, 120
Downing Street Declaration 191
Draft Orders 131
Dudgeon, J. 123

eastern Europe 19, 20, 35, 176
Economic and Social Committee 13
economies of scale 105, 106
economy 38–70, 179
  Agricultural Development Operational Programme (ADOP) 58–9
  Common Agricultural Policy 63–7
  Community Support Framework programme 59–63
  employment 44–6
  expenditure levels 47–9
  gross domestic product 40–2, 44–6
  Industrial Development Operational Programme 57–8
  Structural Funds 46–7, 49–56
  trade 67–8
  unemployment 42–4
electoral isolation 21–2
electricity interconnection 101–2
employment 5, 6, 38, 42, 44–6, 58–9, 60, 61, 62
  rural economy 72, 73, 74, 75, 77, 91
energy 118
England 27, 28, 84, 129
environment 5, 14, 79–80
Environment and Heritage Service (EHS) 134, 135, 138, 140, 141, 143, 144, 146, 147
environmental assessments 141–2
Environmental and Cultural Landscape Payments 91
environmental regulation 32
Environmentally Sensitive Area (ESA) Scheme 80, 142, 145
equality 118–19
Ergo 120

ETA 18
ethnic identity 19–20
Eurobarometer survey 171, 172, 173, 174, 177, 180, 181
Europe of the Regions 155
European Agricultural Guidance and Guarantee Fund 47, 48, 55, 64, 65
European Anti-Poverty Network 124–5
European Commission 5, 7, 11, 14, 31, 40
  Common Agricultural Policy 63, 75
  Directorate General for Regional Affairs 54
  environment 130, 132, 135, 138, 139, 140, 141, 144, 147
  'Future of Rural Society, The' 86
  Northern Ireland problem 150, 151, 152, 158, 164–5, 166
  rural economy 91
  Structural Funds 47, 52, 56
European Council 31
European Court of Justice 134, 144, 159
European Free Trade Area 39, 67, 170
European Monetary Union (EMU) 171, 177
European Parliament 12–13, 31, 154, 155, 164, 165
European Poverty Programme 120
European Regional Development Fund (ERDF) 46, 47, 48, 55, 57, 117
European Sites 141
European Social Fund (ESF) 46, 47, 48, 55, 57, 117
European Social Policy Forum 121
European Treaties 12
Exchange Rate Mechanism (ERM) 42–3, 82, 85, 176, 177, 186
  shock 178, 179, 180, 182

Executive Commission 156
expenditure 47–9, 62, 63
  see also public expenditure
exports 45, 60, 67, 68, 81, 94, 97, 99, 103
  rural economy 72–3, 78
external economic links 94–114
  co-operation policy measures with Republic of Ireland 100–2
  cross-border trade 103–4
  economic background 95–7
  interregional links at firm level 104–9; external ownership, extent of 104–5; inter-firm linkages at all-Ireland level 105–9
  trade, level and geographic distribution of 98–9
external ownership 97
external sales 99
external trade 6

farm households 85–6
farm price policies 81
Farrows, M. 36
Faulkner, B. 151
federalism 26, 28
Fell, Sir D. 162
Fianna Fail 152
Fine Gael 152
Finland 40, 96
fishing 101
FitzGerald, G. 150, 153, 161, 162, 167, 168
Fitzpatrick, J. 112
Flanders 19, 20, 26
Flynn, P. 121
Foix, M. 36
food processing 64, 66, 67, 69, 108
foreign relations 26
forestry 101
Fothergill, S. 69
Four Motors 33–4
Foyle Fisheries 101
Framework Document 100, 102, 154, 159, 163

Index 201

France 24, 25, 27, 33, 40, 63, 81, 96, 120, 176
Franco, General 25
Franco–German border 33
Franco–German reconciliation 170
French overseas territories 46
frontier tax 81
funding 11, 25, 126, 182–3

Galicia 26
Game Laws 129
Garmise, S. 36
General Agreement on Tariffs and Trade (GATT) 68
geo-political sensitivities 115
geographic distance 19
Germany 15, 19, 28, 33, 40, 63, 81, 96, 176
Gilbreath, G. 92
Gillespie, P. 168
Gore, T. 69
government agencies 38
grants 44, 49
Gray, A. W. 112
Greece 28, 30, 31, 40, 43, 46, 86, 96, 126
'green money' 80–2
'green' rate revaluation 85
gross domestic product 2–3, 4, 6, 39, 40–2, 44–6
  rural economy 72, 73
  trade 94, 96–7, 99
Gudgin, G. 6, 8, 15, 38–70, 94, 113
Guelke, A. 154, 155, 167

Haagerup Report 155
Haase, T. 93
habitat conservation 132–3
Hague Summit 148
Harris, R. I. D. 113
Harvey, B. 127
Haughey, C. 152
headage payments 64
Heath, E. 148, 151, 154
Herrington, P. 69
Hill Livestock Compensatory Allowances 64, 65, 78, 80

Hindley, B. 68, 70
Hirsch, D. 126, 127
Hirst, P. Q. 119
Hitchens, D. M. 111, 113
HM Treasury 54
holdings, size of 73
House of Commons Select Committee on the Environment 144
House of Commons Select Committee on Northern Ireland Affairs 54
House of Lords Select Committee on the European Communities 92
Howarth, R. 70
Howe, M. 68, 70
human resources 56, 57, 62
human rights 123
Hume, J. 13, 155–6, 163

Iceland 94
implementation bodies 102
income 3, 41, 44, 77, 86, 94, 109
Industrial Development Board (IDB) 57
Industrial Development Operational Programme (IDOP) 56, 57–8, 61, 62
Industrial Research and Technology Unit (IRTU) 57
Institute for Advanced Microelectronics 101
Institute of European Affairs 161
institutional links 10
Integrated Operations programme 47
integration 35, 109
integration with Europe and public opinion 169–96
  opinion in Northern Ireland 177–9
  opinion in United Kingdom as a whole 171–7
  Republic of Ireland, Great Britain and Northern Ireland 180–6

integration with Europe and public opinion – *continued*
  specific factors in Northern Ireland opinion   186–96
inter-party talks (1991 and 1992)   156, 159
Intergovernmental Conference   153, 161
International Court of Justice   166
International Fund for Ireland (IFI)   89, 155, 165
INTERREG I and II   33, 47, 56, 89
intervention payments   64
investment   3, 39, 60, 68, 97, 104
IRA ceasefire   191
Ireland, Republic of   1, 10, 12
  agri-food   72
  agri-money   82
  co-operation policy measures with   100–2
  Common Agricultural Policy   77
  employment   45
  environment   140
  European Structural Funds   46, 47
  gross domestic product   40, 41, 45
  and the Northern Ireland Problem   149–54 *passim*, 158–9, 161–4, 166
  public opinion on European integration   187, 195
  regionalisation   30, 31
  rural economy   73, 86
  social impact   118, 122, 123, 126
  social progress   119
  trade   67, 98, 99, 103, 104, 105, 106, 107, 108, 110
Irish Constitution   149, 166
Isles, K.   111
Italy   24, 25, 27, 30, 40, 43, 46, 63, 97

Japan   94
Jeffery, C.   36
Jenkins, R.   151, 167
Jobseekers Allowance   43

Keane, M.   93
Kearney, R.   16, 155, 168
Keating, M.   24, 35
Kennedy, M.   111
Kerr–Millan Agreement   54
King, T.   124
Kinsella, R.   112
Kirchner, E.   37
Kirke, A.   93
Kogan, N.   35

Labour government   27, 53, 170
Ireland, Republic of   152
Lal, D.   110
land prices   83, 84
Lander   28, 30
LEADER programmes   88–9, 119, 123
Leda   120
Lega Lombarda   21
Lega Nord (Italy)   18, 19, 21, 22
Lemass, S.   100
Leonardi, R.   36
Less Favoured Areas   78, 80
Lewis-Bowen, J.   58, 70
liberalisation   35, 67, 68
living standards   41, 69
lobbying   29, 33
Local Action Groups (LAGs)   88
local authorities   27, 28, 33
Local Enterprise Companies   90
Local Enterprise Development Unit (LEDU)   38, 57
local government   22–3, 24, 31, 102, 119
Logue, H.   168
Lombardy   33
Lough Neagh   134
Luxembourg   94, 97
Lynch, J.   148, 149, 151

Maastricht Treaty   43, 172, 179, 180, 182
MacEnroe, G.   103, 113

Mack, N. 93
MacSharry, Commissioner R./reforms 1992 64, 80
Madrid agreement (1989) 171
Madrid summit 176
Majone, G. 36
Major, J. 54
manufacturing 3, 6, 41, 44–5, 58, 60, 67, 68, 73
  trade 94, 98, 99, 103, 104, 105, 106, 107
Marine Nature Reserves 136, 140
Marks, G. 35, 36
Matthews, A. 90, 92, 93, 112
Mayhew, Sir P. 156
McCarthy, R. 36
McClelland, A. 196
McEldowney, J. 57–8, 70
McEniff, J. 112
McGumaghan, M. 112
Meat Industry Employment Scheme 82
Mény, Y. 35
mergers 104, 105, 106, 108
Mezzogiorno 46
Michie, J. 104, 110, 113
Mid Wales Development 90
migration 45–6, 94, 109
Milk Marketing Board 76
Milk Marketing Scheme 76
milk production quotas 64, 65, 75, 76, 83
Millward, A. 168
Minimum Income Requirement (MIR) or poverty line 86
Minimum Wage 94
Ministerial Council 102, 121
Ministry of Agriculture, Fisheries and Food 77
Mitchell, D. 36
Mitchell, Senator G. 102
Mitterrand, F. 24
Monetary Compensatory Amounts (MCAs) 81, 82
Morata, F. 37
Morgan, K. 36
Moss, J. E. 58, 70, 80, 92
Moxon-Browne, E. 168
multi-level governance 18
multinational sector 104
Munck, R. 111

Naples 47
national government 88
National Parks and Wildlife Service 140
nationalism 20, 187–8
nationalists 11, 166, 190, 191, 194–5
Natura 2000 sites 137
Nature Conservation and Amenity Lands (Northern Ireland) Order 1985 130–1, 133, 134, 136, 137, 140
negative integration 29, 32, 33, 34
Netherlands 63, 97, 99, 106
networking 11
New Framework for Agreement 159
New Ireland Forum 152, 161, 166
New Zealand 71
non-additionality 55
non-discrimination 118–19
non-governmental organisations (NGOs) 121, 122, 123, 124
non-manufacturing 99
North Atlantic Treaty Organisation (NATO) 26
North Sea Oil 40
North-Schleswig (Germany) 20
North–South body 160, 163, 167
North–South Ministerial Council 120
Northern Ireland Assembly 102, 120, 131
Northern Ireland Centre in Europe 13
Northern Ireland Economic Council (NIEC) 110, 111, 112, 113
Northern Ireland Economic and Research Council (NIERC) 56, 58, 59
Northern Ireland Partnership Board 120

Northern Ireland problem 115, 148–68
Northern Ireland Social Attitudes (NISA) surveys 177, 183, 184, 185, 186, 188, 189, 190, 191
Norway 106, 115

Objective One status 4, 6, 12, 30–1, 46–7, 49, 52, 54, 182
 rural development 88
 social impact 115, 122
O'Day, A. 167
Oil Producing and Exporting Countries (OPEC) 38
O'Kennedy, M. 162–3, 168
Operational Programmes 55, 56, 57
Opsahl Commission 153
Orders-in-Council 130, 131
O'Reilly, M. 68, 70, 103, 113
Organisation for Economic Cooperation and Development (OECD) 119

Pallarés, F. 36
Papadas, C. 92
Paris summit meeting (1972) 5
Parliamentary Assembly 156
partnerships 104, 118, 123–4, 125, 127
 for progress 119–20
Patterson, H. 111
Patton, M. 82, 83
PDS (Germany) 18, 21, 22
peace partnerships 123
Periodic Report on the Region (EC) 40
Perulli, J. 37
Physical and Social Environment Programme 56, 57, 62
pigmeat and eggs 79
Plaid Cymru 22
Planning Service 141, 142
Political Affairs Committee 154
political intervention 10
political movements 19, 21
political situation 4, 10
political violence 38

Pollitt, M. 101–2, 112
Pollution Control and Local Government (Northern Ireland) Order 1978 144
Poole, W. 103, 113
Portugal 28, 30, 31, 40, 43, 45, 46, 97, 126
positive integration 29, 30, 32, 33, 34
poultrymeat 79
poverty 91
private sector 44
privatisation 38
production platforms 104
productive capacity 60, 61
productivity 41, 69
Protestantism 109, 150
public expenditure 7, 8, 24, 41, 49, 50–4, 89
Public Expenditure Report 54

quasi-non-governmental agencies 27

Rafferty, M. 108, 113
Ramsar Convention 129
Ramsar Site 134, 136
Rasmussen, J. 35
rebate mechanism 8
RECHAR Scheme 54
reciprocal fishing rights 101
Referendum Campaign (1975) 170
regional assemblies 24
regional authorities 24, 29, 33
regional development 3, 12
regional government 8, 13, 119
regional input 15
regional institutions 24
regional mobilisation 15, 18, 19, 20, 22, 24, 30, 35
regional reform 25
regionalism 11, 12, 17–37
 dyamics 18–22
 regional government, growth of 22–9
 territorial politics 29–32
 transnational relations, new perspectives for 32–4

regionalist parties 21, 22
regulatory competition 29–30
Republicanism 149
research and development 104, 105
Rhone-Alpes 33
Richard, Lord I. 151
Robinson, A. 36
Rokkan, S. 35
Rotfeld, A. D. 168
Rowthorn, R. 111
Royal Society for the Protection of Birds 134
Rural Community Network 88
rural development 71, 86
Rural Development Council 87, 88, 89
Rural Development Division 87
Rural Development Incentives 91
rural development partnerships 123
Rural Development Strategy (1994–9) 88
rural economy 71–93
　agri-food 72–5
　agri-money 80–2
　agricultural land market 82–4
　Common Agricultural Policy 75–9
　development 87, 88–90
　and environment 79–80
　farm households 85–6
　future of 75, 86
　institutional arrangements 87–8
　subsidies, dependence and instability 84–5
Ruzza, C. 35

Sabel, C. 119
Sardinia 19, 20
Saunders, C. M. 90, 93
Scandinavia 28, 103
Schienstock, C. 36
Schmidtke, O. 35
Schmitter, P. 36
Scotland 14, 19, 21, 26, 27, 28, 74, 75, 124, 129

Scott, J. 37
Scott, R. 57–8, 70, 103, 113
Scott, S. 112
Second Programme of the European Communities to Combat Poverty 120
Secretary of State for Northern Ireland 2
sectoral programme 55
security situation 4
semi-state organisations 102
Sheehan, M. 104, 110, 113
Sheep Annual Premium 64
sheepmeat sector 78
Shortall, S. 87, 90, 93
Single European Act 29, 46, 171
Single European Currency 43, 101, 193
Single European Market 9, 29, 30, 39, 76, 82, 153
Single Programming Document (Single Programme) (SPD), 1994–9 88, 117, 118, 120, 182
Site of Special Scientific Interest (SSSI) 133
social cohesion 125
Social Democratic and Labour Party (SDLP) 152, 153, 155–8, 159, 161, 164
social deprivation 3
Social Exclusion Unit 124
Social Fund 116
social impact 115–27
　civil dialogue 120–1, 124–5
　codification of rights 123
　partnerships 119–20, 123–4, 125
　rights, equality and non-discrimination 118–19
　social inclusion and combating exclusion 120, 124
　transnational exchanges and networks 121–2, 125
social inclusion 118, 120, 124, 127
Social Policy Forums 125
social sector 11
Socrates 120

South America 94
South Slesvig (Denmark) 20
South Tyrol (Austria) 20, 32
sovereignty 170–2, 175–7, 183, 185–7, 190–1, 195
Spain 15, 25–6, 27, 30, 40, 43, 46, 97, 126
Special Areas of Conservation 137–9, 140, 141, 145
Special Protection Areas (SPAs) 133, 134, 135–7, 138
Special Support Programme for Peace and Reconciliation (SSPPR) 4, 10, 13, 47, 48, 49, 54–5, 69, 118, 119, 121, 124, 127
 Consultative Forum 121, 124, 127
 District Council Partnership Boards 88
 Northern Ireland Partnership Board 120
 Northern Ireland problem 165
 rural development 89
 Rural Regeneration strand 90
 social impact 117, 118, 122
 social progress 119
 Structural Funds 55
species conservation 131–2
Stainer, T. F. 80, 92, 93
STAR 47
Stevenson, J. 167
stocking rate limits 80
Strangford Lough 136
Streeck, W. 36
Structural Funds 4, 6, 7–8, 10, 12, 182
 economy 39, 46–7, 48, 51, 55, 68–9
 Northern Ireland problem 155
 Plans 1994–9 (Common Chapter) 122
 regionalisation 30–1
 rural economy 71, 88
 social impact 115, 117, 123
 spending 49–56
Sturm, R. 36
sub-city partnerships 123
subsidiarity 12

subsidies 44, 49, 64, 65, 66, 67, 69, 81
rural development 84–5, 89, 91
subvention 50–1, 94
Suckler Cow Premium 64
Sunningdale Agreement 151
supranational agencies 102
Sweden 40, 97, 106
Sweeney, K. 196
Switzerland 106, 115

Target 2001 135, 138
Targeting Social Need 124
Taylor, J. 110
Teague, P. 111
terrorism/violence 11, 29–32, 38, 148, 149, 151
Thatcher, M. 27, 122, 125, 126, 152, 171
Third European Poverty Programme 120
Thomas, D. 36
three strand multi-Party agreement 100
Thrift, N. 36
Tourism Operational Programme 56, 57, 62, 101
Tovey, H. 93
trade 67–8
 liberalisation 67, 68
 see also external economic links
Training and Employment Agency (T&EA) 57
transnational exchanges and networks 121–2
transnational partnershipping and exchanges 125
transnational relations, new perspectives for 32–4
Transportation Operational Programme 56, 57, 62, 63, 118
Treaty of Accession 148
Treaty of European Union (1993) 171, 176
Treaty of Rome 118, 150, 151
Trimble, M. 70
Tugendhat, Lord C. 152

UK Intervention Board of the
   Ministry of Agriculture
   Fishing and Forestry   64
UK Permanent Representation   13
Ulster Bank   107
unemployment   2–3, 5, 6, 38,
   39, 41, 42–4, 45, 46, 60
   trade   96, 109
Unionism   11, 100, 102, 108
   European integration and
      public opinion   187–8,
      190, 191, 194–5
   Northern Ireland Problem
      150, 154, 155, 156, 162
United Dairy Farmers   76
United Nations   150
   Convention on the Human
      Environment   5
   Security Council and General
      Assembly   149
United States   94, 108, 123, 124,
   125, 126, 170
Urban Renewal Regulation 1983
   47, 48, 54, 117, 154
Urwin, D.   35

Valles, J.   36
vision partnerships   123
voting patterns   109

Wagner, K.   113
Wales   14, 19, 20, 26, 27, 74, 75,
   124, 129
Wallace, M.   92
Wallonia   20, 26
Wayne, N.   111
welfare benefits   86, 94, 126
Wild Birds Protection Act
   (Northern Ireland)   1931
   128, 129, 130, 132
Wildlife and Countryside Act
   1981   130, 131
Wildlife (Northern Ireland) Order
   1985   130–1, 132, 136
Wildlife Refuge   132
Willis, K. G.   90, 93
Wilson, T.   111
Witte, E.   36
Woltess, M.   37
World Bank   125